BIBLICA ET ORIENTALIA

(SACRA SCRIPTURA ANTIQUITATIBUS ORIENTALIBUS ILLUSTRATA)

21

ROMAE
E PONTIFICIO INSTITUTO BIBLICO
1969

NICHOLAS J. TROMP, M.S.C.

PRIMITIVE CONCEPTIONS
OF DEATH AND THE NETHER WORLD
IN THE OLD TESTAMENT

ROME
PONTIFICAL BIBLICAL INSTITUTE
1969

TYPIS PONTIFICIAE UNIVERSITATIS GREGORIANAE - ROMAE

" The last enemy to be destroyed is Death ".

1 Corinthians 15,26

Preface

This dissertation was substantially finished in the autumn of 1966 and defended in Rome on April 12, 1967. From that time the labourers in the biblical vineyard have not been standing idle in the market-place. Since April, 1967, however, I have been able to introduce only changes of a relatively minor nature into this book. An occasional bibliographical reference has also been added with regard to material published after the study was finished, but such references are by no means to be taken as covering all new sources. Meanwhile some names, or rather, some persons the names evoke, were not obliterated from my memory; among them my director, M. J. Dahood S.J. stands in the first rank; but I want to mention also my Professors of the Biblical Institute together with Professors Cl. Westermann and G. von Rad of the University of Heidelberg. My gratefulness also extends to Prof. C. H. W. Brekelmans (Tilburg), who was so kind as to peruse this study.

For the edition of my manuscript in its present form I am much indebted to my director, M. Dahood, to J. Swetnam, managing editor of the series " Biblica et Orientalia " and his assistant, Miss Mary Grosvenor, who carefully improved my English, checked the references and endeavored to achieve consistency in bibliographical citations. Also to Signorina M. Grazia Franzese, who patiently prepared the final typescript.

The ready assistance of the library staffs of the Pontifical Biblical Institute in Rome, of the Canisianum at Maastricht, and of the Alttestamentliches Seminar, University of Heidelberg, was of considerable help. Finally, this dissertation could not have been accomplished without the generosity of my Superiors and the sympathy of colleagues, relatives and friends. I hope they will accept my thoughts for thanks; I have no words.

Tilburg, March 1969   NICHOLAS J. TROMP MSC

Table of Contents

Abbreviations

AJSL	American Journal of Semitic Languages and Literatures
ANEP	Ancient Near East in Pictures relating to the Old Testament (edited by J. B. Pritchard; Princeton 1954)
ANET	Ancient Near Eastern Texts Relating to the Old Testament (edited by J. B. Pritchard; 2nd. ed.; Princeton 1955)
AOT	Altorientalische Texte (edited by H. Gressmann; Tübingen 1909)
ARI	W. F. Albright, Archaeology and the Religion of Israel
ASTI	Annual of the Swedish Theological Institute
ATD	Das Alte Testament Deutsch (Göttingen)
BASOR	Bulletin of the American Schools of Oriental Research
Bib	Biblica
BA	Biblical Archeologist
BDB	F. Brown – S. R. Driver – C. A. Briggs, A Hebrew and English Lexicon of the Old Testament (Oxford 1959)
BH	Biblica Hebraica, 3rd. ed.
BiOr	Bibliotheca Orientalis
BJ	(Bible de Jérusalem) La Sainte Bible traduite en français sous la direction de l'École Biblique de Jérusalem (Paris 1956)
BK	Biblischer Kommentar (Neukirchen)
BZ	Biblische Zeitschrift
BZAW	Beihefte zur Zeitschrift für die alttestamentliche Wissenschaft
CAD	Chicago Assyrian Dictionary (edited by A. L. Oppenheim)
CBQ	Catholic Biblical Quarterly
CIS	Corpus Inscriptionum Semiticarum
CL	Collective Lament
CMAL	G. R. Driver, Canaanite Myths and Legends
colon	" For convenience we may call each half line a colon and each line a bicolon; the terms hemistich and stich (or stich and distich) are used to denote the same verse units " (Albright, Archaeology of Palestine, 231)
DJD	M. Baillet – J. T. Milik – R. de Vaux, Discoveries in the Judean Desert of Jordan. Vol. III : Les petites grottes, (Oxford 1962)
ET	Expository Times
Fs	Festschrift

FSAC . . . . . . W. F. Albright, From the Stone Age to Christianity (2nd
ed.; Garden City, N. Y., 1956)

GK . . . . W. Gesenius – E. Kautsch, Hebräische Grammatik (28th
ed.; Leipzig 1909)

GB . . . . W. Gesenius – F. Buhl, Hebräisches und aramäisches
Handwörterbuch über das Alte Testament (16th ed.;
Leipzig 1915)

HAT . . . . . . Handbuch zum Alten Testament (Tübingen)

HTR . . . . . . Harvard Theological Review

HUCA . . . . . Hebrew Union College Annual

ICC . . . . The International Critical Commentary (Edinburgh)

IDB . . . . . . Interpreter's Dictionary of the Bible. 4 vols. (New York –
Nashville 1962)

IL . . . . Individual Lament

Inf . . . . Inferno

ITh . . . . Individual Thanksgiving Psalm

JAOS . . . . . . Journal of the American Oriental Society

JBL . . . . . . Journal of Biblical Literature

JCS . . . . . . Journal of Cuneiform Studies

JQR . . . . . . Jewish Quarterly Review

JEOL . . . . . . Jaarbericht ... Ex Oriente Lux

JNES . . . . . . Journal of Near Eastern Studies

Joüon . . . . . . P. Joüon, Grammaire de l'hébreu biblique (2nd ed.;
Roma 1947)

JPOS . . . . . . Journal of the Palestine Exploration Society

JRAS . . . . . . Journal of the Royal Asiatic Society

JSS . . . . Journal of Semitic Studies

KAI . . . . . . H. Donner – W. Röllig, Kanaanäische und aramäische
Inschriften (Wiesbaden 1960-1964)

KAT . . . . . . Kommentar zum Alten Testament (Gütersloh)

KB . . . . L. Koehler – W. Baumgartner, Lexicon in Veteris Testa-
menti Libros (2nd ed.; Leiden 1958)

KJ . . . . King James Version of the Bible

OTS . . . . . . Oudtestamentische Studiën (Leiden)

PEQ . . . . . . Palestine Exploration Quarterly

PL . . . . John Milton, Paradise Lost (H. C. Beeching, The English
Poems of John Milton [London 1963])

RB . . . . Revue biblique

RGG[3] . . . . . . Die Religion in Geschichte und Gegenwart. 6 vols. (edited
by K. Galling; 3rd ed.; Tübingen 1957-1965)

RHR . . . . . . Revue de l'histoire des Religions

RP . . . . Revised Psalter (London 1964)

RSV . . . . . . Revised Standard Version

ThPs . . . . . . Thanksgiving Psalm

ThWNT . . . . . Theologisches Wörterbuch zum Neuen Testament, edited
by R. Kittel

TLZ . . . . . . Theologische Literaturzeitung

TM . . . . Textus Massoreticus

TRu	Theologische Rundschau
TZ	Theologische Zeitschrift
UHPh	M. Dahood, Ugaritic and Hebrew Philology
UL	C. Gordon, Ugaritic Literature
" ULex "	M. Dahood, " Ugaritic Lexicography "
VD	Verbum Domini
UT	C. H. Gordon, Ugaritic Textbook
VT(S)	Vetus Testamentum (Supplementum)
ZA	Zeitschrift für Assyriologie
ZAW	Zeitschrift für die alttestamentliche Wissenschaft
Zor	F. Zorell, Lexicon hebraicum (Rome 1957)
WUS	J. Aistleitner, Wörterbuch der ugaritischen Sprache

Quotations

1. Biblical Books

Gn – Ex – Lv – Nu – Dt – Jos – Jud – 1/2 S – 1/2 K – 1/2 C – 1/2 Mc
– Is – Jr – Lam – Ez – Dan – Hos – Jl – Am – Ob – Jon – Mic – Nah –
Hab – Zeph – Hagg – Zach – Mal – Jb – Ps – Prv – Qoh – CC – Sir –
Wisd – Mt – Lk – Rom – 1/2 Cor – Eph – Col – 1/2 Tim – Hebr – Rev
For transliterations the system of CBQ has been adopted.
The sign ' stands for aleph; ' for 'ayin.

2. Ugaritic Texts

Scholars are inexhaustible in inventing new numberings of these texts: we
mention Virolleaud, Driver, Gordon, Eissfeldt, Herdner; in a lesser degree
this is also true for transliterations. In this study Gordon will be followed
for both.

3. Gordon and Aistleitner

When Gordon, *Ugaritic Textbook*, Glossary is quoted, we will simply write
UT Gloss; Aistleitner's *Wörterbuch* will be referred to as *WUS*. In either
case the number of the item only will be given, not that of the page. The
latter principle also applies to the use of Dahood's *Ugaritic and Hebrew Philology* (*UHPh*).

Bibliography

Abel, F.-M., *Géographie de la Palestine* (Paris 1933-1938), cited as *Géogr.*

Aistleitner, J., *Wörterbuch der ugaritischen Sprache* (Berlin 1963 ; edited by O. Eissfeldt).

Albright, W. F., *Archaeology and The Religion of Israel* (2nd ed. ; Baltimore 1946) German translation : *Die Religion Israels im Lichte der archäologische Ausgrabungen* (München 1956).

———, " A Catalogue of Early Hebrew Lyric Poems " ([Ps 68] *HUCA* 23 [1950-1951] 1-39).

———, *From the Stone Age to Christianity* (2nd ed. ; Garden City, N. Y. 1957).

———, *The Archaeology of Palestine* (Penguin Books, 1960).

Alfrink, B., " L'expression *ŠKB 'M 'BWTYW* " (*OTS* 2 [1943] 106-118).

———, " L'expression *N'SP 'L-'MYW* " (*OTS* 5 [1948] 118-131).

Alonso Schökel, L., *Estudios de poética hebrea* (Barcelona 1963).

Anwander, A., *Zum Problem des Mythos* (Würzburg 1964).

Barr, J., *The Semantics of Biblical Language* (Oxford 1961), cited as *Semantics.*

Barth, C., *Die Errettung vom Tode in den individuellen Klage- und Dankliedern des Alten Testaments* (Zollikon 1947), cited as *Errettung.*

———, *Einführung in die Psalmen* (Biblische Studien 32 ; Neukirchen 1961), cited as *Einführung Pss.*

Baumgartner, W., " Rasch Schamra und das Alte Testament " (*TRu* 12 [1940] 163-180 ; 13 [1941] 1-20 ; 85-102 ; 157-183).

Boman, T., *Das Hebräische Denken im Vergleich mit dem Griechischen* (3rd ed. ; Göttingen 1959).

van den Born, A., *Bijbels Woordenboek* (2nd ed. ; Roermond en Maaseik 1957) [German : H. Haag and A. van den Born, *Bibellexikon* (Einsiedeln 1951)].

Brede Kristensen, W., *Het Leven uit den Dood* (Haarlem 1926).

Brekelmans, C. H. W., " Pronominal Suffixes in the Hebrew Book of Psalms " (*JEOL* 17 [1963] 202-206).

Childs, B. S., *Memory and Tradition in Israel* (London 1962).

Coppens, J., *Het onsterfelijkheidsgeloof in het Psalmboek* (Brussel 1957), cited as *Onsterfelijkheidsgeloof.*

Cross, F. M., Jr., " Yahweh and the God of the Patriarchs " (*HTR* 55 [1962] 225-259).

Cross, F. M., Jr. - Freedman, D. N., *Early Hebrew Orthography* (New Haven 1953), cited as *EHOrth.*

Dahood, M. J., " Ancient Semitic Deities in Syria and Palestine " (*Le antiche divinità semitiche,* edited by S. Moscati [Roma 1958] 65-94) cited as " Ancient Semitic Deities ".

———, " Qoheleth and Recent Discoveries " (*Bib* 39 [1958] 302-318).

————, " The Value of Ugaritic for Textual Criticism " (*Bib* 40 [1959] 160-170 [Studia Biblica et Orientalia, Rome 1959, vol. I, 26-36]).

————, " Northwest Semitic Philology and Job " (*The Bible in Current Catholic Thought*, edited by J. L. McKenzie [*Fs Gruenthaner*; New York 1962] 55-74), cited as *Job*.

————, " Ugaritic Studies and the Bible " (*Gregorianum* 43 [1962] 55-79).

————, *Proverbs and North West Semitic Philology* (Roma 1963), cited as *Prov.*

————, " Hebrew–Ugaritic Lexicography " (*Bib* 44 [1963] 289-303; 45 [1964] 393-412; 46 [1965] 311-332; 47 [1966] 403-419; 48 [1967] 421-438) cited as " HULex ".

————, " Ugaritic Lexicography " (*Mélanges Eugène Tisserant* [Studi e Testi 231; Città del Vaticano 1964] vol. I, 81-104).

————, *Ugaritic–Hebrew Philology. Marginal Notes on Recent Publications* (Biblica et Orientalia 17; Roma 1965).

————, *Psalms I* (Pss 1-50) (The Anchor Bible 16; Garden City, New York 1966), cited as *Psalms*.

Dalman, G., *Arbeit und Sitte in Palästina*, 7 vols. (Gütersloh 1928-1935), cited as *Arbeit u. Sitte*.

Daube, D., *The Sudden in the Scriptures* (Leiden 1964).

Dhorme, É., " Le séjour des morts chez les Babyloniens et les Hébreux " (*RB* 4 [1907] 59-78).

————, *Le Livre de Job* (2nd ed.; Paris 1926), cited as *Job*.

Dietrich, M. – Loretz, O., " Zur Ugaritischen Lexikographie, I " (*BiOr* 32 [1966] 127-133).

Donner, H. – Röllig, W., *Kanaanäische und aramäische Inschriften*, 3 vols. (Wiesbaden 1962-1964).

Drijvers, P., *Over de Psalmen, een inleiding tot hun betekenis en geest* (5th ed.; Utrecht 1964), cited as *Psalmen*.

Driver, G. R., " Hebrew Studies " (*JRAS* [1948] 164-176).

————, *Canaanite Myths and Legends* (Edinburgh 1956), cited as *CMAL*.

————, " Plurima Mortis Imago ", in *Studies and Essays in Honour of A. A. Neuman* (Philadelphia 1962) 128-143.

————, " Resurrection of Marine and Terrestrial Creatures " (*JSS* 7 [1962] 12-22).

Driver, S. R. – Gray, G. B., *A Critical and Exegetical Commentary on the Book of Job* (ICC; Edinburgh 1950 [= 1921]), cited as *Job*.

van Dijk, H. J., *Ezekiel's Prophecy on Tyre* (Ez 26,1 – 28,19) (Biblica et Orientalia 20; Rome 1968).

Ebeling, E., *Tod und Leben nach den Vorstellungen der Babylonier*, I (Berlin–Leipzig 1931).

Eichrodt, W., *Theologie des Alten Testaments* (Stuttgart–Göttingen, vol. 1, 6th ed. 1959; vol. 2, 5th ed. 1964), cited as *TAT*.

Eliade, M., *Das Heilige und das Profane. Vom Wesen des Religiösen* (Hamburg 1957), cited as *Das Heilige*.

————, *Le Mythe de l'Éternel Retour* (Paris 1949), cited as *Mythe*.

————, *Images et Symboles* (Paris 1952).

————, *Traité d'histoire des religions* (Paris 1949).

Falkenstein, A. – von Soden, W., *Sumerische und Akkadische Hymnen und Gebete* (Zürich–Stuttgart 1953), cited as Falkenstein – von Soden.

Fohrer, G., *Das Buch Hiob* (KAT 16 ; Gütersloh 1963).

de Fraine, J., " 'Entmythologisierung' dans les Psaumes " (R. de Langhe, editor, *Le Psautier* [Leuven 1962] 89-106), quoted as " Entmythologisierung ".

Frazer, J. C. – Gaster, T. H., *The New Golden Bough* (Garden City, New York 1961).

Gaster T. H., *Thespis. Ritual, Myth, and Drama in the Ancient Near East* (2nd ed. ; Garden City, New York 1961) cited as *Thespis*.

Ginsberg, H. L., *The Legend of King Keret* (BASOR SS 2-3 ; New Haven 1946).

Gordon, C. H., *Ugaritic Literature*. A Comprehensive Translation of the Poetic and Prose Texts (Rome 1949).

———, *Ugaritic Textbook*. Grammar, Texts in Transliteration, Cuneiform Selections, Glossary, Indices (Analecta Orientalia 38 ; Rome 1965).

Gray, J., *The Legacy of Canaan*. The Ras Shamra Texts and Their Relevance to the Old Testament (Leiden 1957), cited as *Legacy*.

———, *The Canaanites* (London 1964), cited as *Canaanites*.

Guerber, H. A. – van den Bergh, O. – van Eysinga, H. W., *Noorse Mythen uit de Edda's en de Sagen* (7th printing ; Zutphen 1951), cited as Guerber.

Gunkel, H., *Schöpfung und Chaos* (Göttingen 1895).

———, *Genesis* (HAT 1/1 ; 6th ed. [= 3rd ed.] ; Göttingen 1964).

———, *Die Psalmen* (HAT 2/2 ; 4th ed. ; Göttingen 1926), cited as *Psalmen*[4].

Gunkel, H. – Begrich, J., *Einleitung in die Psalmen* (Göttingen 1933).

Haag H. – Van den Born A., *Bibellexikon* (Einsiedeln–Zürich–Köln 1951).

Harris, Z. S., *A Grammar of the Phoenician Language* (New Haven 1936), cite l as *Grammar*.

Haussig, H. W., *Wörterbuch der Mythologie* (Stuttgart s.a.), cited as Haussig.

Heidel, A., *The Gilgamesh Epic and Old Testament Parallels* (5th impr. Chicago–London 1965), cited as Heidel.

Heiler, F., *Erscheinungsformen und Wesen der Religion* (Stuttgart 1961).

Herdner, A., *Corpus des Tablettes en cunéiformes alphabétiques découvertes à Rash Shamra–Ugarit de 1929 à 1939*, 2 vols. (Paris 1963), cited as *Corpus*.

Honeyman, A. M., " Merismus in Biblical Hebrew " (*JBL* 71 [1952] 11-18).

Hooke, S. H., " Israel and the Afterlife " (*ET* 76 n. 8 [May 1965] 236-239).

Jahnow, H., *Das Hebräische Leichenlied* (BZAW 36 ; Giessen 1923), cited as *Leichenlied*.

Jean, Ch.-F – Hoftijzer, J., *Dictionnaire des inscriptions sémitiques de l'Ouest* (Leiden 1965), cited as Jean–Hoftijzer.

Johnson, A. R., " Jonah 2,3-20. A Study in Cultic Phantasy " (in H. H. Rowley, editor, *Studies in Old Testament Prophecy* [Edinburgh 1950] 82-102.

———, *Sacred Kingship in Israel* (Cardiff 1955), cited as *Sacr. Kingship*.

Joüon, P., *Grammaire de l'Hébreu Biblique* (2nd ed. ; Rome 1947), cited as Joüon.

Kaiser, O., *Die mythische Bedeutung des Meeres in Aegypten, Ugarit und Israel* (BZAW 78 ; Berlin 1959), cited as *Bedeutung des Meeres*.

Kapelrud, A. S., *The Ras Shamra Discoveries and the Old Testament*, translated by G. W. Anderson (Norman, Oklahoma 1963 = Oxford 1962), cited as *Discov.*

Kittel, R., *Geschichte des Volkes Israel*, I (Gotha 1912).

Kosmala, H., " Mot and the Vine : the Time of the Ugaritic Fertility Rite "
    (*ASTI* 3 [1964] 147-152).
Kraus, H. J., *Psalmen* (Neukirchen 1959-1960), cited as *Psalmen.*
Kristensen, B. W., *Het leven uit den dood* (Haarlem 1926).
Kroll, J., *Gott und Hölle. Der Mythos vom Descensuskampfe* (Leipzig–Berlin
    1932), cited as *Gott u. Hölle.*
van der Leeuw, G., *De primitieve mensch en de Religie* (Groningen 1937).
———, *Phänomenologie der Religion* (2nd ed. ; Tübingen 1956), cited as *Phäno-
    menologie.*
Lisowsky, G., *Konkordanz zum Hebräischen Alten Testament* (Stuttgart 1958).
Maag, V., " Syrien–Palästina ", in H. Schmökel *Kulturgeschichte des Alten Orient*
    (Stuttgart 1961) 448-605, cited as *Kulturgesch.*
———, " Tod und Jenseits nach dem Alten Testament " (*Schweizerische Theo-
    logische Umschau* 34 [1964], 17-37), cited as " Tod und Jenseits ".
———, " B^elīja'al im Alten Testament " (*TZ* 21 [1965] 287-299).
Martin-Achard, R., *De la mort à la résurrection d'après l'Ancien Testament* (Neu-
    châtel–Paris 1956) (English translation : *From Death to Life*) [Edinburgh–
    London 1960], cited as *From Death...*).
Moscati, S., *Il sistema consonantico delle lingue semitiche* (Roma 1954).
Mowinckel, S., *Psalmenstudien*, 3 vols. (Kristiania 1921-1923).
———, *The Psalms in Israel's Worship* (Oxford 1962), cited as *Psalms in
    Worship.*
Mulder, E. S., *Die Theologie von die Jesaja Apokalipse* (Groningen–Djakarta
    1954), cited as *Theol. Jesaja Apok.*
Nicolsky, N., *Spuren magischer Formeln in den Psalmen* (BZAW 46 ; Giessen
    1927), cited as *Spuren magischer Formeln.*
Noth, M., *Die Israelitische Personennamen in Rahmen der gemeinsemitischen
    Namengebung* (Stuttgart 1928), cited as *Personennamen.*
———, *Die Welt des Alten Testaments* (2nd ed. ; Berlin 1953).
———, *Geschichte Israels* (3rd ed. ; Göttingen 1956).
Pauly, A. – Wissowa, G., *Real-Encyclopädie der klassischen Altertumswissen-
    schaft* (Stuttgart 1893), cited as *Pauly–Wissowa.*
Pedersen, J., *Israel, Its Life and Culture*, I-II/III-IV (London 1964 [identical
    reprint of 1926] ; 1963 = 1959), cited as *Israel.*
Pope, M., *El in the Ugaritic Texts* (VTS 2 ; Leiden 1955), cited as *El.*
———, " The Word *šaḥat* in Job 9,31 " (*JBL* 83 [1964] 269-278).
———, *Job* (The Anchor Bible 15 ; Garden City, New York 1965), cited as *Job.*
Procksch, O., *Die Theologie des Alten Testaments* (Gütersloh 1949).
von Rad, G., " 'Gerechtigkeit' und 'Leben' in den Psalmeni" (*Fs Bertholet* ;
    Tübingen 1950) 418-430 [= *Gesammelte Studien*, 2nd ed. ; München 1961,
    225-247].
———, *Das erste Buch Mose* (ATD 2/4 ; Göttingen 1953).
———, *Theologie des Alten Testaments*, 2 vols. (München 1960).
Renckens, H., *Israëls visie op het verleden* (2nd printing ; Tielt–den Haag 1957)
    (= *Urgeschichte und Heilsgeschichte* [2nd ed. ; Mainz 1961]).
Reymond, Ph., " L'eau, sa Vie et sa Signification dans l'Ancien Testament "
    (*VTS* 6 ; Leiden 1958), cited as " L'eau ".
Rin, S., " The *mwṭ* of Grandeur ", *VT* 9 (1959) 324 f.

Rin, Svi – Rin, Shifra, " Ugaritic–Old Testament Affinities ". I (*BZ* 7 [1963] 23-33); II (*BZ* 11 [1967] 174-192).

Roscher, W. H., *Ausführliches Lexicon der Griechischen und Römischen Mythologie*, (Leipzig 1886-1890, 1890, vol. 1/2), cited as *Lex. Myth.*

Rost, L., " Die Bezeichnungen für Land und Volk im Alten Testament " in : *Das kleine Credo und andere Studien* (Heidelberg 1962), 76-101, cited as *Bezeichnungen.*

Rowley, H. H. (editor) *Studies in Old Testament Prophecy* (Edinburg 1950).

Russell, D. S., *The Methods and Message of Jewish Apocalyptic* (London 1964).

Sarna, N. M., " The Interchange of the Prepositions *Beth* and *Min* in Biblical Hebrew " (*JBL* 78 [1959] 310-316).

——, " The Mythological Background of Job 18 " (*JBL* 82 [1963] 315-318).

Schilling, O., *Die Jenseitsgedanke im Alten Testament* (Mainz 1951).

Schmidt, H., *Die Psalmen* (HAT 1/15 ; Tübingen 1934).

Schmidt, W., *Königtum Gottes in Ugarit and Israel. Zur Herkunft der Königsprädikation Jahwes* (BZAW 80 ; Berlin 1961), cited as *Königtum.*

Schottroff, W., *Die Wurzel ZKR im Alten Testament* (Mainz 1961).

Schwally, F., *Das Leben nach dem Tode* (Giessen 1892).

van Selms, A., *Marriage and Family Life in Ugaritic Literature* (London 1954), cited as *Marriage and Family Life.*

Smith, W. R. – Cook, S. A., *Lectures on the Religion of the Semites* (3rd ed. ; London 1927), cited as *Religion Semites*[3].

Stade, B., *Geschichte des Volkes Israel*, I (Berlin 1881).

Stade, B. – Bertholet, A. D., *Biblische Theologie des Alten Testaments*, II (Tübingen 1911).

Strack, H. L. – Billerbeck, P., *Kommentar zum Neuen Testament aus Talmud und Midrasch*, IV/2 (München 1956), cited as Strack–Billerbeck.

Sutcliffe, E. F., *The Old Testament and Future Life* (London 1946).

Tallqvist, K. L., *Sumerisch-akkadische Namen der Totenwelt* (Studia Orientalia V/4 ; Helsinki 1934), cited as *Namen der Totenwelt.*

Thomas, D. W., " A Consideration of Some Unusual Ways of Expressing the Superlative in Hebrew " (*VT* [1953] 209-224).

——, " Ṣalmāwet in the Old Testament " (*JSS* 7 [1962] 191-200).

Vincent, H., *Canaan d'après l'exploration récente* (Paris 1907), cited as *Canaan.*

Vriezen, T. C., *De literatuur van Oud-Israël* (2nd ed. ; Den Haag 1961).

Wellek, R. – Warren, A., *Theory of Literature* (New York 1959).

Wensinck, A. H., *The Ocean in the Literature of the Western Semites* (Verhand. Kon. Acad. Wetensch., Afd. Letterk, Nwe Reeks dl. 19/2 ; Amsterdam 1918), cited as *Ocean.*

Westermann, C., *Das Loben Gottes in den Psalmen* (3rd ed. ; Göttingen 1963), cited as *Loben Gottes.*

Widengren, G., *The Accadian and Hebrew Psalms of Lamentation as Religious Documents* (Stockholm 1937), cited as *Acc. and Hebr. Pss.*

Wohlstein, H., " Zu den altisraelitischen Vorstellungen von Toden- und Ahnengeistern " (*BZ* 5 [1961] 30-38).

Wolff, H. W., *Dodekapropheton*, I. *Hosea* (BK 14/1 ; Neukirchen 1961), cited as *Hosea.*

Wright, G. E. (editor), *The Bible and the Ancient Near East* (*Fs Albright*; London 1961), cited as *Fs Albright*.

Zandee, J., *Death as an Enemy according to Ancient Egyptian Conceptions* (Leiden 1960), cited as Zandee.

Zimmerli, W., *Ezechiel* (BK 13 ; Neukirchen 1956-).

INTRODUCTION

CHAPTER 1: METHODOLOGICAL PRINCIPLES

Death is a vital issue in the Old Testament. This appears both from the innumerable allusions to the reality of death and its consequences, and from the numerous studies devoted to the subject since the rise of modern critical exegesis. As the results of this research are sufficiently well known, a summary of them is not called for; and a fresh analysis of established positions would amount to a series of repetitions.

A new approach is imperative to justify another study of our theme. This fresh starting-point was found in Ugaritic literature.

As the documents found at Ras Shamra belong to an environment where culture was geographically widespread but not subject to frequent changes, an affinity with Old Testament times and culture is obvious [1]. In spite of sceptical voices it can hardly be denied that students of Ugaritic have contributed not a little to a better understanding of the text of the Old Testament as handed down by the Massoretes. The special value of the Ugaritic texts consists in their language, which shows a remarkable similarity with biblical Hebrew, both in vocabulary and style [2].

A limited approach to our subject, however, by no means implies a silent rejection of previous studies which treat the same theme along different lines; it rather presupposes their results which it does not want to disavow but to supplement. An honest and critical application of new acquisitions should not be understood as a repudiation of other approved methods or as an effort to claim a monopoly position for a new approach. This dissertation intends to show how the application of the fruits of Ugaritic scholarship can make a valuable contribution to the study of Israelite conceptions about Death and the Hereafter.

[1] See now M. Dahood, " HU Lex ", *Bib* 48 (1967) 421-423.
[2] See M. Dahood, " Ugaritic Studies and the Bible ", *Gregorianum* 43 (1962) 55-79; C. H. W. Brekelmans, *Ras Sjamra en het Oude Testament.* (Nijmegen s.a.); E. Jacob, *Ras Shamra et l'Ancien Testament* (Neuchâtel–Paris 1960); A. S. Kapelrud, *The Ras Sjamra Discoveries and the Old Testament* (translated by G. W. Anderson, Oxford 1962 = Norman 1963).

In the first place this contribution is of a linguistic nature: it attempts to use the results of philological research on the Ugaritic texts and its application to biblical literature. Secondly, it tries to obtain a better perspective of Israelite views on Death and the Beyond with the help of conceptions found in these texts.

Above all things, this study attempts to take advantage of the results obtained by the philological research of the Ugaritic texts and its application to biblical literature. It is a public secret that this research and its fruits are not welcomed with general applause. Indeed, not all the fundamental questions involved have been treated exhaustively; e.g., it would seem that the presence of so-called dialectical traces of the Ugaritic, Phoenician, and Punic languages in the Bible has been demonstrated with plausible certainty; but on the other hand it remains to be shown if these traces occur with any regularity in certain authors, in well-defined traditions, redactions, or literary genres. This is a question of vital importance. If the alleged dialectical elements occur indiscriminately in the OT, it becomes necessary to find out whether the same is true for the texts where the elements under discussion are found. A negative answer to the latter question would make their very presence in the biblical texts doubtful.

Besides, this kind of solution of seeming anomalies in the Hebrew text is often only partially successful. Not only because little clarity can be derived from obscure extra-biblical texts (although two small rays of light may reinforce each other), but also because sometimes the process involved calls for no less strain and ingenuity than the proposals made before. Not rarely also, an explanation of some surprising feature in the Hebrew text applies to a limited number of instances only; then it must be asked if the element under discussion does really sound as strange in Hebrew as we supposed it does. What may seem surprising to us, may after all be of normal occurrence. So the existence of biblical *gam* with the meaning of Ugaritic *gm*, "in a loud voice", may seem more doubtful when it is shown to be a key to a restricted number of cases only. For all these reasons a critical attitude is required. Finally, elements of a more literary nature prove to be an essential supplement to the strictly philological approach (see below, p. 5).

For two reasons, parallel lines in the strict sense of the word cannot be established for our subject. In the OT the myth is a broken one; it is reduced to scattered motifs and allusions.

On the other hand, the Ras Shamra evidence hardly contains any direct information as to human death and afterlife; relevant material is mainly found in the Baal-cycle, where the death of that vegetational god is described. It is clear, however, that these passages reflect conceptions of human death.

On a very modest scale the conclusions of historians of religion are referred to ; they suggest that most of the motifs in question are of an archetypal nature. Moreover they prevent us from thinking in the restricted terms of a direct or indirect dependence which is hardly a relevant approach (³). Although stray remarks are not lacking in the writings of Ugaritic and biblical scholars, no consistent discussion of our theme from this point of view is found there ; in fact, of the numerous Ugaritic studies only a relatively small number proved important for us.

This study concerns biblical motifs of Death and the nether world, more specifically those motifs originating from myth as an effort to give expression to the primary mysteries connected with human life and its end by means of a symbolism which combines contradictory elements and which consequently cannot be expressed in conceptual language ; which suggests what cannot be fully said ; which brings home to man a concrete totality, a living and transcendent reality. A few quotations from modern literature show that these representations are practically indispensable and not tied to a certain time or culture.

This limitation to mythical motives has its consequences.

1. Our theme is Death and Sheol as the Israelite *eschata* ; the problems of immortality, resurrection, and the like will not be discussed.

2. Traces of mythological language about Death and the Beyond are found throughout the OT. Seeing that they appear as soon as reflection on these mysteries shows itself in the Bible, they should not be labelled as " late " (⁴).

In fact the OT does not dispose of any categories other than the mythological to describe Death and the hereafter. As to their literary expression, scholars of as different trends as Albright and Gaster on the one hand, and Tournay and Deissler on the other, agree that virtually all close stylistic and verbal parallels between the Israelite and Canaanite literature belong to the exilic and post-exilic time, " the product of a general archaeological revival which swept the whole of the Near East in the fifth–sixth centuries B.C. " (⁵).

(³) The passage on the use of ancient parallels owes much to Cl. Westermann, " Sinn und Grenze religionsgeschichtlicher Parallelen ", *ThLZ* 90 (1965) 490-496 ; and to his forthcoming commentary on Genesis, as reflected in his course at the University of Heidelberg, Summer 1966. See bibliography s.v. Eliade, Brede Kristensen, Zandee ; for detailed evidence see the works of J. G. Frazer.

(⁴) There are voices now claiming a pre-exilic date for Job.

(⁵) Gaster, *Thespis* 142. Cf. also the remarks made in passing by W. F. Al-

It seems that this somewhat artificial explanation is based on an hypothesis rather than well-established facts. Affinities between " Phoenician " and Hebrew literature were probably never lacking. In suggesting that all these correspondences are post-exilic and that, consequently, the renaissance is an evident and necessary fact, its defenders are reasoning in a vicious circle. Moreover, unless one is to assume that the Israelites did not reflect on human destiny and the Beyond before that time, it seems rather rash to suggest that all mythological traces in these conceptions necessarily date from that " archaizing period ". Of course Ugarit was at its zenith in a region and a period distant from the biblical ones, and we do not propose an identification of the two; on the other hand it is undeniable that culture in those days was more universal in time and space than ours is. Gerhard von Rad, e.g., found identical stylistic forms in an Egyptian sapiential document of the early 13th century B.C. and chapter 38 of Job ([6]). Besides, Canaanite influence on the Israelite society was more profound than biblical writings confess: Is 18,19 suggests that Hebrew was closely related to the Canaanite language. Further historical developments will receive scant consideration in this study. More recent literature, e.g. the NT, shows how tenacious the life of these categories could be.

3. As this dissertation regards motifs, it cannot boast of an intrinsically necessary structure, though of course an attempt at a logically coherent exposition is made. The amazing number of biblical names for the nether world is taken as a starting-point; these not only show that reflection on this reality was hardly as marginal in Israelite thought as is often supposed, but also give a good indication of its nature. The three chapters of the first part are not sharply distinct from each other; the division mainly serves the purpose of easy survey. In chapter I the local aspect of the names is the predominant common element, the second chapter is characterized by the relation to the dead implied in them, which is suggested by the title " milieu ", while chapter III collects the names suggesting a conception of Death as a personal reality. Part II studies the implications of these names and epithets as elaborated in other biblical descriptions of reality after death, which in that way act as explanations of the view obtained in part I. In that manner the discussion of the Israelite conceptions of Death and Sheol is rounded off.

4. Our evidence is drawn mainly from poetical books, but in view of our approach it has appeared impossible to discuss poetry

bright, *The Archaeology of Palestine* 230-236; R. Tournay, *RB* 70 (1963) 591 f.; 72 (1965) 144; A. Deissler in *Fs H. Junker* (Trier 1961) 50 f.

([6]) G. von Rad, *Gesammelte Studien* (München 1961) 268.

as such. This would require an analysis of the poems as totalities, because only in that way can the import of a motif in its context be duly appreciated. On the other hand, the study of the literary genres has proven of vital importance. This point of view is a welcome supplement to the philological method, because a consideration of the genre in question and an analysis of its vocabulary provide us with more concrete norms for the suitability of proposed meanings in particular cases. In this way the choice of an interpretation can be justified better and the element of arbitrariness and confusion, which a merely philological approach might imply, is considerably reduced.

Finally, some remarks about the bibliography. The bibliography is not intended to be exhaustive, but merely serves the practical purpose of simplifying the reading of this study. As a rule books and articles quoted not more than once are referred to in the relevant passage only. The choice of books and their translations was not rarely influenced by their accessibility in concrete circumstances.

CHAPTER 2: UGARITIC EVIDENCE ABOUT DEATH AND THE UNDERWORLD

Interesting evidence about Ugaritic conceptions of death and the nether world is found mainly in the Baal-cycle ([1]).

Baal, the god of rain, strives for supremacy in the universe; after defeating his competitors Yam, god of subterranean waters, seas, and wells, and Athtar, god of springs and wells, he faces the arch-enemy himself, i.e. Mot, god of death and drought. Relevant passages will be quoted here and commented upon as far as our purpose requires it.

Our first text describes the mission of Baal's two messengers to the abode of Mot, the nether world (*UT* 51 : VIII) ([2]).

1	*idk.al.ttn.pnm*	Then of a truth do you set your faces
	'm.ġr.trġzz	towards the mount of Targhuzi
	'm.ġr.trmg	towards the mount of Tharumagi,
	'm. tlm.ġsr.arṣ	toward the two hills bounding the nether world ([3]).
5	*ša.ġr. 'l.ydm*	Lift up the rocks on your two hands
	ḫlb.lẓr.rḫtm	and the woodland on to your two palms,
	wrd.bt ḫpṭt	and go down to the charnel house of the
	arṣ.tspr.by	nether world ([4]). Be counted among them
	rdm.arṣ	that went down ([5]) into the nether world.

([1]) For introductions, see Gordon, *UL* 3 ff.; Driver, *CMAL* 10 ff.; Jacob, *Ras Shamra et l'A.T.* 47-52; Kapelrud, *Discov.* 37-51; for translations also Gaster (*ANET* and *Thespis*); Virolleaud (see Driver, *CMAL* xi); J. Aistleitner, *Die mythologische und kultische Texte aus Ras Shamra* (Budapest 1959); A. Jirku, *Kanaanäische Mythen und Epen aus Ras Schamra–Ugarit* (Gütersloh 1962); J. Gray, *The Canaanites* (London 1964); R. de Langhe, *Les Textes de Ras Shamra–Ugarit*, 2 vols. (Paris 1945); M. Liverani, *Storia di Ugarit nell'età degli archivi politici* (Roma 1962); A. F. Rainey, " The Kingdom of Ugarit ", *BA* 18 (1965) 102-124; C. Brockelmann, in B. Spuler, *Handbuch der Orientalistik*, III. *Semistik*, 1 (Leiden 1953) 45 f.; M. Dahood in *Or* 34 (1965) 36; A. Haldar in *BiOr* 21 (1964) 267-277 (see Dahood, *UHPh* 6.26).

([2]) Ugaritic texts are quoted according to Gordon's *UT*; the translations are based on Gordon, Driver, and Gaster.

([3]) It is a common conception among the western Semites that these hills are at the entrance to the Beyond; see Wensinck, *Ocean* 34 and Gilgamesh Epic IX : ii : 1-5 (see A. Heidel, *The Gilgamesh Epic and Old Testament Parallels* [Chicago–London 1963] 65).

([4]) See the discussion below, on pp. 157-159.

([5]) For the past tense, see below, pp. 33 f.

10	*idk.al.ttn*	Then, indeed, set face [towards El's Son
	pnm.tk.qrth	Mot], midst his city
	hmry.mk.ksu	"Slushy". Ruin is the throne ([6])
	ṯbth.ḫḫ.arṣ	where he sits, infernal filth ([7])
	nḥlth.wnǵr	his inheritance. But be on your guard,
15	*'nn.ilm.al*	look you, gods, come you not
	tqrb.lbn.ilm	near to the son of El ([8]),
	mt.al.y'dbkm	Mot. Let him not make you
	kimr.bph	like a sheep in his mouth,
	klli.bṯ ! brn	you be carried both away like a kid
20	*qnh.*	in his jaws ([9]).

Lexicographically this small fragment contains quite a number of revealing items.

First of all it is indisputable that *arṣ* stands for the nether world here; in fact the Hebrew Sheol is missing in Ugaritic. Moreover this *arṣ* occurs in a phrase which is found with several variants in the Old Testament: "Be counted among those who went down to the nether world". Sometimes the Old Testament reads: "Go down to Sheol" (e.g. Ps 55,16), which at the same time establishes the equivalence of *arṣ* and Sheol ([10]). It should not pass unnoticed that the Ugaritic expression in our case contains an unmistakable example of enclitic *mem*: *yrdm arṣ* ([11]).

Unfortunately the exact meaning of *bt ḫpṯt* remains baffling, but on the other hand the description of the nether world as Mot's City is beyond doubt; it will return in the Old Testament. The word

---

([6]) For "ruin" see pp. 72 f. — *mk ksu ṯbth / ḫḫ arṣ nḥlth*. This division of the text is unobjectionable in view of '*nt* IV : 15 f. (*UL* 23 ; *CMAL* 91B). The word *mk* derives from the verb *mkk* ("to sink down, to be low ", *KB* 521B) which, in Qoh 10,18, refers to house-timber. Consequently, *mk ksu* may mean : "Ruin is the throne ... " (Pope, *Job* 73). Of course translations such as " pit " (*Thespis* 200) and the like cannot be discarded. Dahood now translates *mk* as " sinkhole " and finds it in Am 3,11b (" HU Lex ", *Bib* 40 [1967] 425 f.).

([7]) Others translate *ḫḫ* as " thorns " (*WUS* 1015).

([8]) Or : " divine "; Mot appears some 40 times in Ugaritic literature (*WUS* 1704).

([9]) Interpretation of Dahood, " The Etymology of *maltā'ôt* (Ps 58,7) " CBQ 17 (1955) 180-183 ; see Aistleitner, *WUS* 2834, p. 332.

([10]) See below, p. 32 f. *Arṣ* = nether world occurs about 12 times in Ugaritic texts (*CMAL* 135B ; B II : vi : 25 probably stands for vii : 52 ; 49 : v : 4 should be added). The division is : *ḫrt ilm* (!) *arṣ*, 4x ; *yrd* (*b*) *arṣ*, 4x ; *n'my arṣ*, 2x ; *ḫḫ arṣ*, 1x ; *ms' larṣ*, 1x.

([11]) See Rin in *BZ* 11 (1967) 191 ; we also find *ilm arṣ*.

characterizing this town, *hmry*, derives from a root which belongs to the same *Ideenwelt* in biblical Hebrew ([12]).

To the affinities with the Old Testament belong also the representation of Mot's city as Ruin ([13]), of Mot himself as a voracious monster with his dangerous jaws ([14]) and of the two hills at the entry of the nether world([15]). Finally the Ugaritic text shows unambiguously the subterranean situation of the nether world in the Canaanite tradition.

The following scene is pictured in Text 67, which ranks among the most difficult of the cycle and whose translation, therefore, remains tentative.

UT 67 : I : Mot addresses Baal.

1	*ktmḫṣ.ltn.bṯn.brḥ*	When thou smotest Leviathan the slippery serpent
	tkly.bṯn.ʿqltn	and madest an end of the wriggling serpent,
	šlyṭ.d.šbʿt.rašm	the tyrant with seven heads ([17]),
	tṯkḫ.ttrp.šmm.krs	. . .
5	*ipdk.ank ispi.uṭm*	. .; I myself was ([18]) swallowed up like funeral meats
	ḏrqm.amtm.lyrt	. . .; I died. Verily thou must descend
	bnpš.bn ilm.mt.bmh	into the throat of divine Mot, into the miry
	mrt.ydd.il.ǵzr	gorge of the hero loved of El.
18	*hm imt imt.npš.blt*	Lo ! truly, truly my life is spent
	ḥmr pemt.bklat ([16])	. . ., truly with both
	ydy ilḥm...	my hands I am eating mud.

So some time Mot, the Swallower, himself was swallowed ; Death himself died, i.e. was affected in his fulness of life ([19]).

Lines 6 f. contain a variation of the formula, found in *UT* 51 : VIII : 8 f. ; now the nether world is personified ; in 7 f. the word *mhmrt* returns : in view of the parallelism Driver's translation is a happy one.

([12]) See below, pp. 54 ff.
([13]) Below, pp. 72 f.
([14]) Below, pp. 104 f.
([15]) Below, p. 55.
([16]) For this reading see Herdner, *Corpus* I, 33.
([17]) Cf. Is 27,1.
([18]) Final *amtn* implies understanding *ispi* as a passive.
([19]) See below, p. 172.

Line 18 seems to repeat the idea, expressed by *amtm* in line 6, but its translation is not quite certain, as may appear from Aistleitner's interpretation : " Gras ist das Begehren des Gaumen des Esels "[20], although the repeated *imt* rather suggests that the chain of comparisons is finished here.

If lines 19 f. may be rendered this way, they contain a reference to mud as the quintessence of the nether world [21].

The Ugaritic text continues (67 : II) :

1	. . . *k.lmt.m*	Even as Mot has
	ltᶜt[22]*.larṣ.špt.lšmm*	jaws (reaching) to earth, lips to heaven,
	wlšn.lkbkbm.yᶜrb	and a tongue to the stars, Baal
	bᶜl.bkbdh.bph yrd	will enter his stomach and go down into his mouth
5	*kḫrr.zt.ybl.arṣ.wpr*	as the olive, the produce of the earth and the fruit
	ᶜṣm.yraun.aliyn.bᶜl	of trees is swallowed. Shall the victor Baal be afraid of him,
	ṯtᶜ.nn.rkb.ᶜrpt	the rider on the clouds fear him ?
	tbᶜ.rgm.lbn.ilm.mt	Depart, tell Mot son of El,
	ṯny.lydd il ǵzr	repeat to the hero loved of El
10	*ṯḥm.aliyn.bᶜl.hwt.aliy*	the message of the victor Baal, the word of the valiant
	qrdm.bhṯ.lbn.ilm.mt	victor, (saying) : " Hail, Mot son of El !
	ᶜbdk.an.wdᶜlmk	I am thy servant and thine for ever ".
	. . . .	
20	. . . *šmḫ.bn.ilm.mt*	. . . Mot son of El did rejoice,
	yšu.gh.waṣḥ.ik.ylḥn	he lifted up his voice and cried : " How shall
	bᶜlm.	Baal understand ? " [23].

The first lines portray the traditional voracity of Mot; this appears in *UT* 52 : 27 f., where the same image is " translated " afterwards : " ... lips to earth and lips to heaven — and the birds of the heaven and the fishes of the sea verily do enter their mouths ... and they cannot be satisfied " [24].

In Gaster's translation line 12 reads :

[20] *WUS* 527.
[21] For *ḥmr*, " mud ", see *CMAL* 139 A (with Albright).
[22] Text restored (*CMAL* 104).
[23] See *CMAL* 104 f.
[24] *Ibid.* 122 ff.; the image returns in Ps 73,9.

" I am thy perpetual bondman " ([25]); the correctness of this interpretation may be illustrated by Job 40,28, where the parallelism is
to be noted:

> Will he make a covenant with you,
> to take him for your servant for ever?

Mot is considered as a personal reality throughout the poem; in keeping with this a familiar formula returns here in the words: " to go
down into the mouth of Mot ".

In another text Baal, about to descend to the nether world, is
advised by an unnamed speaker, probably his sister Anat (67: V):

11 . . . *idk*	" Then
pnk.al ttn.tk ǵr	of a truth do thou set thy face unto a rock
knkny. ša. ǵr 'l ydm	full of graves; lift up the rocks on thy two hands,
ḫlb.lẓr.rḫtm wrd	and the woodland on to thy two palms and go down
15 *bt ḫpṭt.arṣ tspr by*	to ... the nether world, be counted among
rdm.arṣ. wtd' ill	those who went down into the nether world and know inanition ([26]);
kmtt.yšm'.aliy.b'l	for thou wilt have died ". The victor Baal listened.
yuhb.'glt.bdbr.prt	He loved a heifer in the land of decease,
b šd. šḫlmmt....	a cow by the edge of the strand of death... ([27]).

This text shows the affinity between graves and the underworld:
" Sheol is the entirety into which all graves are merged ", as Pedersen puts it ([28]). Because of the same coherence the nether world is
labelled " region of inanition "; this conception recalls the biblical
" pit of destruction " (Is 38,17) and the like.

The area, referred to in the words *dbr* and *šd šḫlmmt*, returns
in 67: VI: 5 f., where for the first expression a more elaborated formula is used: *n'my.arṣ.dbr*, " the fairness of the land of *dbr* " and
ysmt šd šḫlmmt, " the beauty of the fields of *šḫlmmt* ", ironical additions no doubt, as will appear. As, in the latter text, Baal is found
dead there, the connection of this area with Mot's domain seems evi-

---

[25] *Thespis* 207.
[26] For *ill* cf. Hebrew *'ĕlîl* (*CMAL* 136B).
[27] *Ibid.* 106 f.
[28] Pedersen, *Israel* I/II 462.

dent. This is reinforced by *UT* 49 : II : 20 ff., which reports an en-
counter of Mot and Baal in the same surroundings, with fateful consequences for the latter. Because of 67 : V : 18 f. it seems unlikely
that the nether world itself is meant by the terms mentioned. With
Gaster ([29]) we think the desert is intended : this barren and chaotic
reality belongs to Mot's domain.

It may not be fortuitous that *arṣ dbr* can mean both " pasture-
land " and " land of disease and death " ([30]) and that *šd šḫlmmt* reminds one of the " lion that kills ", " die Löwe von Mametu " ([31])
and can be rendered also " the edge of the strand of death " ([32]).

UT 67 : VI : 10 ff. ; Baal is reported dead after his descent to the
nether world. The divine messengers are speaking :

8	... *lbʿl.npl.la*	Verily Baal has fallen
	rṣ.mt.aliyn bʿl	into the nether world ([33]), the victor Baal is dead,
10	*ḫlq.zbl.bʿl. arṣ*	the prince lord of the earth has perished !

In this small fragment with its characteristic tripartite parallelism the verb *ḫlq* appears, which, as both Accadian *ḫalaqu* and the
parallel verbs here indicate, means " to perish " ([34]).

UT 2114 : 10-12 shows that *ḫlq* is not only applied to living
beings :

ap.krmm.ḫlq.qrtn.ḫlq	Also the vineyards are destroyed ; de- stroyed the cities.

Until recently, Hebrew lexicography distinguished two roots *ḥlq* :
I to make smooth ; II to divide ([35]).

As, in Hebrew, this uvular *ḫ* shifts into the laringal *ḥ* ([36]), it is
reasonable to suppose that Hebrew *ḥlq* also contains Ugaritic *ḫlq*.

It has been demonstrated in fact that the verb means " to perish "

([29]) *Thespis* 125 § 3 ; 132, n. 19.

([30]) *CMAL* 154 s.v. ; n. 29.

([31]) *WUS* 2589.

([32]) *CMAL* 107 ; Scandinavian mythology knows a " strand of the corpses "
(Guerber, 181). For *šdmt* see below, pp. 50-53 ff.

([33]) *CMAL* 106 f. ; he reads : " Fallen to the ground ". The verb *npl*
has a pregnant meaning here ; see Ps 5,11 (Dahood, *Psalms* 36) and Jr 23,12,
where also *ḫlq* occurs. See also Van Dijk, *Ezekiel's Prophecy* p. 90.

([34]) *UT* Gloss 969 ; *WUS* 1038 ; Dietrich–Loretz, *BiOr* 23 (1966) 130 A.

([35]) *KB* 305B.

([36]) Terminology : Moscati, *Il Sistema consonantico delle lingue semitiche*
57-59.

in several biblical texts, e.g. in Lam 4,16 and Jb 21,17 ([37]) ; in Ps 5,10 ; 12,4 ; 17,14 ; 36,3 ; Hos 10,2 ([38]). Some other texts will be treated explicitly elsewhere in this study ([39]).

Consequently lexicographers will have to insert *ḥlq* III, " to per-ish ". Ugaritic also possesses the root *ḥlq*, namely in the noun *ḥlqm*, which probably means " ring " ([40]). In this case its relation to Hebrew *ḥlq* I is unquestionable ([41]).

The passage picturing El's mourning for Baal (*UT* 67 : VI : 11-23) is a striking example of Canaanite mourning customs. It is quoted here in Gaster's translation ([42]) :

> Thereupon the gentle-hearted El
> comes down from his throne and sits upon the footstool,
> and down from the footstool and sits upon the ground.
> Ashes (?) of mourning he strews upon his head,
> dust wherein mourners wallow on his pate ;
> for raiment he dons a loincloth.
> Then he wanders in mourning o'er the upland,
> in the manner of a ... through the woods.
> Cheek and chin he gashes ;
> he scores the forepart of his arm ;
> he furrows his chest as ' twere a garden,
> scores his back as ' twere a valley.
> he lifts his voice and cries :
> " Baal is dead ! "

Anat behaves in the same way ; moreover she descends into the nether world to retrieve the corpse of her brother Baal (*UT* 62 : 8-18) :

... *'mh.trd.nrt*	With her went down Shapash (the Sun),
ilm.špš.'d.tšb'.bk	the divine luminary while she sated herself with weeping,
10 *tšt.kyn.udm't.gm*	drank tears like wine. Aloud
tṣḥ.lnrt.ilm.špš	she cried to the divine luminary Shapash :
'ms m'.ly.aliyn b'l	" Load, pray, upon me the valiant Baal ! "
tšm'.nrt.ilm.špš	Shapash the luminary of the gods listened,

([37]) Dahood (in review B. Albrektson, *Studies ... Book of Lamentations* [Lund 1963]) *Bib* 44 (1963) 540.

([38]) Dahood, *Psalms* 35.

([39]) Below, pp. 83 f.

([40]) *WUS* 1038.

([41]) See also Dahood, *UHPh* 969a.

([42]) *Thespis* 212 f. ; see Jr 6,26 ; Lam 2,10 ; Ez 27,30. etc.

tšu aliyn.b'l.lktp	lifted up the valiant Baal on to the shoulders
15 *'nt.ktšth.tš'lynh*	of Anat. When she put him there, Anat
bṣrrt.ṣp(')n tbkynh	took him up to the recesses of the north ([43])
wtbqrnh.tštnn.bḫrt	and buried him; she wept for him, she put him in a hole of
ilm.arṣ...	the earth-gods.

This text offers a remarkable example of the necessity of burial for ancient peoples: even Baal, who stays in the nether world itself, cannot be in peace unless he is decently interred.

In lines 17 f., the " hole " obviously stands for the grave; consequently the " gods " are chthonic deities or ghosts of the dead ([44]). It is hard to render *arṣ* adequately here, as its meaning seems to be floating between earth and nether world. The idea is that Baal, who died as a man does, must be buried properly to be well at home in Mot's kingdom, as is true for man.

Meanwhile Baal's throne is vacant; the terrible Athtar is appointed Baal's successor, but unfortunately his stature proves too small. The text continues (*UT* 49 : I : 35-37) :

yrd.'ṭtr.'rẓ.yrd	And the terrible Athtar came down, came down
lkḫṭ.aliyn.b'l	from the throne of the valiant Baal
wymlk.barṣ.il.klh	and became king on earth, god of it all.

Dahood proposes to render *arṣ* by " nether world " in this text, as the interpretation which takes *arṣ* for simple " earth " " overlooks the consideration that this was Baal's domain " ([45]).

It is not obvious, however, that Athtar, simply because of his incapacity to occupy Baal's throne, supplants Mot from his dais in the nether world ! It seems more likely that the text says how Athtar leaves the heights of the Canaanite Olympus to exercise on earth a more limited degree of sovereignty ([46]).

([43]) On " recesses " see below, pp. 181 f.
([44]) " The grave as a hole in the ground is part of the domain of the earth-gods " (Van Selms, *Marriage* 131). For the importance of burial, see Heidel, 155-166.
([45]) Dahood, *Psalms* 111.
([46]) Gaster, *Thespis* 218 f.

Anat longs for her brother. " She grasps Mot by the hem of his robe, holds him tight by the edge of his cloak, then she lifts her voice and cries : " Thou Mot, surrender my brother ! " But the godling Mot keeps retorting : " What is it that thou art asking of me, O Virgin 'Anat ? " ([47]).

But Anat cannot be put off with fair words. When the opportunity presents itself, she grasps Mot again, but now less peacefully (*UT* 49 : II : 30-35) :

30	... *tiḫd*	She seizes
	bn.ilm.mt.bḥrb	the divine Mot; with a sword
	tbqʿnn.bḫṯr.tdry	she rips him up; in a sieve she scatters([48])
	nn.bišt.tšrpnn	him; in a fire she burns him;
	brḥm.tṯḥnn.bšd	with two millstones she grinds him; over the
35	*tdrʿnn.* ...	fields she strews him....

This description can hardly be dissociated from harvest customs, found in many ancient or primitive cultures (see J. G. Frazer and T. H. Gaster, *The New Golden Bough* [Garden City 1961] 243-253). In the harvest season " the corn-spirit is slain, either in the cut corn or in the human representative " (*ibid.* 250), and in the latter case often in mimicry. The corn (i.e., the spirit) is cut, threshed, burnt, winnowed; human victims are hewn to pieces, killed " with hoes or spades or by grinding him between stones " (*ibid.* 248), ashes or other remnants are scattered on the fields, etc. In this way the human representative " is seized and treated as the corn-spirit himself " (*ibid.* 249).

UT 49 prompts the conclusion that Mot is taken for the spirit of the corn. This opinion was voiced by R. Dussaud, who wrote : " Donc Mot est l'esprit de la végétation, plus spécialement du blé " ([49]). He points to Lv 2,14 in this connection. Similarly Pedersen ([50]) and Albright ([51]). The latter writes : " In view of what we have said above about the fluidity of mythological conceptions among the Canaanites, as well as about the dual functions of such gods as Resheph, we may safely infer that Mot is also treated as though he were a god

---

[47] *UT* 49 : II : 9-14 ; Gaster, *Thespis* 221.

[48] Translation with Gaster, *Thespis* 221. The verb *dry* means : " to winnow, scatter, hack to pieces " (*UT* Gloss 702) ; the meaning of *ḫtr* derives from postbiblical *ḥšr*, " to sift " (*ibid.* 1027). Aistleitner (*WUS* 790) and Driver (*CMAL* 111) agree with Gaster.

[49] *RHR* 52 (1931) 309.

[50] *Israel* III/IV 794.

[51] *ARI* 86 f.

of fertility ". More explicitly Kapelrud ([52]): " He [Mot] represents the dry season of the year, summer, with its drought, but also with the ripening fruit and corn ". In other words, " the god of the under-world was at the same time a chthonic deity, that is, he was the lord of the ground and of its productive faculties " ([53]). In Egypt Osiris is treated in the same way ([54]).

This position is supported by the evident affinity of Mot and Tammuz which appears in a tenth century text by Ibn en Nedim: " The women bewail him, because his lord slew him so cruelly, ground his bones in a mill, and then scattered them to the wind " ([55]).

Greek Adonis is closely related to Tammuz; the self-mutilating Eshmen belongs to the same category ([56]). Similar dual functions are found in Osiris, king of the dead and god of fertility ([57]) and others ([58]). As to Mot's relation to Baal, Kapelrud notes : " He [Baal] and Mot alternated in the same way as, for instance, the perennial antagonists Horus and Seth in Egyptian religion " ([59]).

Similar motifs occur in biblical texts and may have the same background; see Ps 141,7; Is 29,5; 41,15 f.; perhaps also Ps 1,4; 35,5; Jb 21,18. Gaster quotes an Accadian curse saying: " May he kill thee like death, and grind thee in a mill " ([60]).

Baal, alive again, takes his revenge (*UT* 49 : V : 1-4) :

yiḫd.b'l.bn.aṯrt	Baal seized the sons of Athirat ;
rbm.ymḫṣ bktp	he smote the mighty One with a sword,
dkym.ymḫṣ.bṣmd	smote the Pounder with a mace ;
ṣḥr mt.ymṣi.larṣ	and Mot did gape open that they might go right into the nether world.

Unfortunately the translation of the last line is far from cer-tain; in fact Driver stands alone in this interpretation ([61]). The affin-ity of the picture with Old Testament representations of Sheol is obvious ([62]).

([52]) *Discov.* 49.
([53]) *ARI* 81.
([54]) Frazer–Gaster, *New Golden Bough* 250 f.
([55]) J. G. Frazer, *Adonis, Attis, Osiris. Studies in the History of Oriental Religion* (London 1906) 131; cp. Gray, *Legacy* 57 f.
([56]) Dussaud, *RHR* 52 (1931) 407.
([57]) Frazer, *Adonis* 280 f.
([58]) Dussaud, *art. cit.* 407
([59]) *Discov.* 49.
([60]) *Thespis* 224 note.
([61]) *CMAL* 113B.
([62]) Cf. below, pp. 26 f. etc.

Finally Baal and Mot come to close quarters with each other; the latter gets the worst of it.

A small fragment in *UT* 52 (Shachar and Shalim) again connects Mot with agriculture:

mt.w šr.yṯb.	Death-and-Rot sits:
bdh.ḫṭ.ṯkl.	in his hand the rod of bereavement,
bdh/ḫṭ.ulmn.	in his hand the rod of widowhood [63];
yzbrnn.zbrm gpn	they prune him, those pruning the vine;
yṣmdnn.ṣmdm.gpn.	they bind him, those binding the vine.
yšql.šdmth/km.gpn	He is felled in his field (*šdmth*) like the vine [64].

Powerless Mot is here identified with the vine, which is harshly treated in spring in order to be fruitful afterwards. For our purpose it is significant that the word *šdmt* here indicates a barren field and contains a clear allusion to Mot and his condition [65].

The *waw* in Death and Dissolution apparently is an appositional one, the second word being a further qualification of the first one [66]. It is remarkable that biblical Abaddon, which is equivalent to Ugaritic *šr*, is used in a similar way [67].

It would not be correct to say that the Baal-cycle does not yield any information as to human death and beyond on the grounds that it directly concerns only such natural processes as rain and drought. One may safely maintain that on the one hand man serves as a model for Baal's vicissitudes, while on the other hand Baal himself looks like a personification of man's fears and hopes. In the words of Eissfeldt: " Aller Wahrscheinlichkeit nach kommt hier noch Tieferes zum Ausdruck, nämlich der Jammer über des Menschen Vergänglichkeit und der Jubel über sein erhofftes Wiederaufleben, für das der Naturvorgang Symbol und Gewähr ist " [68].

Another piece of evidence about death is found in the legend where Danel is playing the leading part; and, although the boundaries between human and divine are obscure in this case, there certainly

[63] Cp. Is 47,9.

[64] 52:8-11; thus H. Kosmala, *ASTI* 3 (1964) 147-151. Dr. Kosmala kindly sent me an offprint of his article.

[65] See below, pp. 50-53.

[66] Albright, *BASOR* 164 (1961) 36.

[67] See below, pp. 80 f.

[68] *TLZ* 64 (1939) 404.

is a strong influence of human customs and conceptions.   Danel bewails
Aqhat (*UT* 1 Aqht: 146-151):

... *ybky.wyqbr*	He weeps and buries him;
yqbr.nn.bmdgt.bknrt	he buries him in a dark place in a linen shroud ([69]);
wy šu.gh.wyṣḥ.knp.nšrm	and he lifts up his voice and cries:
b'l.yṯbr b'l.yṯbr.diy	" May Baal break the wings of the eagles;
hmt.hm.t'pn.'l.qbr.bny	their pinions may he break, if they fly over the grave of my son
t šḥṭann.b šnth.	and disturb him in his sleep " ([70]).

The categories " dark place " and " sleep " will return in the
same sense in the Old Testament ([71]).

A graphic description of the transition from this world to the
other is found in *UT* 76: II: 24 f., where Baal tells his sister Anat
that he has conquered his enemies and will return to power:

nṭ'n.barṣ.iby	We have planted my enemies in the nether world,
wb'pr.qm.aḫk	those rising up against your brother in the dust.

The pair *arṣ-'pr* in this context clearly has its ominous connotation as in quite a few Hebrew texts.

The form *nṭ'n* is easily recognised as a first person plural qatal
of *nṭ'*, to plant ([72]).   This conception of human death is also found
in biblical Hebrew ([73]).

Moreover it is interesting to notice how the first person singular
possessive suffix in the first line is balanced by " your brother " in
the second; this form of gallant modesty stresses the fraternal relations
between Baal and his sister.   The same reserve is found in the cour-
teous plural of the first line.

[69] *knrt*, " shroud ": Gray, *Legacy* 86 ; Driver, *CMAL* 63 ; *knkn*, " urn "
UT Gloss 1268, *WUS* 1340.
[70] *ḫṭ*: *UT* Gloss 951.
[71] Cf. below, pp. 95 ff. and pp. 185 ff.
[72] *UT* Gloss 1643, differently, *CMAL* 151A and *WUS* 1123, Dahood
(*Psalms* 3) follows Gordon.
[73] Cf. below, pp. 171 f.

Unfortunately the passage about Keret's burial in *UT* 125 : 87-89
is too badly damaged to yield any certain sense ([74]); in the same cycle
Sha'taqat appears as an adversary of illness and death (*UT* 127 : 1 ff.).
The name of this goddess means : " She-who-causes-(sickness)-to-pass-
away ", or, with Aistleitner : " Who prolongs old age " ([75]). In 127 : 1 f.
she is ordered :

mt.dm.ḫt.š'tqt dm	Truly, Death, be scattered ; truly, Sha'taqat,
li.	be victorious !

In Ugaritic literature two demons appear that are associated
with the nether world.
The first is Ḥoron, " the one of the pit ", i.e., of the nether world ([76]).
He is mentioned at the end of the Legend of Keret, where the king
addresses this remark to his rebellious son : " May Ḥoron break, O my
son, may Ḥoron break thy head ! " (127 : 55 f.). The name of this
god " appears in Canaanite personal and place-names from *ca.* 1900
B.C. to 600 B.C. ", as Dahood writes ([77]). Scholars disagree as to the
exact nature of this god. According to some, he was a god of life
and death ; " we note in this connection ", Gray remarks, " that in
the vicinity of Beth-Horon there was a site Yirpeel ' God heals ' (Jos
18,27) " ([78]). Others consider Ḥoron as a chthonic deity, " a virtual
equivalent of Rešep, who in turn is the West-Semitic counterpart of
Babylonian Nergal, the god of the plague and the nether world " ([79]).
In a new text we read that Ḥoron flies the City of Shapash to
take refuge in the country Aršh, where he seeks to obtain recovery.
The text then runs :

ydy b'ṣm 'r'r w bšḫt 'ṣ mt.

This is rendered by Virolleaud : " (Là), il arrache d'entre les arbres
le *'r'r*, et, de la *šḫt*, l'arbre de mort " ([80]).

([74]) Compare Van Selms, *Marriage* 132 with Driver, *CMAL* 42 f. (II : ii :
25 ff.).
([75]) First interpretation : Gordon, *UT* Gloss 1938, ; second : *WUS*, 2661.
([76]) Dahood, *Ancient Semitic Deities* 82 f. ; Albright, *ARI* 81.
([77]) Dahood, *Ancient Semitic Deities* 83.
([78]) Gray, *Legacy* 133.
([79]) Dahood, *Ancient Semitic Deities* 82 ; see Gaster, *Thespis* 155 ; Albright,
ARI 80 f.
([80]) *Comptes rendus du Groupe Linguistique d'Études Chamito-Sémitiques* 10
(1963-66) 64 ; also *Comptes Rendus de l'Académie des Inscriptions et des Belles
Lettres* (1962) 108.

Biblical ʿrʿr, " Juniper " [81], suggests that the Ugaritic word stands for some desert plant, which squares well with the context.

Difficulties start with the second colon. Parallelism suggests that šḫt balances ʿṣm and, consequently, that ʿṣ mt is on a level with ʿrʿr. Virollaud, with a reference to Accadian šaḫatu (some plant), obtains the translation he proposes : he remarks that the sterilized god looks for healing in trees which are related to drought and death. Gordon identifies šḫt with biblical šaḥat, " pit ", but the result for the inter-pretation of the bicolon is doubtful, unless, with Dahood, one explains ʿṣ in the first colon as " hole ", this in the light of Ps 10,10 [82]. The uncertainty of the latter proposal justifies a reluctance to accept this solution, although it obtains a perfect parallelism. Anyway, the vicinity of Ḥoron, and the tree of death, and, possibly, the Pit, is a remarkable fact. It is in keeping with our knowledge of this god.

Finally we mention Resheph, the Canaanite god of war, pesti-lence, and underworld [83]. Here again we find the " tendency to bring opposites together " [84] : " he is both the god of the plague and of well-being " [85]. In *UT* 1001 : 3 he is characterized as *bʿl ḥẓ ršp*, " Resheph, the lord of the arrow ", and in 128 : II : 6 as *ršp zbl*, " Prince Resheph ". His activity is summarized in Krt 19 :

yitsp. ršp. mṯdṯ   Pestilence gathered to himself a fifth.

Several traces of his presence will be discovered in the Old Testa-ment [86].

[81] *KB* 735A, 738A.
[82] Private communication, July 8, 1967.
[83] Gray, *Legacy* 96, n. 2 ; Albright, *ARI* 79 f. ; Dahood, *Ancient Semitic Deities* 83-85, etc. Resheph is closely related to Nergal.
[84] Albright, *ARI* 80.
[85] Dahood, *Ancient Semitic Deities* 84.
[86] See index s.v.

PART I. NAMES AND EPITHETS OF SHEOL

Chapter 1 : LOCAL ASPECTS

1. Sheol

Sheol is " ein den Israeliten eigentümliches Wort für das Totenreich " [1] ; the common north-west Semitic word is *'ereṣ*.

" Sheol " does not occur in Ugaritic, Phoenician, and Punic ; Aramaic literature yields one example only, in the Papyri Blacassiani, probably dating from the fifth century B.C. [2].

As to Accadian, M. Jastrow pointed to the word *šu'alû* occurring four times in a lexicographical text and, with high probability, referring to the nether world [3]. A possible allusion to this name was discovered in an Accadian curse from Ras Shamra [4].

In Arabic the term is unknown.

In the Old Testament " Sheol " is the most common name for the beyond [5]. Its etymology is a matter of dispute [6]. Jastrow derived the Accadian word from the verb *š'l*, which both in Accadian

---

[1] *GB* 796B ; this statement remains fundamentally true.

[2] *wgrmyk l' yḥtwn š'l*, " ossa tua non descendant in orcum " : *CIS* II, t. 1, p. 152, text 145 B 6. The date is proposed by Albright, private letter Nov. 16, 1965.

[3] " The Babylonian Term *šu'alû* ", *AJSL* 14 (1897-1898) 165-170. (Devastating criticism by Heidel, 173). The rare occurrence of the word is ascribed to " the desire to avoid terms that conveyed an ill omen ". The same supposition for Hebrew individual laments is made by Gunkel (*Einleitung Pss* 185-188) and Barth (*Errettung* 111). Gunkel makes a double reservation : psalmists only use the word when they feel themselves approaching Sheol or where they pray not to be delivered to it. These restrictions weaken this explanation seriously and moreover the contrast with individual thanksgiving psalms is false : Sheol occurs four times in the latter, but at least with the same frequency in the former (Pss 6,6 ; 88,4 ; 89,49 ; 141,7.) ; so it is hardly correct to contrast IL and Ith in this respect.

[4] *Palais Royal d'Ugarit III*, 16.157, quoted by Dahood, *Psalms* 212.

[5] More than 60 occurrences.

[6] Recent attempts : L. Koehler, " Alttestamentliche Wortforschung : *sch^{e}'ōl* ", *TZ* 2 (1946) 71-74 ; W. Baumgartner " Zum Etymologie von *sch^{e}'ōl* ", *ibid.* 233-235 ; H. Ferenczy's dissertation : " Scheol. Eine Untersuchung des Begriffs " (Wien 1963) remained inaccessible to me.

and in Hebrew denotes a " religious enquiry ". This interpretation
is supported by Accadian *ḫuršān*, meaning " place of the ordeal " and
" nether world " ([7]). For the Hebrew word, the same etymology
was proposed by Ed. König, who defined it in this way : " Befragung,
metonymisch für Stätte der Befragung " ([8]).

Several modern scholars have taken his side. According to Gaster,
š'l is a *terminus technicus* for questioning a witness in a court of law ;
Eissfeldt defines it as a *terminus technicus* for " making an investigation " ([9]). So Albright writes with good reason : " ... Canaanite-
Hebrew *še'ôl* seems to have etymologically denoted ' examination,
ordeal ' and then ' nether world ' ". And he adds that, in his opinion,
ša'al " was originally the name of an underworld god, presumably
connected with the ordeal of death " ([10]).

This statement accords with the fact that Sheol is used without
the article as a proper name ([11]) ; as, however, it is feminine, the conclusion should be that *ša'al* was a goddess ([12]).

If a plausible etymology for " Sheol " is to be found in this way,
it is necessary to acknowledge the limitations of the result. First
of all, biblical evidence does not show that the Israelites were conscious
of the original meaning of the word : the judgment of the dead in
Sheol is not mentioned in the OT ([13]).

([7]) The import of this word in Accadian and Ugaritic is discussed by M. Pope
El in the Ugaritic Texts 69-71 ; see also von Soden, in *ZA* 51 (1955) 140 f. ;
Albright, in *JBL* 75 (1956) 257 ; *UT*, Gloss. 1018 ; Tallqvist, *Namen* 23.

([8]) E. König, *Hebr. and Aram. Handbuch zum AT* (2nd-3rd. ed. ; Leipzig
1922) 474B.

([9]) T. H. Gaster, " Short notes " (*VT* 4 [1954] 73-79) 73 ; O. Eissfeldt,
" The Alphabetical Cuneiform Texts from Ras Shamra Published in PRU "
(*JSS* 5 [1960] 1-49) 49 ; Dt 13,15 ; cp. Esdr 5,9 f. ; Elephantine (Cowley 16 : 3 ;
20 : 8, etc.) ; add Ps 35,11.

([10]) Albright, letter ; cp. *JBL* 75 (1956) 257 ; Gaster, in *IDB* I 787A.

([11]) Cp. Martin-Achard, *From Death* ... 37 ; of course the article appears
rather late in Hebrew : the first examples belong to the tenth century, and
in the more conservative poetical and liturgical language, much later still. But
biblical Sheol never has an article.

([12]) Sheol is apparently feminine in Is 5,14 ; 14,9 ; and Ps 86,13. Jb 26,6 does
not prove the contrary, as the adjective precedes it ; cp. G. R. Driver, " Hebrew
Studies ", *JRAS* 1948, 164-76 ; in Is 14,9 the logical subject of b-c is masculine.
In Scandinavian mythology also Hell is a goddess. She is a daughter of Loki,
the god of evil, and of Angurbuda, the prophetess of misery ; she is a sister of
the ominous animals Serpent and Wolf, which in Semitic thinking also are akin
to Death (see I : 3 : 3). Hell reigns as a queen in Niflheim (" Foghome ").
See Guerber, 178.

([13]) Jb 31,6 is an allusion to a judgment by Yahweh ; see the illustration
in the Egyptian Totenbuch, *ANEP*, fig. 639.

Here the remarks of J. Barr should be kept in mind : " Etymology is not ... a guide to the semantic value of words in their current usage ", or at least, not necessarily so : " It is quite wrong to suppose that the etymology of a word is necessarily a guide to its ' proper ' meaning in a later period or to its actual meaning in that period " ([14]).

A solid conclusion on the point is hindered by the fact that it is not clear how far Hebrew " Sheol " is related to the Accadian word, nor when it was introduced in Israel : we can say that the word is used there as soon as the thought of the beyond becomes operative in the Bible. As its occurrence presupposes some degree of reflection on the after-life, it seems in the nature of things that the word " Sheol " is more frequent in poetical literature (Psalms, Proverbs, Job, Isaiah) than in the historical books.

Finally, it is not clear why the word, used only exceptionally in Semitic languages, became predominant in Israel.

1.2 'ereṣ (The Nether World)

On the basis of Accadian *erṣetu* meaning " nether world " ([15]), Gunkel, in 1895, recognized *'rṣ* with the same sense in Ex 15,12 ; Is 14,12 ; and Qoh 3,21 ; he also found it in the phrase *taḥtîyôt 'āreṣ* ([16]). Dhorme referred to the Accadian word and Greek *chthôn* to justify the same interpretation for 1 S 28,13 (which occurrence he called a " terme technique ") and Is 26,19 ([17]). *GB* refers to Gunkel but applies this meaning to Jb 10,21 f. only ; *BDB* adds Ps 139,15 and Is 44,23 ([18]). In 1917 W. Baumgartner proposed five more examples ([19]).

The discovery of Ugaritic literature gave a new impetus to this tendency. It appeared that the new language has no word *š-'-l,* but uses *'rṣ* as a name for the nether world ; obviously this is the proper term in North-West Semitic ([20]). A few characteristic examples may be quoted here ([21]) :

UT 51 : VIII : 5-14 reads in Pope's translation :

> Descend to the charnel house of the nether world (*arṣ*).
> Be counted among those who go down into the earth (*arṣ*) ([22]).

([14]) J. Barr, *Semantics* 107-109.
([15]) *CAD* 4 E, 310 ; see Tallqvist, *Namen der Totenwelt* 4,8-16 ; Zandee, 96 ascertains the same double meaning for Egyptian *tȝ*.
([16]) *Schöpfung und Chaos* 18, n. 1.
([17]) *RB* 4 (1907) 61 f.
([18]) *GB* 68A sub 7 ; *BDB* 76A, sub 2. g.
([19]) *BZAW* 32 (1917) 40 : Ps 22,30 ; 71,20 ; 143,3 ; Jon 2,7 ; Sir 51,9.
([20]) See above, pp. 21 ff.
([21]) More examples are listed by Driver, *CMAL* 135B.
([22]) Earth, i.e. nether world.

> Then, indeed, set face
> (Toward El's son Mot),
> Midst his city " Slushy ".
> Ruin is the throne where he sits,
> Infernal filth (*ḫḫ arṣ*) his inheritance ([23]).

In this short fragment *arṣ*, "nether world", occurs no fewer than three times; it is beyond dispute that *arṣ* stands for the domain of Mot.

> *UT*: Aqhat 111 f. runs:
> I shall weep and bury him,
> I shall put him in a hole of the earth-gods (*ilm arṣ*) ([24]).

Here it is evident that by *ilm arṣ* the chthonic or infernal gods are meant.

> *UT* 76 : II : 24 f. reads:
> We have planted my foes in the nether world (*arṣ*),
> and the mud (*'pr*) those who rose up against
> your brother ([25]).

Here it is important to notice the parallelism between " earth " and " mud ", which is also found in the OT.

In view of this evidence a more frequent usage of *'rṣ* in this sense may be expected in the OT. In fact more than 20 occurrences have been found and proposed by biblical scholars ([26]).

Strangely enough this development is ignored in the lexicon of Koehler (1958) and also by Gordon in four successive editions of his glossary (1940-1965). Recently F. Gössman has taken their side; he writes: " Im Gegensatz zu Babylon (*irṣitu*) und Ugaritic (*'rṣ*) bezeichnete ... in Israel das Wort *'aeraeṣ* allein nur die Erdoberflache " ([27]).

This statement has the merit of formulating clearly what in the past was commonly thought of as the only meaning of the word. For the rest the present writer doubts whether Gössman is right; this may

---

([23]) Pope, *Job* 73.
([24]) Driver, *CMAL* 63 ; Van Selms, *Marriage and Family Life* 131.
([25]) Dahood, *Psalms* 144.
([26]) Barth, *Errettung* 83 ; U. Cassuto, *Commentary on Exodus* (Jerusalem 1951) 22 ; *JNES* 14 (1955) 247 ; Gray, *Legacy* 193 ; Martin-Achard, *From Death...* 38 ; Dahood, *Bib* 40 (1959) 165 f. ; *id.*, *Job.* 61 ; *id.*, *Psalms* 106 ; *id.*, *Prov.* 52, n. 1 ; Schmid *RGG*³ VI, 912 ; Eichrodt, *TAT* II, 58.
([27]) *Augustinianum* 5 (1965) 204. In view of parallelism, Semitic poetry cannot do with just a single word.

appear from the title of the first part of this study, which counters
his assumption that for Hebrew " das bequeme und eindeutige Wort
Šeʾôl " was sufficient, and from the following analysis of texts where
ʾrṣ = " nether world " is said to occur.

Gn 2,5 f. (Cross–Freedman) :

> There was no man to till the ground and to lift the primordial
> river from the " earth " and to water the whole surface of
> the ground ([28]).

It would hardly make sense here to understand ʾrṣ = earth with
F. Gössmann as denoting " surface of the earth " only : the water is
to be taken *from* the earth for the irrigation of the surface of the ʾădāmâ,
i.e. the ground as " tilled, yielding sustenance " ([29]). Apparently
water is not found on the surface here : it is to be lifted " to it " from
a deeper level. It is also clear that the ʾēd is not flowing on earth
(cp. v. 10 ff.) but in it.

This text is good example of the connotations of ʾrṣ : it denotes
the whole structure which is covered by the surface as by a roof and
at whose other extreme are the subterranean waters.

" Earth " comprises the massive reality, in all its layers, which
is under our feet. In general this is not true for ʾădāmâ. Moreover
we see here, that this " earth " can have a merely " cosmological "
meaning, without any reference to the abode of the dead ([30]).

Ex 15,12 (Gunkel) :

> Thou didst stretch out thy right hand :
> the underworld swallowed them.

On a divine command the " earth " opens its mouth and devours the
Egyptians. To all appearances, the enemy vanishes into the sea,
is swallowed by the waves ; these billows, however, acquire extraordinary dimensions and become " mighty waters " (15,10 and *infra*).
In the hymnic description this is the end of the Egyptians ; they were

---

([28]) *wayyăʿălê* is understood as hiphil ; for the interpretation of ʾēd see
Albright, quoted by W. Kaiser, *Bedeutung des Meeres* 101 f.

([29]) *BDB* 9B.

([30]) Where " nether world " is merely understood as the " ground level "
of the universe (consisting of heaven–earth–underworld), the chaotic part of
the world, this conception is called " cosmological " ; where there is also a reference to the abode of the dead, the epithet " anthropological " is used. Cp.
Reymond, " L'eau " 201.

covered by the sea, the waters of chaos, i.e. they were swallowed by the nether world: they are in the land of no return [31].

In fact there is a correspondence between Ex 14,21b (where the sea is drained by a strong wind: J, cp. 15,8) and 15,10 (the sea returns because of Yahweh's mighty breath). The same remark applies to 14,21a.26 (the sea is divided by the outstretched hand of Moses: E) and 15,6.12 (according to which the outstretched right hand of Yahweh causes the "earth" to swallow the enemies). So both the causing and the removal of the "path through the mighty waves" are described in two corresponding ways signifying one and the same event. Consequently the mighty waters (15,10) must be identical with the 'rṣ (v. 12) and the latter cannot be understood as referring to the mere surface of the earth.

Num 16,30-32:

30   If the ground ('ădāmâ) opens it mouth (pāṣ'tâ .. 'et-pîhā) and
      swallows them up (bl')
      and they go down alive into Sheol
      then you shall know that these men have despised Jahweh.
31   And as he finished speaking ... the ground under them
      split asunder;
32   and the earth ('rṣ)
      opened its mouth (ptḥ)
      and swallowed them up.

Here we find 'rṣ and 'dmh as equivalents (vv. 30.32; cp. Dt 11,6); the expressions "opens its mouth" and "swallows" imply that this reality has been personified: the earth is a voracious monster. This strongly reminds us of Ugaritic representations of Mot with his jaws reaching to earth, his lips to heaven and his tongue to the stars [32]:

      Come not near to Mot son of El,
      let him not make you like a sheep in his mouth ... [33].

There is an obvious difference: in Nu 16 the earth, not Mot, opens its mouth. In this respect the OT is consistent. It may be argued

---

[31] The motif of "the land of no return" will be discussed below (cf. pp. 189 f.).

[32] UT 67: II : 1 ff. (see above, p. 9).

[33] UT 51: VIII : 15 ff.; cp. the description of Mot's appetite in 67: I: 5-8. (See above, pp. 7 and 8).

that, in Nu 16,30, the " ground " is not identical with Sheol, as it apparently constitutes a higher level: because the " ground " clears the way Dathan *cum suis* can go down to " Sheol ". On the other hand the personification of the ground (" mouth ", " swallow up ") brings out its affinity with Sheol ([34]).

UT 67 : I : 6 f. in fact suggests that to go down and to be swallowed imply going the same way, and an infernal way at that:

Truly, I have gone down into the throat of divine Mot.

As in Ugaritic texts one is swallowed by Mot's mouth to go down his throat and to enter his stomach, so here the Ground opens its muzzle (which logically is continued by other members !), gulps its victims down to receive them in its belly, here called Sheol. " The pit ... was imagined as a vast subterranean cave with a narrow mouth like a well " (G. A. Cooke, *Ezekiel* in ICC [1936] 293). The continuity between ground and nether world is undeniable; this connotation of " ground " should not be overlooked. There is a striking affinity between Nu 16,30 ff. and Ex 15,12 (*'rṣ; bl'*).

The same conception is found in Gn 4,11:

Now you (Cain) are cursed from the ground (*'dmh*),
which has opened its mouth to receive your brother's blood.

For the equation *'rṣ-'dmh* = nether world, compare also the goddess's name *'edom* = *'arṣay*: The One of the Nether World ([35]).

1 S 28,11-13 (Dhorme):

Saul at Endor. The woman asks: " Whom shall I bring up for you ? " and soon she exclaims: " I see a ghost coming up out of the earth ". Twice *'lh* is used, in hiphil (v. 11) and qal (v. 13).

In that way the true shade of *'rṣ* is clear: the verb *'lh* quite naturally requires a *terminus a quo* on a deeper level; moreover the verb is often connected with Sheol and the like for indicating a process similar to that described here (cp. Ps 30,4, etc.). Apparently the starting-point must be identical: *'rṣ* = Sheol. As to this use with *'lh*, one might compare *yrd* connected with *'rṣ* (Jon 2,7).

Jonah 2,7 (Cross–Freedman):

Jon 2,1-7 is impregnated with conceptions of after-life; the expression relevant here runs:

([34]) See below, pp. 99 ff. (Sir Death); on *bl'*, see pp. 126 f.
([35]) This is the name of one of Baal's daughters; Dahood, " HULex ", *Bib* 45 (1964) 292; cp. Cross, *HTR* 55 (1962) 46 f.

> I went down to *hā'āreṣ* whose bars
> closed upon me for ever.

Both the connection with *yrd* and the context firmly establish that *'rṣ* stands for the nether world. Besides, " the bars " of the country strongly indicates an interpretation which understands *'rṣ* as Sheol, " la città dolente " (Inferno III, 1) with its fortified walls (cp. Jr 15,7). So it seems preferable to translate :

> I went down to the nether world whose
> bars closed upon me for ever.

Is 14,12 (Gunkel) :

> How you are fallen from heaven,
> brilliant star [36], son of Dawn !
> How you are cut down to the nether world,
> you who laid the nations low !

In this way the king of Babylon is welcomed in Sheol by the choir of his fellow kings. The meaning of *'rṣ* is made clear by the parallel 11a : " Your Eminence is brought down to Sheol ! " and is required by the opposition within v. 12. The overbearing tyrant is brought low : toppled from the heights to the depths of the universe.

Is 21,9 :

> Babylon is fallen, is fallen ;
> and all the graven images of her gods
> he hath broken unto the ground. (KJ)

According to Cross–Freedman, *'rṣ* " ground ", stands for the nether world here. This implies that they think the usual translation less satisfactory. There is no difficulty, however, in *'rṣ* meaning " surface of the earth " [37] ; and the preposition *l^e* connected with it is quite normal in the sense of " down to the earth " [38]. As *šbr*, strictly speaking, does not denote a movement, it is to be taken pregnantly, in this way : " the idols are smashed and thrown down to the earth " [39]. This makes good sense.

---

[36] " Brilliant star ", cp. P. Grelot, " Sur la vocalisation de *hyll* (Is. XIV 12) ", *VT* 6 (1956) 303 f. ; " Crescent Moon ", cp. *CMAL* 137B. Same opposition in Mt 11,23.

[37] *BDB* 76, *sub* 3 a.

[38] *Ibid.*, 511, *sub* 1 g.

[39] Or : " broken from top to bottom ".

Of course *'rṣ* is ambivalent and the nuance underworld may contribute to its effect in this text; but it is unlikely that this meaning is predominant. That translation would not remove any difficulties. The text does not show that the writer considered the idols as living beings that can be done to death.

Is 26,19 (Dhorme): *'āreṣ rᵉpā'îm tappîl*

Verse 19 is a short *Heilsorakel* announcing a return of the dead to life. The words quoted can be translated in different ways. *La Bible de Jérusalem* links *'rṣ* and *rp'ym*: " ... le pays des ombres enfantera "; RSV translates *npl* in the light of the preceding dew: " ... on the land of the shades thou wilt let it fall ".

We understand *npl* as in 18d, where its qal means " to be born " [40], and as *'rṣ* itself is a name for the nether world, *rp'ym* is better taken as the complement of the verb. In this way the translation reads: " ... the earth will give birth to the *rephaim* ".

It needs not to be argued that *'rṣ* means underworld here: it undoubtedly stands for the abode of the dead [41]. The association with Mother Earth is evident [42].

Is 29,4, part of a *Unheilsprophetie* announcing a siege of Jerusalem, describes the subsequent humiliation of the city in these words:

> Then deep from the earth you shall speak,
> from low in the dust your words shall come;
> your voice shall come from the earth like the voice of a ghost,
> and your speech shall whisper out of the dust.

The ominous connotation of this " earth " and " dust " in the first two cola is not only suggested by the adverb " deep ", which excludes a too superficial understanding of " earth " and calls for the interpretation " nether world ", but also by the latter two cola.

In fact the addition of v. 4b shows how spontaneously the pair " earth–dust " is associated with the thought of the dead. It seems evident that in this text " earth " is to be understood as the abode of the deceased.

---

[40] See *KB* 625, qal 5; hiph. 8.
[41] Dahood deriving *tpyl* from *npl = nbl*, " to wither " (cp. *id., Prov.* 24). Dahood reads: " For your dew is the dew of the fields, but the Land of the Shades will be parched " (*id., Psalms* 222 f.). I doubt if this is a better sense.
[42] Cp. below, pp. 122 ff.

Is 44,23 runs :

> Sing, heavens, for Yahweh has done it ;
> shout, o depths of the earth !

Here the opposite extremes of the universe represent its totality ; the whole world (cp. v. 24) is called to testify to the glorious deeds of its Creator in history ; there can be no doubt that here the totality, rather than the representative extremes themselves, is stressed [43]. If, therefore, the word 'rṣ itself stands for " nether world ", " depths of the earth " must denote its farthest extremity [44] which is the abode of the dead. But as in our text 'rṣ is used in a cosmological sense, it seems preferable to understand it as " earth ", the compound referring to the nether world. For these reasons this text should not be interpreted as an invitation to the dead to praise Yahweh [45].

Jer 15,7 (Dahood) [46] :

> I have winnowed them with a winnowing fork
> at the gates of the nether world.

In the preceding verse Yahweh threatens his people with total destruction ; this thought is set forth in v. 7. The process of winnowing (Jr uses the verb zrh) is found in connection with death in *UT* 49 : II : 30 ff [47].

It is not easy to establish the relation between Jr 15 and the Ugaritic text ; indeed, the background of the former may be mythological, but this remains a mere possibility [48].

One might further argue that it is not customary for lands to have gates and that consequently the current translation " gates of the land " is a surprising phrase. On the basis of Sheol being represented as a fortified city [49], the interpretation given above removes

---

[43] See A. M. Honeyman, " Merismus in Biblical Hebrew ", *JBL* 71 (1952) 11-18 ; P. Boccaccio, " I termini contrari come espressioni della Totalità in Ebraico ", *Bib* 33 (1952) 173-190.

[44] Below, pp. 180 ff.

[45] C. R. North interprets this verse thus : " The present passage is in line with Ps 139,7-9 where heaven and earth and sea, and Sheol are all within his domain ". (*Second Isaiah* [Oxford 1964] 143). See below, p. 197 ff. Our text is an affirmation of Yahweh's omnipotence.

[46] in *Bib* 40 (1959) 164 ff.

[47] See above, p. 14.

[48] The imagery may be merely agricultural.

[49] Below, pp. 152 ff.

this difficulty by rendering the phrase as " the gates of the nether world ".

In its turn, however, this new interpretation creates fresh difficulties. Apart from being uncertain, the relation to the Ugaritic myth does not contribute to a better understanding of the text. It is not clear what process at the gates of the nether world Jeremiah refers to.

As *'rṣ* itself also stands for " city ", i.e. " city-state " ([50]), it seems preferable to translate " gates of the city " and to understand the text as referring to the sentence which Yahweh will execute there, winnowing his people " in chastisement " ([51]).

A session of a court in the threshing floor at the gates of city is mentioned in 1 K 22,10.

Jr 17,13 (Baumgartner):

Those that turn away from him shall be enrolled in hell ([52]). RSV reads " shall be written in the earth ", an impressionistic saying, which could make sense as a symbol of complete oblivion, and so a prelude to a " name writ in water ".

It seems, however, that the prophet aims at a more terrible destination for the wicked; his intention must have been immediately clear to his hearers and less whimsical than the idea of persons written in the earth.

Dahood's main arguments for the proposed translation are the following. He compares Ps 88,5 : *nḥšbty 'm ywrdy-bwr* and 51 : VIII : 8 f. : *tspr byrdm 'arṣ* — " you will be reckoned among those who descend into the nether world ".

So we find the related verbs : *ḥšb – spr – ktb* ; so very likely the meaning of the expressions is similar as well. Moreover *ktb* has an eschatological connotation in :

Ez 13,9   They shall not be enrolled in the register of the house of Israel ;

Ps 69,29   Let them not be enrolled among the righteous ([53]).

([50]) Cp. Dahood, *Prov.* 62 ; *id.*, " HULex ", *Bib* 44 (1963) 297 f. Moreover E. C. John brought Nah 3,13 to my notice : " The gates of your city are wide open to your foes ; fire has devoured your bars " ; here TM has *'rṣ* for " city " also. For *UT* 1001, cp. below, p. 154.

([51]) *BDB* 279A, *ZRH* qal 2.

([52]) For the 3rd masc. sg. suffix -*y*, see F. M. Cross, Jr. – D. N. Freedman, " The Pronominal Suffixes of the third Person Singular in Phoenician ", *JNES* 10 (1951) 228-230 ; M. Dahood, " Qoheleth and Northwest Semitic Philology ", (*Bib* 43 [1962] 349-365) 353 ; other examples in Jr are 23,18 ; 31,3 ; 48,5.

([53]) Dahood in " The Value of Ugaritic for Textual Criticism " (*Bib* 40 [1959] 160-170) 165 f.

Ps 7,6 (IL) reads:

> Let the foe pursue and overtake me,
> Let him trample my vitals into the nether world,
> Let him cause my liver to dwell in the mud. (Dahood)

The psalmist, in a confession of his innocence, puts his sincerity to the test by summoning an enemy and invoking upon himself a violent and premature death.

The sinisterly anonymous enemy can be no other than Death himself: in spite of his innocence the psalmist avoids his ominous name [54]. No doubt *lā'āreṣ* primarily means " down to the earth, to the ground " [55], but in view of the self-imprecation it is likely that the nether world is referred to.

This supposition is backed up by the verb *škn*, which is currently used to describe the stay in Sheol [56] and by the parallel " dust ", a characteristic element there [57].

Ps 22,30 (IL):

> *'klw wy šṯḥww kl-dšny-'rṣ*
> *lpnyw ykr'w kl-yrdy 'pr.*

A good spring-board for an interpretation of this difficult verse is found in its second part. It can be rendered as follows:

> before Him will kneel all those who go down into the dust.

The expression *yrd 'pr* is clear; " dust " refers to the dust of the grave / nether world, a normal meaning of *'pr* (*GB* 608A). This is confirmed by related formulas [58]:

yrd š'wl: Ps 55,16: Let them go alive into Sheol (etc.).

---

[54] In Accadian incantations demons are often said to pursue their victims: Falkenstein – von Soden, B 49 : 11 (312); B 67 : 5 f. (340); B 70 : 8 (345).

[55] *BDB* 511A, sub lg.

[56] *BDB* 1015A, qal 2-b. Cp.: Ps 94,17 (*dûmâ*); Ps 139,9 (*'aḥărit yam*); Is 26,19 (*'pr*). For Ps 68,19b Dahood proposes: " But Yahweh God really entombed the stubborn ", interpreting the lamed as emphaticum and deriving *škn* from *miškān* " mansion, tomb " (see *id., Psalms* 299). The references given above in this note show that this etymology of *škn* as a denominative is hardly imperative. Of course *piel* must be read.

[57] See above, pp. 85 ff.

[58] In Ugaritic we find : *yrd arṣ* (*UT* 51 : VIII : 8 f.; 67 : VI : 26); *yrd bnpš bn ilm mt* (into the throat of divine Mot, 67 : I : 6 f.); *bph yrd* (into his mouth, 67 : II : 4).

> Jb 17,16 : It (my hope) will descend into the hands of
> Sheol, when we descend together upon the dust ([59]).

Here we notice the parallelism dust / Sheol.

yrd šḥt :   Ps 30,10 : What profit is there in my weeping ([60]),
> in my going down to the pit ?
> Will the dust praise thee ?

In this case " dust " is equivalent to *šḥt*, another name for the Beyond.
Consequently it seems right to put *yrd 'pr* on a par with *yrd šḥt*.

yrd bwr : occurs more than ten times ; it means " to go down to
the pit " and again refers to death : in Ez 26,20 it is identified with
'rṣ tḥtyt ; Ez 31,14 reads : " For they are all given over to *death*, to
the *nether world* among mortal men, with those who go down to the
Pit ".   Here again, parallelism is significant.

yrd 'l 'rṣ tḥtywt : Ez 32,24 ; 26,20.

yrd l'rṣ : This expression can safely be translated by " To go down
to the nether world " now ([61]). both in the light of the preceding expressions with *yrd* and of the meaning of the verb *yrd*, which supposes some level, lower than the starting-point.   Qoh 3,21 : " Who
knows whether the spirit of man goes upward and the spirit of the
beast goes down to the nether world ? "

We conclude that *yrd 'pr* means " to go down to the grave / the
nether world ".

The expression " all those going down ... " is not equivalent to
" all mortals ".   Compare Ps 88,5 where this interpretation would
be preposterous : " I am counted among those who went down into
the Pit ".   See also Is 38,18 :

> For Sheol cannot thank thee,
> those who go down to the pit cannot hope for thy faithfulness.
> The living, the living, he thanks thee .... (RSV)

Moreover these two examples, which could be multiplied ([62]), show
that instead of the vague and dubious present of some translations,

---

([59]) Dahood, *Job* 62.
([60]) For *dommî*, infinitive construct with pronominal suffix, from *dmm*,
" to weep ", see Dahood, *Psalms* 183 f. A close parallel is Is 38,10.
([61]) This is the common formula in Ugaritic and in Accadian. For the
latter cf. *ana irṣiti ūrīd*, " [Istar] descended into the nether world " (Tallqvist,
Namen der Totenwelt 9).   For *yrd dwmh* see below, p. 76.
([62]) See Westermann, *Loben Gottes* 120.

the participle is to be understood as referring to the past. The phrase *kol-yôrᵉdê ʿāpār*, as all related formulas, is a designation of the dead. For Is 38,18 this is beyond dispute because of the opposition to " the living ". And as to the background of Ps 88,5 it may suffice here to say that for the Israelite a diminution of life implies a real contact with Death ([63]).

This is relevant for the interpretation of the first colon. As parallelism is synonymous throughout this psalm, it is obvious to identify *'rṣ* in 30a with *ʿpr* in 30b; this is confirmed by the identical *kol* in both.

The exact import of " going down " rules out the translation " pingues terrae ", a doubtful hapaxlegomenon, which can hardly denote the reduced existence of the dead.

Tournay renders " ashes " as in Jr 31,40 (where, however, a singular form without any further determination is found); he explains it thus : " = mortui qui in et per posteritatem Deum laudant " ([64]).

The interpretation " ashes of the earth " is far from evident. It would seem desirable to look for a better translation of *dšny*.

The emendation to *yšny*, " those sleeping ", yields excellent sense, in perfect harmony with the biblical conception about the condition of the dead : the sleep of death is mentioned also in Ps 13,4 and Dn 12,2.

It is a question, however, if the emendation is necessary : we think that the text can be retained without altering the proposed meaning.

The form can be analysed as *d-šny*.

As to *d-*, Dahood adduces an " impressive list of dialectical pairs involving the *d-z* sounds " ([65]). So in this case *d-* may be considered identical with *z*, the demonstrative / relative pronoun *zû*, Ugaritic *d* (in a quadrilingual vocabulary vocalised as *du-û*), Aramaic *dî*, West Semitic *z-* ([66]).

Secondly the root *yšn* is really present here, but by contraction *y-* has disappeared. Dahood remarks : " The same phenomenon may

---

([63]) See below, pp. 129 ff. and 68 n. 213.

([64]) " Relectures bibliques concernant la vie future et l'angélologie " (*RB* 69 [1962] 481-505) 499 ff. ; P. Nober derives *dšn* from Accadian *dušmu*, " slave born in the house ", " Notae philologicae " (*VD* 39 [1961] 109-113), " Ps 22,30 : 'venae Inferorum' (?) " 111-113.

([65]) Dahood, *Job* 72.

([66]) For *zû* : *KB* 252 B ; for Ugaritic *d-* : Gordon, *UT* 632, p. 382 f. ; Driver, *CMAL* 153, n. 22 ; for West Semitic in general : Jean–Hoftijzer, 70 f.

be of greater frequency in the Bible than noted before ", and he quotes
Ugaritic *bd*, for *byd*, as in *UT* 68 : 13 *bd b'l*, " from the hands of Baal "([67])
and *wld* for *wayaladû* ([68]).   As to biblical usage he refers to Ps 16,4
mdm, " from my hands " ([69]) ; Is 1,27 *wšbyh* instead of *wyšbyh* (cp.
Ps 23,5) ; Is 37,27 *wbšw* for *wybšw* (cp. *BH* apparatus) ([70]).

It appears therefore that syncopation was not exceptional nor
restricted to fixed compounds.   As to the vowel sequence, we have
ay-a in *bd* ; *i-y-a* in *mdm* ; *a-y-ē* in *wbšw* ; *a-y-ô* in *wšbyh* ; here it
would be *î/û-y-ô*.

Ergo : " Yes, to him will bow down all those who sleep in the
nether world " ([71]).

In this way an all-encompassing choir is invited to sing Jahweh's
praise ; the community (v. 26), the poor (v. 27), the ends of the earth
(v. 28), the dead (v. 30), a people yet unborn (v. 31 f.).

" Sogar die Toten werden in die grosse Huldigung eingeschlossen.
Nun ... ist die Schranke (between dead and Jahweh) durchbrochen " ([72]).

Ps 41,3 (ITh) :

> May Yahweh protect him, give him long life, bless him.
> Into the nether world do not put him, into the maw of his
>   foe ! ([73])

This reading supposes that *'rṣ* is on a par with *npš*, etc. ; the *waw*
before *'al* is considered an emphaticum.   Dahood moreover argues
that the syllabic count is 6 : 8/8 : 6 ([74]).   Although the numbers look
rather like 6 : 7 / 8 : 7, this interpretation certainly obtains a perfect
balance between the two cola.

([67]) " ULex " *sub* 1166, 1241, *UHPh sub* 9.48.
([68]) Dahood, *Psalms* 88.
([69]) Dahood, *Psalms* 88.
([70]) *Ibid.* 148.
([71]) *'klw* is read *'ak lô* ; the wrong vocalization is quite understandable as
very often in ancient texts no matres were written at all, e.g. in 10th and 9th
century Phoenician and in the Gezer calendar : Cross–Freedman, *EHOrth* 14-
23, 46.   The following *waw* can be maintained as pleonastic, see P. Wernberg-
Møller " Pleonastic *waw* in classical Hebrew ", *JSS* 3 (1958) 321-326 ; L. Prijs
" Ein waw der Bekräftigung ? " in *BZ* 8 (1964) 105-109 and Dahood, *UHPh
sub* 13.103, p. 40.
([72]) Kraus, *Psalmen* I 183 ; cp. Gunkel, *Psalmen*⁴ 94.
([73]) Dahood, " HULex I ", *Bib* 44 (1963) 297.   See also C. Brekelmans,
" Pronominal Suffixes in the Hebrew Book of Psalms ", *JEOL* 17 (1963)
202-206.
([74]) Private communication.

There are serious difficulties, however. Not only is this emphatic
waw before the negative particle rather curious, but the construction
of the second colon seems somewhat laborious. In our opinion these
objections counterbalance the arguments in favour of the new reading.
Consequently we prefer to retain a more traditional interpretation:

> May Yahweh protect him, keep him alive;
> may he bless him on earth;
> do not put him into the maw of his Foe! ([75])

The division now is tripartite, the count being 6 : 4/3 : 3/5 : 6 :
the blessing of Yahweh is now the central element in the verse.

The third verb *y'šr* is read as a piel; indeed, it is more likely that
the three stand on a level. As the person in question is seriously
ill (v. 4) and consequently within the sphere of death, the wish is related to recovery. This situation justifies the translation of the final
words: *'ōy^ebāyw* is interpreted as a plurale excellentiae (for which see
the parallelism in Ps 18,4-5); for *npš* throat, consult the lexica ([76]),
and for ampler evidence see below ([77]).

Ps 44,26 (CL; Barth):

> Our soul is brought low, even unto the dust:
> our belly cleaveth unto the ground. (RP)

Those praying here are afflicted and oppressed and feel forgotten by
God (v. 25); the sentiment runs parallel with texts as Ps 88,4-8.
Of course the obvious sense of v. 26 is:

> We are " floored " by the enemy and
> shamefully lying in the sand;

but there is an undeniable suggestion of a deeper understanding. As
will be clearer after our treatment of *'pr*, the pair earth–dust has a
particularly ominous sound: those endangered feel that they are in
Sheol already, they become rigid in the grip of the Enemy:

> We are humiliated to the dust,
> our body is stuck in the nether world.

([75]) Cp. 67 : I : 6 f.: *lyrt bnpš bn ilm mt*: " In truth, I have gone down
into the maw of divine Mot " (Dahood).
([76]) *Zor* 527B, *sub* 7; *KB* 626B-27A.
([77]) Pp. 104 f.

See also the characteristic use of the verb *hrg* in v. 23 ([78]).

Ps 61,3 (IL; H. Schmidt):

> From the edge of the nether world I call to you
> when my courage fails.
> Onto a lofty rock lead me from it ([79]).

In his commentary on Psalms (1934) Schmidt translated: " Vom Ende der Unterwelt her ". He added: " Diese Bedeutung ist ... gerade in dem Klagegebet des Einzelnen, wie es hier vorliegt, zu erwarten ". Although the core of this pregnant exegesis was not made fully clear till Barth's study, to appear in 1947, it contains the decisive argument for the interpretation of *'rṣ* as " nether world " in this case. Elsewhere the phrase *miqᵉṣê hā'āreṣ* and its variants denotes an extreme distance on earth or a totality; Ps 61,3 is the only occurrence in an individual lament, and for that very reason a reference to the nether world is to be expected ([81]).

Several other considerations support this exegesis. One of them is given by Kraus, although he does not adopt Schmidt's view, where he writes: " Ṣûr als sicherer Platz, den die Wasser des Verderbens nicht erreichen, ist (mythologischer) Bezeichnung des Urgrundes und Benennung des heiligen Ortes " ([82]). In other words: there is a clear antithesis between the unsteady mire of the nether world and the safe rock.

In this light it is also reasonable to suppose that the enemy in v. 4 is the arch-enemy, Death, himself ([83]).

Finally in v. 5 " *sēter* " of Yahweh's wings is mentioned: this no doubt is another opposition to the nether world, which is also called a *sēter* ([84]).

Ps 63,10 (ITh; Barth):

> ... shall go down into the depths of the nether world.

See under Is 44,23 ([85]).

([78]) Cp. pp. 129 ff.
([79]) Cp. Dahood, *Psalms* 260.
([80]) H. Schmidt, *Psalmen* 116.
([81]) Cp. C. Barth, *Errettung*, and below, pp. 129 ff.
([82]) H. J. Kraus, *Psalmen* 433; below, pp. 205 ff.
([83]) Cp. below, pp. 110 ff.
([84]) Below, pp. 46 f.
([85]) Verse 11 runs: " They shall be given over to the power of the sword,

Ps 71,20 (IL; Barth):

RSV reads: " From the depths of the earth thou wilt bring me up again ". This, however, is a rather colourless rendering of TM *t^ehōmôt hā'āreṣ*; but most likely it is based rather on the apparatus of Kittel's *BH* (F. Buhl) than on TM.

But the " emendation " to *taḥtîyôt* is unnecessary and therefore cannot be justified; in fact, the nether world is very often portrayed as *t^ehôm* and the like, as will be shown below. Besides, the verb *'lh* (parallel: to revive) also belongs to the vocabulary of the Errettung aus dem Tode: consequently *'rṣ* is to be understood as " nether world " here.

Explaining the plural as a *plurale excellentiae*, we read:

> From the bottomless abyss of the nether world thou wilt bring me up again.

Ps 95,4 (Barth):

> In his hand are all the deep places of the earth:
> and the heights of the mountains are his also. (RP)

First of all there is no reason whatsoever to change *mḥqr* into *mrḥq* ([86]). *BDB* ([87]) correctly refers to Jb 38,16, " Have you walked in the recesses of the deep? ", where the same term (*bḥqr thwm*) serves to express the same conception. *BDB* translates *mḥqr* as " range (as place to be explored) "; the verb means " to search, explore ".

The expression used here is a polar one, like the opposition " sea — dry land " found in v. 5. Two extremes are put forward: the superlative height of the mountain peaks and the unfathomable depths of the nether world; the totality called " universe " is in Yahweh's power.

We translate:

> In his hands are the unfathomable depths of the nether world.

they shall be the prey for jackals ". These bicola refer to the execution of the psalmist's enemies (below, p. 181; Jb 15,22) and the shameful destination of their corpses (cp. Jr 7,33; Ps 44,20).

([86]) *KB* 514 B.

([87]) 350 B.

Though the reference is doubtless to the nether world, our translation may very well be a pleonasm; perhaps "depths of the earth"
should be read. The difference is negligible; in any case the continuity of earth and nether world is apparent.

Ps 106,17 (Barth):

> The earth opened and swallowed up Dathan,
> and covered the company of Abiram.

Compare Ex 15,12 and Num 16,30 ff.: Death, a rapacious monster,
is hidden behind "the earth" that opens its mouth and swallows
Dathan ([88]). The verb used is the characteristic *blʿ* ([89]).

Ps 141,7 (IL; Dahood):

> *kᵉmô pōlēaḥ ûbōqēʿa bāʾāreṣ*
> *nipzᵉrû ʿăṣāmênû lᵉpî šᵉʾôl*

The meaning of the line is not obvious. First the dubious elements
are analysed here:

([88]) The verb *ksh*, to cover, has a sinister connotation in this case. In a
paper, read at the Journées Bibliques de Louvain on August 24, 1967, Dahood
assumed the same meaning for Ps 143,9: *haṣṣîlênî mēʾoyᵉbay yhwh*; *ʾēlî kî
kussētî*; "Save me from my enemies, Yahweh; my God, truly I am covered".
The apparatus in *BH*³ sufficiently shows that the Masoretic pointing is not above
suspicion; St. Jerome apparently read *kussētî*, "protectus sum". Dahood recognizes in *yhwh ʾēlî* the poetic device of stereotyped phrases, broken up into their
two components (see Pss 69 f. etc.); moreover he obtains an expressive quad-
ruple succession of *kî* (8a; 8b; 9; 10). In this way a passage of real poetic
value is revealed by a sound interpretation of the Hebrew text. It must be
shown, however, that this meaning of *ksh* was so generally known as to be a
technical sense, recognizable in a discreet allusion as found in Ps 143,9. In
the present writer's opinion relevant examples are found in Ps 44,20 (CL):
"You covered us with total darkness" (*ṣalmāwet*); Ps 55,6 (IL): "Horror
covers me"; Ps 106,11: "The waters covered their adversaries" (cp. Ps 106,17;
Ex 15,5.10; and for chaos, Ps 104,6.9). Some difficulties are undeniable:
a) The particle *kî* is followed by an expression of confidence in the other
cases, v. 9b being an exception. b) It may be questioned if *ksh* really
belongs to the *Wortfeld* of death and the underworld. This last objection, however, may be answered by a reference to the numerous allusions to the nether
world occurring in vv. 3-7 and in general it must be acknowledged that strong
arguments are in favour of this happy interpretation of a difficult colon.
    ([89]) For Ps 139,15 see below, pp. 123 f.

$k^e m\hat{o}$: " when ", as in Gn 19,15 (*KB* 441 B). — *plḥ*: read *pelaḥ*, " mill-stone ". — *û*: pleonastic *waw*. — *bq'*: " to rip open ". For this verb, see 49 : II : 32 (⁹⁰), where the verb *bq'* in line 32 and the description in line 34 should be noticed ; both elements return in Ps 141,7. All this, however does not prove that *'rṣ* stands for " underworld " here. In view of the customs referred to above (⁹¹), it seems clear that the harsh treatment takes place on earth ; besides, the presence of millstones in the nether world is not mentioned elsewhere. — *'ṣmynw*: " their bones " (RSV ; RP). The suffix *-ynw* is 3rd person plural in : 2 K 22,13 : " Written upon it " (TM *'ālênû*) ; Jb 24,24 " They are exalted a moment, and are gone " (⁹²), where TM has *w^e'ênennû*. Perhaps this form is related to the 3rd pers. plural suffix *-n* which was found by Milik in the Copper Scroll of Qumran (⁹³).

These considerations result in the following translation :

> When a millstone rips them open on earth
> their bones are scattered in the mouth of Sheol (⁹⁴).

This verse is to be compared with Is 21,9 and Jr 15,7.

Ps 143,3 (IL ; Baumgartner) :

> For the Enemy has pursued me ;
> he has smitten (⁹⁵) my life into the nether world ;
> he has made me sit in darkness like (⁹⁶) those long dead.
> My spirit faints ....

The dark situation outlined here is not obscure : the Arch-enemy drags the psalmist into Sheol. The tormented man feels crumbled in the clutches of Death. See Ps 7,6.

(⁹⁰) See above, p. 14.
(⁹¹) Above, pp. 14 f.
(⁹²) Pope, *Job* 170.
(⁹³) *DJD* III, 231 *sub* 16 (four times).
(⁹⁴) Perhaps a precative perfect is to be understood here ; for v. 6, see p. 106, n. 35.
(⁹⁵) Or : crushed my life in ... (for this meaning of *dk'/dkk/dkh*, see *GB* 161B ; *WUS* s.v. *dk*, 739). Parallelism and the use of the preposition *l^e* favour a slight preference for " smitten ".
(⁹⁶) The preposition *k^e* is used for variety's sake after *b^e*, but has the same value according to H. van Dijk, *Ezekiel's Prophecy* 43-45.

Ps 147,6 (Cross–Freedman):

> Jahweh lifts up the downtrodden,
> he casts the wicked as far as the underworld.

The preposition '*ădê* obtains its full force if we interpret '*rṣ* as "nether world", commonly the portion of the wicked. Yahweh punishes the impious people by a premature death.

"He casts them to the ground" (RSV) is a possible translation. Then we are reminded of the traditional *Sitz im Leben* of the poor: the Dust (1 S 2,8, etc.). But we shall see that even in this case Sheol is denoted as well.

Ps 148,7 (Cross–Freedman):

> Praise the Lord from the earth,
> you sea monsters and all the chaotic waters!

In the first part of this psalm the heaven and its contents are invited to praise the Lord; in the second this task is assigned to the "earth" and its components. Now, the *tannînîm* and *tᵉhōmôt* are most likely to be located in the nether world and as they are classified under the heading "earth", '*rṣ* must be more than the surface only. The structure of the universe is bipartite in this psalm: heaven and earth; and the "earth" is to be understood in its widest sense.

Jb 10,21 f. (Dahood):

21   ... before I go, never to return,
       to a land of darkness and gloom,
22   a land of utter darkness,
       of gloom without order.... (Pope)

It is manifest that Job is haunted by the vision of the nether world, the land of no return, the land of darkness and chaos. In the present writer's opinion, however, it is less obvious that '*rṣ* itself stands for "nether world" here. It might as well mean "country, area, region", which is specified as infernal by the epithets added to it.

For this idea, we may refer to Dn 12,2 "the land of the dust": here '*rṣ* stands for "country" rather than for "earth", the "earth of the dust" hardly making sense. Often this distinction is too subtle to be possible. In Jb 10,21 the interpretation "ein Land" seems preferable to "die Erde"; for this, we could point to the verbs *hlk* and *šwb* which denote a kind of emigration to the "land of no return" with its bolted boundaries. Also an implicit opposition with "the land of the living " and the " light of the living " might be present. But all this is rather tenuous.

Job 12,8 (Dahood):

> 7a But now ask the beasts, and they will teach you ;
> 7b and the birds of the heavens and they will tell you ;
> 8a or speak to the nether world, and it will teach you ;
> 8b and the fishes of the sea will inform you.

" If *'ereṣ* is here understood as ' nether world ' .., a quadripartite division of the universe comes to the fore " ([97]).
We find :   earth 7a
  heavens 7b
  nether world 8a
  sea 8b.
For this " conversation ", Dahood refers to *'nt* : III : 19-21 : " ... converse of the heavens with the nether world, the deep with the stars ". The suggested rendering was accepted by Pope ([98]).

Job 15,29 (Dahood):

> He will not be rich, nor his wealth endure,
> nor his possessions reach the nether world. (Pope)

The interpretation " nether world " is evident and needs no further proof. It is corroborated by " darkness " in 30a : " He will not escape from Darkness " ([99]).

Prv 11,31 (Dahood):

> If the virtuous is requited in the nether world
> how much more the wicked and the sinner !

The preceding verse shows that the context requires an eschatological sense :
> The fruit of the virtuous is the tree of life,
> and the wise man attains eternal life ([100]).

([97]) Dahood, *Job* 58.
([98]) Pope, *Job* 88.
([99]) For further explanation see Dahood, *Job* 60 f. See also below, pp. 187 f.
([100]) *Id., Prov.* 25.

" The biblical writer is evidently reacting against the traditional view that an equal lot in Sheol awaits all men and argues, *dato non concesso*, that if all men, virtuous and vicious alike, are to be consigned to Sheol, the punishment of the latter will be much greater than that of the former " ([101]).

Here the addition " *dato non concesso* " is necessary indeed. Unfortunately, through it the interpretation itself becomes doubtful, as in this way the translation loses the clear and obvious meaning which would recommend it. No doubt " earth " offers fewer difficulties.

Prv 25,3 (Dahood):

> As the heavens for height, and the earth for depth,
> so the mind of the king is unsearchable.

The idea of the nether world's inscrutability is proverbial in the Old Testament (e.g., Ps 95,4). Moreover the opposition heaven/nether world is perfect in this verse.

Sir 51,9 (Baumgartner):

> *w'rym m'rṣ qwly, wmš'ry š'wl šw'ty* ([102])

The man saying this prayer is in urgent need; he says:

> My soul approached death, and my life the depths of Sheol (v. 6);

and in the line quoted above we hear the same theme:

> I raised my voice from the Nether City
> from the gates of Sheol my cry.

Context and parallelism show that *'rṣ* stands for the nether world; more precisely, " gates " insinuates that this reality is thought of as a city here. For this meaning of *'rṣ* see above ([103]).

([101]) *Ibid.* 25 f.

([102]) Hebrew text: J. Knabenbauer, *Comm. in Ecclesiasticum* (Paris 1902) lxxxi.

([103]) On Jer 15,7, pp. 30 f.

Conclusion

We have found that 'rṣ, standing for " nether world ", in fact has three connotations; its concrete meaning is specified by the context: I, earth; II, country; III, city.

I. Most often this 'rṣ is to be classified under the primary meaning of the term, i.e. " Erdboden der den Füssen des Menschen Stand gewährt und über den sich Bauten erheben " ([104]). In fact this definition is a happy one, for it leaves room for a wide extension of this " floor ", which cannot be limited to a mere surface. Our study of single texts shows indeed, that 'rṣ, apart from its meaning " surface ", has a widely varied range of connotations. The main distinction within 'rṣ = nether world is between its cosmological and anthropological meanings.

1. Cosmologically, 'rṣ signifies a material reality under our feet, extending to incalculable depths. It contains the waters which have a vital function in relation to the inhabited world: they represent the primeval force in its negative and positive aspects. Creation means a victory of order over chaos, over chaotic waters, which on the one hand are essential for the vitality of the earth, but on the other hand continually threaten to make the cosmos relapse into chaos. A text like Gn 2,5 shows that these vital sources are considered to have ramifications extending up to the surface of the earth.

2. As to the anthropological meaning, 'rṣ, apart from its relation to the grave, has a deep and fundamental connection with the " cosmological " nether world; the dead leave the divinely established order of creation and return to the chaotic situation they were taken from. In this way the nether world is the abode of the dead. Throughout this study we hope to offer some more information about this reality.

Different meanings of 'rṣ apparently pass into each other and very often a clear distinction cannot be made. Surface itself, for instance, unavoidably implies some depth: matter is necessarily three-dimensional. In other words: a " pure " surface is an abstraction; and consequently it is hard to say where the surface ends and where the depth starts. The same phenomenon, noted in Accadian already, is found in Greek as well. And we are told that χθόνιος can be a qualification of gods having a relation to the earth or to the nether world ([105]).

Sometimes 'rṣ implies mass, including surface and depth. Then

---

([104]) L. Rost, *Bezeichnungen* 82. The assumption that in our case 'rṣ fundamentally means " ground " is confirmed by its partial synonymity with 'dmh.
([105]) W. Brede Kristensen, *Het Leven uit den Dood* 173 f.

we cannot but translate " earth ", but it is an inadequate rendering.
By way of example we quote Ps 18,8 :

> The earth trembled and quaked :
> the very foundations of the hills shook and were moved. (RP)

As the roots of the mountains are in the underworld ([106]), parallelism
suggests that this meaning is present in the first colon also.

And when the springs of the waters were seen, and the foundations of the world uncovered, God " reached from on high, he took
me, he drew me from the many waters " (v. 15 f.). The earthquake
opens the earth, unlocks the prison from which the oppressed psalmist
could not escape. Then God stretches out his hand and saves hell's
victim.

" Earth " may have the same sense in Hab 3,9 " Thou didst
cleave the earth with rivers ". Duhm comments : " Wahrscheinlich
denkt sich Hab., da er vom Regen erst später spricht, dass aus den
Rissen des aufgespalteten Landes das unterirdische Wasser hervor-
bricht " ([107]). This may remain true even if, with Albright, we have
to read 10a – 10c – 10b – 9c ("The clouds streamed with water, the
rivers which cleave the earth ") ([108]).

Just because of this osmosis, which is possible in Hebrew and
not always in our languages, translating 'rs is sometimes a delicate
task, so a certain scepticism as to the examples given above is understandable. " Each word is the centre or focus of a whole circle of
meaning, and the circles in several languages may overlap but seldom
coincide. The difficulty which this makes for a translator lies in
the fact that the whole range of meaning covered by such a term ...
is present, at least potentially, in the mind of the writer who uses it
on any occasion " ([109]).

This difficulty is more perceptible still in the texts we are generally dealing with. In the words of T. Gaster : " Hence, it is reasonable to suppose that here ... the poet chose his words carefully
in order to convey at one and the same time both a concrete and figurative sense " ([110]).

([106]) Jon 2,7 ; Is 24,18 ; 32,22 ; for the foundations of earth see Ps 18,16 ;
Is 24,18 ; Jr 31,37 (cp. Ps 95,4) ; Mi 6,2.

([107]) B. Duhm, *Das Buch Habakuk ...* (Tübingen 1906) 87.

([108]) " The Psalm of Habakkuk " (in H. H. Rowley, *Studies in Old Testament Prophecy presented to Th. H. Robinson* [Edinburgh 1950] 1-18) 11 ff.

([109]) C. H. Dodd, *Bible Translator* 11 (1960) 5 f.

([110]) *Thespis* 172 note.

Is 25,12 might serve as an example of the use of a double meaning:

The high fortifications ... he will ... cast to the
earth, even to the dust.

Because of the general idea and the appearance of the sinister
couple earth-dust the suggestion of " nether world " is strong in 'rṣ.
But the translation " nether world " would certainly not do [111].

II. Sometimes, as in Jb 10,21 and Is 26,19, 'rṣ is applied to the
nether world with the meaning " country, land ".

III. As Sheol is commonly represented as a fortified city [112],
the application of 'rṣ in this sense to the nether world is hardly surprising. It is found in Jon 2,7 and Sir 51,9.

Strictly speaking 'rṣ II and III denote the nether world, i.e.
as a country or a city; but the word itself does not mean (nor should
it be translated) " nether world " here.

Finally, it needs no proof that in cases II and III the word is
used to design Sheol exclusively as the abode of the dead [113].

1.3. The Hidden Place (ṭāmûn - sēter)

Humans have no right to call God to account or to question the
justice of his actions. To show Job that he cannot put himself on
a level with his Creator, God challenges him:

40,12   Glance at every proud one and humble him:
           tread down the wicked where they stand.
   13   Bury them in the dust together;
           bind them in the infernal crypt. (Pope)

[111] Cp. Ez 28,17; Lam 2,11.
[112] Dahood, *Prov.* 62 f.
[113] Also Rost, *Bezeichnungen* 85. As to the expression " land of the living ",
GB lists it under 'rṣ 7 = " Land der Finsternis für Scheol Hi 10,21 f ' (68A);
and no doubt " land of the living " denotes the earth " as distinguished from
the realm of the dead " (C. A. Briggs, *Psalms* I in ICC [1906] 242). As the
corresponding contrary formula is missing (land of death – of the dead?),
the import of ḥym cannot be established with certainty (see Zor 234B); but in
any case 'rṣ ḥym implicitly refers to another 'rṣ, as appears from Ez 32,24 (opposition 'rṣ tḥtywt and 'rṣ ḥym). The latter text justifies a certain reluctance
to accept Dahood's translation " land of life eternal " (Dahood, *Psalms* 170).
In Accadian the name irṣit mītutī, " land of the dead ", is found (Tallqvist,
Namen der Totenwelt 36).

" Bind them in *ṭāmûn* ". Parallelism with *'pr* shows that this " hidden place ", where man has no power, must be Sheol ([114]). The reference clearly is to the nether world as a prison : see the idea of " binding " ([115]).

The same idea is evoked by the word *sēter* in Ps 139,15, as appears from the contents of the verse, the formation of an embryo in the womb of the nether world, and from parallelism with a certain name of Sheol :

> ... I was made in the Secret Place,
> woven in the depths of the nether world ([116]).

1.4 The Broad Domain (merḥab)

The nether world is a wide country. Babylonians called it KI.GAL and in Egypt Osiris complains : " Oh Atum, whereto go I ? There is no water, there is no air, it is very deep, dark and extensive " ([117]). The question may be asked if these conceptions are also found in the OT, concretely, if derivates of the root *rḥb* are used to denote the nether world.

The proposal was made by E. de Marcellis and accepted by M. Dahood for Ps 18,20 ; 31,9 ; with reserve for Ps 118,5 ; and finally for Jb 38,18.

Ps 31,9 reads :

> *lō' hisgartānî bᵉyad 'ôyēb*
> *heᵉᵉmadtā bammerḥāb raglāy :*
> you did not incarcerate me in the hand of the Foe ([118])
> nor set my feet in the Broad Domain ([119]).

([114]) Pope, *Job* 268. In Egypt the dead are sometimes called " those hidden of place " (Zandee, 97). In the Judenfriedhof at Worms the writer found that most epitaphs start with the words *pô ṭāmûn* (Here has been buried). Perhaps the name " Hidden Place " was derived from the grave.

([115]) This interpretation sheds new light on Jb 3,21, which at least contains an allusion to this name of Sheol. M. Dahood proposes the following translation : " Who waits for Death that it might annihilate him, and that the Hidden Place might bury him ".

([116]) For *str* in Is 45,19 see below, p. 97.

([117]) Zandee 9 f. See also Accadian *irṣitu rapaštu*, " the broad nether world " (Tallqvist, *Namen der Totenwelt* 14 f.).

([118]) See below, pp. 106 f. and 154 ff.

([119]) Dahood, *Psalms* 185.

As synonymous parallelism characterizes this psalm, it is reasonably supposed that the negation on the first colon covers the second as well; the phenomenon is not unknown in biblical Hebrew (120).

As to both texts, however, there are some facts exhorting to discretion.

First of all there is the use of the verb *rḥb* in hiphil as the expression of deliverance from need in an individual lament. Here certainly the opposition *rḥb – ṣr* should not pass unnoticed.

Ps 4,2 runs: " In distress set me at large (121) ". Besides, the same remark may be made for *yš*, whose original sense " to be capacious " is visible in the (thanksgiving) Psalm 107, v. 13: " He delivered me from distress (122) ".

Ps 18,20 reads:

> *wayyôṣî'ēnî lammerḥāb*
> *yᵉḥallᵉsēnî kî ḥāpēṣ bî*

The first colon is translated: " He brought me out of the broad domain (123) ". This rendering rests on the following arguments:

— The preposition *lᵉ* is not uncommonly equivalent to " from " in our languages (124); and, more specifically, connected with the hiphil of *yṣ'*, it is argued to have this sense in Ps 66,11 f.:

> You brought us out into the wilderness,
> you laid a heavy load upon our loins.
> You let men ride over us, we went through fire and water,
> after you had let us out of abundance (*wattôṣî'ēnû lārᵉwāyâ*)(125).

Four clauses describe the sufferings of the Israelites after their flight from Egypt (126); consequently it would seem likely that the last also

---

(120) Joüon, 160q; *GK* 152z.

(121) See *rḥb* in Ps 18,37 and *mrḥb* in 2 S 22,37.

(122) Cp. Barth, *Errettung* 127.

(123) Dahood, *Psalms* 111.

(124) Gordon, *UT* 10.1. " It is now clear that where our idiom demands ' from ', Hebrew (Canaanite) and Ugaritic idiom employed ' in ', ' in regard to ', and ' upon ' ". Thus W. Moran in *Fs Albright* (ed. G. E. Wright) p. 61. Further, Moran says: " The writer agrees with Sutcliffe (*VT* 5 [1955] 436-439) that we should not say that these prepositions mean ' from ' " (69, n. 79). A similar use is found in French: ' boire dans un verre ' (cf. Am 6,6), ' fumer dans une pipe ', ' manger dans une assiette ', ' prendre quelque chose dans l'armoire '.

(125) Dahood, *UHPh* 29 *sub* 10.1.1.

(126) The fire stands for lightning: Wisd 16,16 f.; cp. Is 43,1 f. (New Exodus).

refers to them, i.e., to the fleshpots of Egypt the wanderers were han-
kering after in the desert (Num 11,5).

This interpretation, however, is not unexceptionable.   About the
necessity of a new translation judgments may differ, but some objections are obvious. The translation of the *waw* as " after " shows
that its author saw the difficulty of the position of the sentence in
this interpretation : logically one would expect it at the beginning
of the series not at its end ! Moreover Hebrew syntax is not in favour
of this rendering : about the form *wayyiqtōl* Joüon writes : " s'emploie
surtout dans la sphère du passé pour une action unique et instantanée :
le *waw* ajoute surtout l'idée de succession " ([127]). The last few words of
this quotation are of vital importance in our discussion. Besides, Ps 66,8-
12 is a *Volkslobpsalm* ([128]). At the very end of such a psalm an element
of praise, existing " in einem einfachen Aussagesatz " ([129]), is far more
likely.

The use of *yṣ'* will be discussed below.   With more certainty the
postulated linguistic phenomenon occurs in Ps 68,21 : *lammāwet tôṣā'ôt*,
" escape from death ([130]) ".

— As far as the contents of Ps 18 are concerned, the interpretation proposed by M. Dahood fits into the context well :

vv. 8-20   describe Yahweh's intervention in favour of the psalmist ;
v. 18   the deliverance from death ; v. 19 the imminence of death ;
v. 20   deliverance from Sheol ([131]).

— Finally, the hiphil of the verb *yṣ'* is employed, twice in an
IL and once in a ThPs, to denote a release from need, here again in
an explicit opposition to words which express the absence of room and
capacity. Ps 143,11 reads : " In thy righteousness bring me out of
trouble (*ṣrh*) ([132]) ".

Summarizing : both grammatically and lexicographically the interpretation proposed by M. Dahood is unexceptionable. Our last considerations, based on a special consideration of the genres involved,
however, do not support it.   It appears that the verbs expressing the
idea of deliverance into " free space " as opposed to " confined space ",

---

([127]) Joüon, 118c.
([128]) Westermann, *Loben Gottes* 62 ff.
([129]) *Ibid.* 64.
([130]) Albright, *HUCA* 23 (1950-1951) 48.
([131]) Cp. Drijvers, *Psalmen* 188.
([132]) See also Pss 107,28 ; 142,8.

have a favourable sense in IL and ThPs. More specifically this is true
for the hiphil of the verb *rḥb*.

As Ps 18 is an ITh and Ps 31 an IL, it is less likely that the idea
of space has the gloomy sense of Broad Domain = Sheol there. This
is specially true for Ps 31, which, being IL with *mrḥb*, is directly affected by Ps 4,2 (IL, verb *rḥb*).

Ps 118,5 is also mentioned in this connection. It is a compact
bicolon; " I cried to Yahweh in straitened circumstances, " *'ānānî*
bammerḥāb yâ. As being in need implies a staying in Sheol, the
following translation is possible: " and Yahweh heard me, who was
in the Broad Domain ". Apart from Ps 118 being an ITh, we think
that, in view of *mēṣar* in the first colon, contrasting *merḥab* stands for
something quite different; we should prefer the rendering: " Yahweh
answered me from his broad habitation ([133]) ".

Finally, *raḥab* is used as a substantive and applied to the nether
world in Jb 38,18:

> Have you examined the vast expanse of the nether world?
> Tell, if you know all of it.

" All of it ", *klh*, is the same qualification as the one found in *UT*
49: I : 37, quoted above ([134]). The whole passage runs a smoother
course in Jb 38, if the " broad planes of the nether world " are understood here:

> v. 16: abysmal depth ;   v. 17: death-darkness ;
> v. 18: " wide nether world "; v. 19: light-darkness.

The literary genre is a different one here and the connotation of this
" nether world " is exclusively cosmological.

1.5 š\ᵉdēmôt (Field of Death)

The main lexica maintain that *šᵉdēmâ* is a feminine singular
meaning " cultivated field ", the singular occurring once only (Is 37,27),
the plural five times.

M. R. Lehmann ([135]) critically analysed this statement, and indeed

---

([133]) Ps 18,7 offers a strict parallel : " In my distress I called upon Yahweh...
from (*min* [*sic*]) his temple he heard my voice ". The second *yâ* in Ps 118,5
may be explained as a superlative (cp. CC 8,6): " from his immensely broad
habitation ".

([134]) Cp. Dahood, *Job* 73 ; *id.*, *Psalms* 111 ; above, p. 13.

([135]) M. R. Lehmann, " A New Interpretation of the term *šdmt* ", *VT* 3
(1953) 361-371.

it appears to be highly contestable.   He proved that in fact TM regards
šdmt as a masculine singular, the Isaian *šdmh* being an anomalous
fem. sg. derived from the reputed fem. pl. *šdmt*.   Our lexica continue
the ancient and erroneous tradition.

a) As argued by Lehman, two texts clearly show that TM takes
šdmt for a singular : Is 16,8, a prophecy against Moab : *kî šadmôt ḥešbôn
'umlāl, gepen šibmâ*.   The singular verbal form certainly favours the
interpretation of *šdmt* as a singular [136].   The text is a lament ; the
parallelism with *gpn* is a fixed one : cp. Hab 3,18 ; Dt 32,32.   The
canticle of Habakkuk mentions in 3,17 the following calamity : *šᵉdēmôt
lō' – 'āśâ 'okel*.   Here again it is clear that one must assume harmony
between subject and verb, in other words, that *šdmt* is a masc. sg.
It is rather too much to suppose that both cases where the word is a
subject, are exceptions to the correspondence between subject and
verb.

b) Moreover the word occurs in Dt 32 and 2 K 23, which makes
the common rendering " cultivated land " look doubtful.   Dt 32,32
says about the enemies :

> Their vine (*gpn*) comes from the vine of Sodom,
> and from the *šdmt* of Gomorrah.

The biblical writer hardly refers to the " cultivated fields " of Gomor-
rah here.   According to 2 K 23,4, a historical text, vessels made for
the cult of Baal *cum suis* are to be burnt in the *šdmwt qdrwn*.   In this
place are the graves of the common people (v. 6).   So it is hardly farm
land.   Lehmann merely says about these texts that there our word
has a connotation of pagan cults and peoples.

c) To these arguments the following may be added.   In a word
of Yahweh about Sanherib we read that the king, by order of Yahweh,
was to destroy cities while their inhabitants were " like grass on the
housetops and *šᵉdēmâ lipnê qāmâ* " (Is 37,27).   This *šdmh* is troublesome and suspect.   The singular is surprising, its meaning remains
obscure.   So it was for others before us : 1 QIs reads *hn šdp lpny qdym*,
" scorched by the eastern wind " and 2 K 19,26 has *w šdph lpny qmh*.
Either reading confirms the questionable character of Is 37,27.

It looks as if *šdmh* in Is 37 is a comparatively recent and anomalous singular, created by an author who understood *šdmt* as a plural.
As in Is 16,8 and Hab 3,17 the Massoretes do not propose a different

---

[136] 1 QIs reads feminine singular : *'mllh*. The right understanding had
already been lost.

qerē for the masculine singular verb, they may have understood *šdmt* correctly.

These are new arguments for Lehmann's position.

Now the question about meaning and composition of the word can be broached.

Lehmann simply translates " fields of Mot ", but with Croatto and Soggin ([137]) the peculiar *šd* (not: *śd*) should be emphasized; nor-ally Ugaritic *šd* passes into Hebrew *śd*.

There cannot be any reasonable doubt that Ugaritic and Hebrew *šdmt* are identical; this is stressed by the context in 52 : 11 to be quoted below.

Now Ugaritic *šd* / field always becomes *śd* in Hebrew, apart from our case. This suggests that Canaanite *šdmt* was adopted by the Hebrews as an established technical term.

From the reading *šdmth* in *UT* 52 : 11, the possessive suffix being added to -*mt* and not to *šd*-, some ([138]) deduce that the compound was regarded as an indivisible unity. This argument, however, is far from cogent, as Ugaritic quite normally attaches the possessive suffix to the *nomen rectum* in a construct chain ([139]).

But the statement remains true : both in 52 : 11 and in 137 : 43 there is no word divider between the two components ([140]), so we are entitled to consider *šdmt* as a unity with a technical sense. In this way only could it one day be taken for a plural; the anomaly of Is 37 is quite understandable now : *šdmt* was an archaic term.

Finally, *mt* (*mutu*) is the common spelling for Mot in Ugaritic; so the translation " fields of Mot " is a literal and sound one. The question is, how this is to be understood.

Obviously this technical and archaic term must be connected with cultic custom. This is most likely in the light of *UT* 52 : 8-11 :

> Death-and-Rot sits —
> in his hand the rod of bereavement,
> in his hand the rod of widowhood,
> they prune him, those pruning the vine,
> they bind him, those binding the vine.
> He is felled in his field (*šdmth*) like the vine. ([141])

([137]) J. S. Croatto – J. A. Soggin, " Die Bedeutung von *šdmt* im Alten Testament ", *ZAW* 74 (1962) 44-50.

([138]) M. R. Lehmann, *VT* 3 (1953) 364; Croatto–Soggin, *art. cit.*

([139]) *UT* Gramm. 13.22.

([140]) As appears from Herdner, *Corpus* II, fig. 67.

([141]) See above, p. 16.

For our purpose it is significant that the barren field of the last line is called *šdmt* with a clear allusion to Mot and his condition. Similar undertones are heard in biblical usage, and not unlikely an echo of cultic custom is perceptible in Is 16,8; Hab 3,17; and Dt 32,32. All these texts contain both *šdmt* and *gpn* and pertain to a literary genre (curse, lament) in which the after effects of archaic cultic formulas would not be surprising ([142]).

As to the real impact of *šdmt* it is to be noticed that Mot is the god of " the torrid summer heat " ([143]) and that in oriental idiom, " dead land " is uncultivated, waterless land ([144]).

This interpretation perfectly suits our texts where the " fields " appear to be barren and waste. It is confirmed by the response in *UT* 52 : 13 : " Now the field is a divine field, a field of Asherat and the Virgin (= Anat) ". Gaster correctly remarks that " divine field " means " fertile land " and points to the " garden of Yahweh " (Gn 13,10 ; Is 51,3) as parallels ; but he overlooks the opposition between *šdmt* and *šd ilm* in our text. After ceremonial ploughing the soil is fertile again ([145]).

So *šdmt* is not a designation for the nether world in as far as it is the abode of the dead. But our analysis shows that the universal conception of chaos embracing the uncultivated land, is found also in Canaan ([146]). Waste fields and deserts belong to the *Machtsbereich* of the Arch-enemy.

([142]) Cp. 2 S 1,19-29 ; Gaster, *Thespis* 357 n. ; H. Jahnow, *Leichenlied*.

([143]) Gaster, *Thespis* 125, par. 4.

([144]) *Ibid.* 132, n. 22.

([145]) *Ibid.* 422, note. Asherat and Anat have the function of Demeter and Kore in Greece. As to ploughing, it is of old a sexual act, because of the relation between woman and earth : G. van der Leeuw, *De Godsdiensten der Wereld*, II (Amsterdam 1941) 11 f.

([146]) " Au limite de ce monde clos, commence le domaine de l'inconnu, du nonformé. D'une part il y a l'espace cosmisé, puisque habité et organisé — d'autre part, à l'extérieur de cet espace familier, il y a la région inconnue et redoutable des démons, des larves, des morts, des étrangers ; en un mot le chaos, la mort, la nuit ". M. Eliade, *Images et symboles* 47 ; see *Le Mythe de l'Eternel Retour* 26 f. ; Joh. Pedersen, *Israel* I/II, 470 f.; G. v.d. Leeuw, *Phäno-menologie* 359 f. The congeries of netherworld conceptions in M. Eliade's statement is fascinating.

1.6   Depths

1.6.1   hāmîr (Miry Depths)

In *UT* 67 : I : 6-8 we read : *lyrt ⁷bnpš ilm mt bmh ⁸mrt ydd il ǵzr* :
" Truly, you will descend into the throat of divine Mot, into the *mhmrt*
of El's beloved, the Hero ". Authors agree about *hmr* meaning to
" pour down " as Arabic *hamara*. And as the prefixed *m-* can be
easily interpreted as forming a local name out of it ([147]), *mhmrt* is safely
rendered by " the place of pouring down " ([148]).

As to further specification, however, scholars disagree. Gray,
Gordon, and Aistleitner rely on parallelism when they translate " gullet " ([149]); Driver and Pope take the local character of the word
more largely when they render by " watery abyss " and " wässrige,
morastige Tiefe ". For this they refer to the name of Mot's residence " his city, Slushy " (*hmry*) (*UT* 51 : VIII : 11f) ; Pope moreover
quotes Philo's interpretation of the term : " Schlamm, Fäulnis von
wässriger Misschung " ([150]). Both interpretations are philologically
sound and acceptable ; in *UT* 67 the context recommends " gullet ",
in *UT* 51 " watery abyss " looks preferable.

Derivatives from the same root occur also in biblical Hebrew.
Ps 140,11 contains the word found in *UT* 67 : I : 7f, as recognized by
Dussaud and accepted by others ([151]). Cursing his enemies, the psalm-
ist prays : " Let him be thrown into miry depths, no more to rise ! "
Or, with another division of the verse : " From the miry depths may
they not arise ! "

The wish is more radical than traditional translations made us
believe. It is a malediction to death.

Jb 17,2 runs : *'m l' htlym 'mdy | wbhmrwtm tln 'yny*. We now rec-
ognize *hmrt* in the second colon ; it is a dual here, probably referring
to the " Double Deep ", well known in Ugaritic texts ([152]). The verb
lyn is used to denote a stay in the nether world ([153]). In the first colon

([147]) Joüon, 188 L d.
([148]) Gray, *Legacy* p. 47, n. 1.
([149]) Gordon, *UL* 67 : I : 8, p. 38 ; Gray, *Legacy loc. cit.* ; *WUS* 847 p. 91.
([150]) *CMAL*, 159 ; M. Pope in *Haussig* 301.
([151]) See Dahood, *UPHh* 779 ; *id., Psalms* 278.
([152]) According to Driver, *CMAL* 152 B, the sg. is *thmt* ; Aistleitner (*WUS*
2749) is uncertain : *thm* sg. ; *thmt* pl. (?) Most likely the truth is this : *thm* sg. ;
thmtm du. ; *thmt* pl. (*UT* 2537). The name " Double Deep " probably stands
for the upper and lower oceans : Pope, *El* 61-64 ; Gaster, *Thespis* 183 n. (refers
to Albright, *AJSL* 35 [1919-1920] 161-195) ; W. Schmidt, *Königtum* 6 ; V. Maag
in H. Schmökel, *Kulturgesch.* 574 f. ; cp. Wensinck, *Ocean* 26 ff.
([153]) Cf. below, pp. 105 ff.

another netherworld phenomenon quite unexpectedly appears: *tlym*
means the two hills, bordering the entrance of the nether world in
UT 51 : VIII : 4 : *tlm ġṣr 'rṣ* : " the two hills bounding the nether
world " (¹⁵⁴). The motive returns with Ezra Pound, *Canto* XVI :

> And before the hell mouth
> dry plain and two mountains.

In Jb 17, 1f. : parallelism recommends this interpretation, and
so does the preceding verse and the literary genre, the lament :

> My spirit is broken,
> My days are spent ;
> It is the grave for me.
> Indeed the two hills are before me,
> And my eyes pass the night in the twin miry depths.

Ps 46,3 : here occurs the crux *bhmyr 'rṣ*, where *KB*, quite typi-
cally, proposes to read *hāmîš* (¹⁵⁵). Dahood finds here the root *hmr*
again, and refers to the Ugaritic texts quoted above, *hmr* meaning
" gullet " in our case.

The preposition *bᵉ* after the verb *yr'* is uncommon ; it also occurs
in Jr 51,46 and possibly in Ps 49,6. The consideration that *bᵉ* is
often to be rendered by " from " and consequently is practically equivalent to the preposition *min*, which is normal after the verb *yr'* (¹⁵⁶),
makes it reasonable to suppose that in Jr 51 and Ps 49 the construction with *bᵉ* does not merely denote " attendant circumstances ",
but the object of the verb itself. On the basis of these considerations
Dahood proposes the following translation : " Therefore we will not
fear the jaws of the nether world " (¹⁵⁷).

Some remarks should be made. In the first place the -*y*- in *hāmîr*
is not accounted for ; besides parallelism with the infinitive *môṭ* favours the interpretation of *hāmîr* as an infinitive form, v. 3a de-

---

¹⁵⁴) It is a common conception among the western Semites that these hills
are at the entrance to the Beyond, cp. Wensinck, 34 ; for that reason *ġṣr* is
translated " to confine " here with *ARI* 198, n. 1 and *WUS* 2163 and *CMAL*
142B. Pope, however, writes about the mound(s) that plug(s) the nether world :
they " do not appear to be semitic " *JBL* 83 (1964) 276, n. 22. For a different
interpretation of *UT* 51 : VIII : 4, see Dahood, *Prov.* 59. For the literary genre
cp. C. Barth, *Errettung*.

(¹⁵⁵) *KB* 506A.

(¹⁵⁶) *BDB* 431A.

(¹⁵⁷) Dahood, *Psalms* 278 f. Cp. *id.*, *Bib* 40 (1959) 167 f.

scribing a natural phenomenon as v. 3b does. These suspicions find
support in the evident correspondence between vv. 3f. and v. 7:

    4a and 7c. Verb: *ḥmh*; subject: *mayîm* – *gôyîm*.
    3b and 7a. Verb: *mwṭ*; subject: *hārîm* – *mamlākôt*.

Consequently it is tempting to put *hāmîr* (3a) and *tāmûg* (7b) together.
The latter means: "to melt, to sway to and fro" ([158]), so the former
might have a similar meaning. In fact Ugaritic *mr* is rendered
"passed to and fro" ([159]) and "weichen, weggehen" ([160]). Perhaps Ps
46,3 contains this root, the hiphil being similar to the hiphil form of
verbs of movement, *ngš*, *rḥq*, *qrb*, and *qdm* ([161]). This would yield
a perfect sense, the mountains being the foundation of the earth:

> Therefore we will not fear when the earth would waver,
> when the mountains would shake in the heart of the sea.

1.6.2 Various terms

1.6.2.1: Ps 40,3: *ṭîṭ hayyāwēn*: The Miry Bog

This picturesque appellation is paralleled by another characteristic name of Sheol: "He drew me up from the pit of destruction,
out of the miry bog." In the nether world man's feet find no hold,
there is no stability, no safety, and no peace there. Therefore its
opposite is "rock".

1.6.2.2: *meṣûlâ*: deep, depth, vorago (Zor)

This term always refers to an extreme distance. God will cast
our sins "into the depths of the sea" (Mi 7,19), i.e., into chaos, annihilation; the Egyptians went down "into the depths" like a stone
(Ex 15,5), i.e., they vanished completely into the Sea and so to
the nether world (// *teḥôm*); Jonah exclaims: "Thou cast me into
the 'deep', in the heart of the waters" (2,4). In all these cases a
double entendre seems to be intended; the first sense no doubt is
a geographical one, but again and again a deeper, qualitative understanding is suggested: the nether world shines through. In some

---

([158]) *GB* 404A.
([159]) *CMAL* 161B.
([160]) *WUS* 1658; Gordon, *UT* Gloss. 1541 renders "to drive out".
([161]) *GK* 53e.

cases, however, the idea of Sheol, " la livida palude " (Inf. III : 98), is in the limelight :

Ps 69, verse 3 runs :

" I sink in deep mire (y^e*wēn* m^e*ṣûlâ*)
where there is no foothold ;
I have come into deep waters (*ma'ămaqqîm*)
and the vortex sweeps over me ".

The afflicted psalmist feels sinking down into the miry depths of the nether world, into the " bog of the Deep " as he puts it ; we notice the parallels " deep waters " (cp. Ps 130,1) and the " flood ". In v. 15 f. rescue from danger is described in the same terms :

... rescue me from sinking in the mire (*ṭîṭ*) ;
let me be delivered from my enemies and from the deep
[waters (*m'mq*).
Let not the vortex (*šblt*) sweep over me,
or the deep (*mṣlh*) swallow me up (*bl'*),
or the pit close its mouth over me.

This text offers a good survey of different names for the nether world in the OT, interpreting them as " enemies " ; in the light of preceding *bl'* it is natural to understand the pit with its mouth as a personification. The same *Wortfeld* is found in Ps 88,7 :

Thou hast put me in the depths (*taḥtîyôt*) of the pit (*bôr*),
in the regions of darkness, in depths (*mṣlh*).

Ps 68,23 reads :
My Lord says : " I have smashed the Serpent ;
I have muzzled the Deep Sea " (*mṣlh*) [162].

---

[162] Transl. of Dahood, " *Mišmar* ' Muzzle ' in Job 7,12 " (*JBL* 80 [1961] 270 f.) 270 ; *Bib* 42 (1961) 385 (review of H.-J. Kraus, *Psalmen*) : *'āmar 'ădōnāy-m bāšān 'ešōb, 'ešbōm m^eṣullôt yām.* (Ugar. *ṭbb-šbb*, " to shatter "; *šbm*, "to muzzle "; cp. also *id.*, " ULex " 100 f.). Albright translated : " From (smiting) the Serpent I return, I return from destroying Sea ", " A Catalogue of Early Hebrew Lyric Poems — Ps. 68 " (*HUCA* 23 [1950-1951] 1-39) 27. He connected *bšn* with Ugar. *bṭn*, which in 67 : I : 1 and *'nt* III : 38 stands for the chaos monster, the Dragon, and consequently might stand for the nether world in our text. For the dialectial *bšn = ptn* see Dt 33,22 : F. M. Cross and D. N. Freedman, " The Blessing of Moses (Dt. 33,3-5.26-29) " (*JBL* 67 [1948] 191-

In this verse, strongly reminiscent of Ugaritic myth, Yahweh plays the role of Baal, overmastering his enemy Sir Sea, a chaotic Power. A substantial diminishing of life's fullness for the Israelite means that he is in the *Machtsbereich* of Death.

1.6.2.3 : *m'mq*

Barth correctly recognized the deep nether world in Ps 130,1 : " Out of the deep have I called unto thee " ([163]).

m'mq has the same connotation of chaos in Is 59,10 : " Was it not Thou... that didst make the depths of the sea a way, for the redeemed to pass over ? " The miracle consisted in the Hebrews passing unharmed through the depths of the sea which swallowed their enemies. " Crossing of the Red Sea is considered also as the crossing of Tehom " ([164]).

This meaning appears again in Ezekiel's lament on Tyre (27,34) : " Now you are wrecked by the sea, in the depths of the waters " ([165]). The Tyrians were swallowed by the unfathomable throat of Death.

---

210) 208, n. 74a and Garbini, " Note aramaiche. 1" (*Antonianum* 31 [1956] 310 f.) and 2 (*Anton.* 32 [1957] 427 f.) ; P. Nober, " Notae philologicae " (*VD* 39 [1961] 112 f.), and for the shift dragon–sea cp. *UT* 2537. In a Proto-Canaanite inscription Asherah is referred to as *dt btn*, the Serpent Lady. (Cross, " Yahweh and the God of the Patriarchs ", *HTR* 55 [1962] 238, quoting Albright, " The Early Alphabetic Inscriptions from Sinai and Their Decipherment ", *BASOR* 110 [1948] 6-22). Albright's version, however, was hardly a rendering of the actual text. It is rejected by Johnson, *Sacr. Kingship* 73, n. 8 ; Kraus 469-473. Mowinckel (*Psalms in Worship*, I 174) reads : " I bring back from the dragon " and comments : " Every year ... Death ... seeks to overthrow the land of the living but every time Yahweh conquers him ". This interpretation is rather far fetched ; the object of this " bringing back " is not indicated.

([163]) Barth, *Errettung* 109. As in all other instances, *m'mq* is connected with *mayîm* or *yam* it is reasonable to suppose that this verse suggests the same association.

([164]) Wensinck, *Ocean* 55.

([165]) F. Moriarty comments : " Without changing the text the proposed reading is : ' Now you are wrecked by the waters (instrumental use of *min*) in the depths of the sea '. For the last phrase I would read *bema'amaqe* with enclitic *mem*, followed by *yam*. See Ps 18,16 " (" The Lament over Tyre ", *Gregorianum* 46 [1965] 83-88 : 87). Indeed the presence of enclitic *mem* in Ps 18,16 becomes most likely in view of 2 S 22,16 (*ăpîqê mayîm* and *ăpîqê yam* respectively). The author, however, does not justify his translation " by the waters " for *mîyammîm*. As things are, the reading " by the sea " (TM), which perfectly balances the " depths of the waters ", saps the urgency of Moriarty's proposal. Van Dijk, accepting the new suggestion, reads twice " the sea " (*Ezekiel* 90 f.).

1.7 Waters

1.7.1 t^ehôm (Ocean)

As noted by lexicographers, this word never has an article, *nisi a punctatoribus* in Is 63,16 and Ps 106,9 ([166]). This fact was generally attributed to its character of a " mythological name " ([167]), which now can be confirmed by Ugaritic usage. *UT* 51 : IV : 20 ff. contains the normal description of El's abode : " Then surely she (Anat) set her face towards El at the source of the rivers (in) the midst of the channels of the two oceans (*thmtm*) ". The upper and lower ocean are known in the OT also (Gn 1,6 f.) ; there, however, the heavenly waters are called *mabbûl*, the subterranean ocean is labelled *t^ehôm* ([168]).

UT 'nt : III : 19-22 pictures a cosmic conversation : Baal will speak a word to his sister Anat and it will resound throughout the world :

> Speech of wood, whisper of stone, converse of heavens
> with the nether world, the deeps (*thmt*) with the stars ([169]).

A far echo of that ancient text is heard in a modern novel ; the inanimate is intimately related to man. " Stars and trees meet and converse, flowers talk philosophy at night, stone houses hold meetings ... " ([170]).

Hebrew *t^ehôm* is a vigorous and often grim word, which never entirely renounced its mythical past. A primordial strength pervades *t^ehom* throughout. It stands for : *a*) the primeval ocean ; *b*) the waters round the earth after creation, which [continually threaten the cosmos ([171]) ; *c*) these waters as a source of blessing for the earth ([172]). The word denotes chaotic waters, both at the time of creation and after it. This conception is by no means peculiar to Israel, as some quotations from historians of religion may show. " L'océan est un monde négatif, à la manière du Shéol et du désert, et comme tel, il est le monde des morts, le monde où Dieu est absent " ([173]).

([166]) Zor 889A.

([167]) So, e.g., Th. Robinson, *Die Zwölf Kleinen Propheten* (HAT 1/14 ; 3rd ed. ; Tübingen 1964) 98 ; Ph. Reymond " L'eau ", *VTS* 6 (1958) 183.

([168]) Ps 33,7 is an exception for *t^ehôm*.

([169]) Translation from Dahood, *Job* 58.

([170]) Boris Pasternak, *Dr. Zhivago* (Fontana Books ; London 1958) ch. 5 : 8, p. 147.

([171]) Reymond, " L'eau " 168 ; 184 ; Wensinck, *Ocean* 56-65.

([172]) Zor 889A ; Gn 49,25 ; Dt 33,13.

([173]) Reymond, " L'eau " 185.

It is to be remarked that this writer associates chaotic ocean with the world of the dead. This will return time and again.

Wensinck writes : " The reign of chaos is the reign of t^{e}hôm " ([174]). And Eliade : " *Apsû* und *tehôm* symbolisieren sowohl das ' Wasser-Chaos ', die kosmische Materie, die noch keinerlei Gestalt hat, als auch die Welt des Todes, also all das, was dem Leben vorausgeht und was auf das Leben folgt " ([175]).

In Gn 1, the chaotic character of the deep is intensified by the presence of darkness, another infernal element. The Deluge shows that these waters remain threatening cosmos : " The water of the deluge is the return of the primeval ocean " ([176]).

> Umgekehrt versinnbildlicht das Eintauchen in das Wasser die Rückkehr ins Ungeformte, die Wiedereinfügung in den undifferenzierten Zustand der Prä-existenz. Das Auftauchen wiederholt den kosmogonischen Akt der Formwerdung ; das Eintauchen bedeutet die Auflösung der Formen .... Der Sint-flut ... entspricht auf menschlicher Ebene der " zweite Tod " des Menschen (die " Feuchtigkeit " und der Leimon der Unter-welt) oder der Initiationstod durch die Taufe ([177]).

It is remarkable that the view of man is here a cosmic one : moreover it appears that the " Deep " (and equivalents) are qualitative rather than local ([178]) ; the waters are a negative, formless element.

In the Egyptian Book of Gates the dead are called " drowned ones " : " Horus says to the drowned ..., who are in Nun, denizens of the nether world ... " ([179]).

Eliade pictures " water " in this way : " Seine Bestimmung ist, der Schöpfung vorauszugehen und sie wieder auf zu saugen, selbst aber die eigene Modalität nicht verlassen, dass heisst keine Formen annehmen zu können. Das Wasser bleibt immer in einem virtuellen, keimhaften und latenten Zustand. Alles, was Form ist, manifestiert sich oberhalb des Wassers, sich von ihm ablösend ! " ([180]). In Israel

---

([174]) *Ocean* 50.

([175]) *Das Heilige* 25. In Accadian, *apsū* is a name for the nether world ; quite characteristically Ereskigal, the goddess of the nether world, is identified with Tiamat (Tallqvist, *Namen der Totenwelt* 8).

([176]) Wensinck, *Ocean* 13 ; see Gn 7,11 ; 8,2, cp. 1,2.

([177]) Eliade, *Das Heilige* 76.

([178]) For that reason the exceptional Jb 26,5 is not particularly disturbing. In his forthcoming dissertation A. Blommerde translates : " the Shades writhe in pain, the waters ... are crushed (*tēḥat*) ".

([179]) Zandee, 236 ; Eliade, *Das Heilige* 77.

([180]) Eliade, *Das Heilige* 77.

primeval and historical facts merge : the salvation in the Sea of Reeds represents the subdual of the chaotic waters in the beginning : the Hebrews were saved from destruction, the Egyptians (and later enemies) thrown into it, reduced to chaos ([181]).

$T^e h\hat{o}m$ also serves to describe an infernal situation ([182]).

The use of the term in Ps 107,26 suggests a *double entendre* : " They mounted up to heaven, went down to the depths ". Jonah cries out of the belly of Sheol (2,6) : " The deep was around me ". In Ez 26,19, Yahweh threatens Tyre with destruction : he will bring the Deep over it and the mighty waters will cover it : it will be reduced to nothing, to Chaos.

These waters are a mystery ; only Yahweh fathoms them([183]) ; Job, a mere creature, did not walk in the recesses of the Deep ([184]).

Summarizing : " The dynamic nature of Sheol appears ... in the fact that it is often identified with the powers of chaos which constantly threaten creation. The earth is in fact encompassed by noxious waters seeking to submerge it, and in certain respects, the world of the shades is merely one with the Abyss upon it rests " ([185]).

1.7.2 Various terms

In fact $t^e h\hat{o}m$ denoting chaos and nether world has quite a few synonyms in biblical Hebrew. As they often occur together, treating them separately would involve much repetition. The following paragraphs therefore contain a summary, though it will be appreciated that some overlapping is unavoidable.

Baal, in the Ugaritic cycle bearing his name, is threatened by Lord Sea, who is also called Judge (or rather : Prince ([186])) River ; but with the help of the divine Craftsman Kothar, Baal subdues his enemy. In other words : Cosmos wins a victory over Chaos ; chaotic powers are enchained and order reigns ([187]). As Yam-Nahar is most

([181]) Ex 15,5 ($t^e h\bar{o} m\hat{o} t$) ; cp. Is 51,10 ; 63,13 ; Ps 77,17 ; 106,9 (Kraus, *Psalmen* 533, 897).

([182]) Abundant documentation with Barth, *Erettung* 85.

([183]) Sir 42,18.

([184]) Jb 38,16 ; cp. 28,14 ; Hab 3,10 ; Ps 148,7.

([185]) Martin-Achard, *From Death ...* 43.

([186]) Cp. C. Brekelmans, *Rasj Sjamra en het OT* (Nijmegen–Utrecht *s.a.*) 17 f.

([187]) *UT* 137, 132, 68 ; Gordon, *UL* 9 f. ; 13-17 ; Driver, *CMAL* 13 ; 79-83 ; gaster, *Thespis* 153, 71 ; Ginsberg, *ANET* 129 ff.a ; summaries in Gray, *Canaan-*

likely identical with the Dragon under different names ([188]), the resemblance of this myth with the *Drachenkampf* motive is obvious. In mythological figurative speech all cosmic sources were conceived of as dragons, Albright ascertains ([189]).

In addition to this creation motive, vegetation myth is found in the Baal cycle as well ([190]): Baal, the god of rain, life and fertility, is to submit to Mot, the god of death, drought and ripening, and descends into his domain, the nether world from which he is delivered again in due time.

Turning to the OT, we will find traces of the same motives there ([191]); Yam and Nahar, however, are exclusively used in a cosmic sense, so that the original connotation is not entirely lost. The use of such terms as *mayîm* with a nether world connotation is sometimes traced back to the experience of travellers surprised by the sudden rise of *wadi's* ([192]); a similar use of *yam* is explained by a lack of maritime experience among the Israelites ([193]). By now it should be clear that these rationalizing explanations tend to overlook the age-old use and deeper dimensions of this vocabulary and the awe of primordial mysteries expressed in it.

---

ites 127-134 and Kapelrud, *Discov.* 41-44; L. R. Fisher, " Creation at Ugarit and in the OT ", *VT* 15 (1965) 313-324; V. Maag in Schmökel, *Kulturgesch.* 579 f. Scholars disagree as to the cosmogonic character of these texts. D. J. McCarthy writes: " It must suffice to notice that the struggle is between adversaries for control of an apparently organized world, and that there is no hint that the winner constructs a new order as Marduk does ... " (" Creation Motifs in Ancient Hebrew Poetry ", *CBQ* 29 [1967] 393-406: 393, n. 1).

([188]) *'nt*: III: 37 ff.: parallelism *ym-nhr-tnn-bṯn 'qltn* (the seven-headed writhing serpent); the latter is equated with *ltn* in 67: I: 1. *Tnn, ltn* and *bšn* occur in the OT. Gaster (*Thespis*[1] 186): " Leviathan is ... simply another name for the draconic Sir Sea "; in *Thespis*[2] 145, however, he thinks that " they must be clearly distinguished ". See G. R. Driver, " Mythical Monsters in the Old Testament ", *Fs Levi Della Vida* I (Roma 1956) 234-249.

([189]) *Die Religion Israels* 166.

([190]) Maag in Schökel, *Kulturgesch.* 577; Gaster, *Thespis* 201 ff., etc.

([191]) See O. Kaiser, *Bedeutung des Meeres*.

([192]) M. Löhr, in *ThLZ* 42 (1917) 428; Dalman, *Arbeit u. Sitte* I, 1, 211.

([193]) Reymond, " L'eau " 163 f. Of course the connection with experience can hardly be denied: " An element that kills everyone who is immersed in it, is in itself, according to ancient view, an element of death and destruction " (Wensinck, *Ocean* 45).

1.7.2.1 *yam,* etc.

As, in parallelism, *yam* often stands for Chaos, subdued by the creating God ([194]) there is plenty of reason to suppose that *yam* alone could stand for chaos and nether world as well. This conclusion does not hold good, however. It is only very exceptionally that *yam* alone denotes welter or Sheol; in the Psalter, for instance, apart from the cases in which it is balanced by *nhrt, yam* means chaos in 68,23 (*meṣulôt yam*), in 77,20 (+ *mayîm rabbîm*), in 89,10 (+ *rhb* etc), 93,4 (*mšbry ym; //*), 135,6 (*// teḥôm*). In all cases but the last *yam* is singular. We see the strict nether world connotation is extremely weak with *yam.*

In Jonah 2 an accumulation of elements involving water serves to describe the dire straits the prophet is in:

> Thou didst cast me into the Deep,   (*mṣlh*)
> into the heart of the seas,
> and the stream was around me;   (*nhr*)
> all thy breakers and waves   (*mšbr*)
> passed over me ...
> The waters surrounded me   (*mayîm*)
> up to my neck,
> the Deep was round about me....(4.6; RSV 3.5) (*teḥôm*)

There follows a very instructive description of Jonah's situation in terms of nether world. We shall return to this text later.

Another collection of chaos names, but this time without any anthropological connotation, is found in Ps 93,3 f.

> The streams have lifted up, O Jahweh,
> the streams have lifted up their voice,
> the streams lift up their roaring.
> Mightier than the voices of mighty waters,
> mightier than the breakers of the sea,
> mightier than heaven is Yahweh ([195]).

([194]) Ps 74,13; 89,26; 24,2; Nah 1,4; Is 44,27; Hab 3,8; Is 51,10.; historicized in Jr 6,23; Ps 65,8, etc.

([195]) Understanding *b* as *bet* comparativum with Dahood, " HULex ", *Bib* 44 [1963] 299 f.); for *mārôm,* " heaven ", cp. Zor 472B. This psalm is strongly reminiscent of the " Baal-type " of cosmogony in Ugarit: see the judicious remarks of L. R. Fisher, " Creation at Ugarit and in the Old Testament ", *VT* 15 (1965) 313-324. W. Schmidt remarks that the parallelism *nhr/ym* agrees with Ugaritic myth where *nhr/ym* are opposed to Baal (*Königtum* 39).

Here we have *nhr, mym rbym, mšbry-ym*, so this text serves well as a transition to the next item.

1.7.2.2   *mayîm rabbîm*

Since this expression was extensively treated by H. G. May [196] who put forward its cosmic connotations, we can review it concisely here.   It is another chaos name, so we can expect it to stand for nether world as well.   As to its chaotic connotation, this appears, e.g., in the strongly Canaanite Psalm 29:

> The voice of Jahweh is upon the waters,
> the God of glory thunders,
> Jahweh on the mighty waters (v. 3).

This obtains an historical dimension in Ps 77,20:

> Thy way was through the sea,
> thy path through the mighty waters. (cp. Is 8,7)

The same remark holds true for the many occurrences in Ezekiel; on 26,19, W. Zimmerli comments: " Tyrus wird von der Sintflut erschlungen werden " and he adds that *mayîm rabbîm* in Ez most often denotes " chaotische Urwasser " [197].
Finally, it stands for netherworld in Ps 18,17:

> He reached from on high, he took me,
> he drew me out of the mighty waters,

which is echoed in Ps 144,7:

> Stretch forth thy hand from on high,
> rescue me and deliver me from the mighty waters,
> from the hand of aliens ... [198].

Cant 8,7 reads: " Mighty waters cannot quench love, neither can floods (*nhrt*) drown it " which, in the light of the preceding " love is strong as death, jealousy cruel as the grave ", contains a clear allusion to the nether world.

Simple *mayîm*, on the contrary, hardly ever represents chaos and the nether world.   In general it stands for fertility, prosperity, and

---

[196] " Some Cosmic Connotations of *mayîm rabbîm* ", in *JBL* 74 (1955) 9-21.
[197] W. Zimmerli, *Ezechiel* 621.
[198] See Gunkel, *Schöpfung und Chaos* 102-106.

well-being. Lam 3,54 is one of the very rare exceptions: " water closed over my head, I said: ' I am lost ! ' "

In other cases context or added epithets rule out any misunderstanding:

> Then the waters would have swept us away,
> the stream would have gone over us;
> then over us would have gone
> the raging waters. (Ps 124,4 f.)

In view of the preceding considerations Pope's interpretation of Job 33,22 obtains a lucid simplicity:

> His soul draws near the Pit,
> His life to the waters of Death.

Parallelism shows that the reference in the second colon must be to the abode of the dead, a place, or to Death himself. This was felt by the ancient translators, who wrote: " Hades " and " Death ". TM reads *lam^{e}mîtîm*. Without any consonantal change, Pope reads *l^{e}mê māwet-mô*, the last part being the enclitic emphatic particle. " The difficulty " of this enclitic *mem*, however, " is its very ease " ([199]); besides, it is not evident that the reading *māwet* does not imply the addition of a *waw*, which, as *māwet* contains two syllables, should be expected in primitive spelling as well ([200]).

1.7.2.3 Breakers

The word *mšbr* is used five times to describe infernal distress; we already met it in Ps 93,3 and Jon 2,4 where the context shows that it stands for " brechende Wellen, Brandung " (Gesenius). Indeed, roaring surf is overwhelming for those not given to surfing.

" All thy breakers and waves have gone over me " (Ps 42,8). This use is frequent enough to exclude misunderstanding; moreover, the context generally leads to a correct appreciation of the term. There is sufficient evidence to rule out the necessity of offering a new explanation for Ps 88,8 where it is balanced by " wrath " in the second colon. This led G. R. Driver to the translation " outburst (of grief

---

([199]) Cp. Wellek–Warren, *Theory of Literature* 69.

([200]) Unless *māwet* is contracted to *môt*, as in Ugaritic, and in Hebrew status constructus. Simple *mayîm* stands for danger in Ps 88,18. For a different interpretation see now Dahood, " HULex " *Bib* 48 (1967) 435 (*l^{e}mō mōtîm*, " to Death ").

or vexation); outbreaks (of temper) ", which he backs by *nšbr*, " broken, vexed " in Ez 6,9 (and Arabic *'anâ* = " intended, caused to appear ") (²⁰¹). We do not wish to discuss here the rather loose connection between diverse meanings proposed by Driver and the elliptical translation which results from it: " Thou hast caused thy outbreaks to appear ". We quote the preceding line to give this one its natural background and read:

> 7a Thou hast put me in the depths of the Pit,
> b   in the regions dark and deep.
> 8a Thy wrath lies heavily upon me,
> b   " and Thou dost overwhelm me with all thy breakers ".

So 7 a + b clearly refer to nether world; and though 8a makes an approach to " conceptual language ", infernal *mšbr* in 8b is not surprising at all as another image of God's ire. *'nh* can be rendered " humbled, oppressed ", of course; but perhaps another proposal may be made. For Ps 107,10, *'syry 'ny wbrzl*, D. W. Thomas suggested: " shackled by fetters " etc., deriving *'ny*, " fetter ", from Arabic *'aniya*, " became a captive ", and *'ana*, *'anwa*, " imprisonment " (²⁰²). This is rendered the more likely in that 2 S 22,5d contains a similar use: *ăpāpūnî mišbᵉrê māwet, naḥălê bᵉlîya'al yᵉba'ătūnî* " the breakers of death encompassed me; the torrents of Belial assailed me ".

In Accadian *'pp* means " to bind " (²⁰³), which is still visible in Ps 18,5: " the cords of Death bound me ".

So we have:

> Ps 18,5 :   *ḥbl*   + *'pp*
> 2 S 22,5 :   *mšbr*   + *'pp*
> and Ps 88,8 reads : *mšbr*   + *'nh*

So Ps 88,8 reads:

> Thy wrath lies heavily upon me,
> and Thou entanglest me in all thy breakers.

1.8 The Pit (bôr)

Un pozzo assai largo e profondo. (Inferno XVIII, 5)

1. Primarily *bôr* means cistern, i.e., store of caught rainwater:

(²⁰¹) *JSS* 7 (1962) 96.
(²⁰²) *The Text of the Revised Psalter* (London 1964) 45. Cp. E. W. Lane, *An Arabic–English Lexicon* (London 1863 ff.) 2718b.
(²⁰³) *KB* 78 B.

" waterpit, cistern, pearshaped, generally some metres deep, (artificial) hollow in rocky ground, used to store wintry rainwater " ([204]).

2. Then it means: " prison, dungeon " as in Jr 38. From now on, scholars disagree:

3. a) Gesenius, explicitly rejecting the interpretation " nether world " gives as next meaning: " grave " ([205]). b) For *KB*, *bôr* signifies the cistern as entrance to Sheol ([206]). c) According to others, *bôr* can stand for Sheol: *BDB* points to the phrase *yrd bwr* as parallel with *yrd š'wl*, etc. ([207]); Zorell confines the meaning " orcus, infernum " to that phrase; Gunkel comments: " ... der Bedeutungsübergang erfolgt nicht über die Bedeutung ' Grab ', was das Wort niemals bezeichnet ... " ([208]); In Qumran the word occurs in the sense of ' petit réservoir souterrain ' ([209]).

There can be no reasonable doubt now as to *bôr* meaning " grave " ([210]): this interpretation is imperative in Is 14,19: " ... who go down to the stones of the pit ". Vincent remarks how well this queer expression corresponds to palpable facts: in Palestine dead were found buried on a bed of stones ([211]). So there is no reason to change or omit this phrase in Is 14. Nor can the meaning " grave, sepulchre " possibly be denied for this text.

It is clear now that Lam 3,43 must refer to a custom different from the one found in Is 14; Lam 3 recalls rather the use mentioned in 2 S 18,17 (Absalom's last resting-place).

But certainly *bôr* in Lam 3 bears upon the grave:

> They flung me alive into the pit
> and cast stones on me;
> water closed over my head;
> I said: " I am lost ".

The " waters " here suggest a deeper understanding of this verse: the psalmist feels himself in Sheol, and the first two cola are to be understood as referring to a lamentable situation.

As to Zorell's opinion, Ps 40,3 shows that *bôr* is found with Sheol connotation outside of the phrase *yrd bwr*:

([204]) *KB* 114 B.
([205]) *GB* 89B.
([206]) *KB loc. cit.* Compare Accadian *būru* (Tallqvist, *Namen der Totenwelt* 7).
([207]) 92 B.
([208]) *Psalmen*⁴ 121.
([209]) Milik, *DJD* III, 243 *sub* 64.
([210]) *Bôr* is balanced by *šḥt* in Ps 7,16; see also Ps 55,24.
([211]) H. Vincent, *Canaan* 270.

> He drew me up from the pit of destruction,
> out of the miry bog (*tît*).

This is a rather stereotyped locution signifying serious danger and liberation from it; the reference to the nether world and its shifting sand is unmistakable. At the same time, however, there is a clear allusion to the background of this representation: this pit with its miry bog reminds us of Jeremiah's prison (38,6):

> And there was no water in the cistern (*bôr*), but only
> mire (*tît*) and Jeremiah sank in the mire.

KB's statement is hardly in harmony with the evidence. In Is 38,18 parallelism must be observed:

> Sheol cannot thank thee,
> death cannot praise thee;
> those who went down to the pit cannot hope .....

Here *BDB*'s remark about parallel phrases is to the point.

In Ez *yrd bwr* is particularly frequent. It is balanced by *'rṣ tḥtywt* in 32,18.24. Ez 26,20 is a suggestive text:

> And you will perforce descend ([212]) to those who are descended ([213]) into the pit, to the people of old, and I will make you dwell in the depths of the nether world as in ([214]) primeval ruins with those who are descended into the pit so that you will not return nor stand in the land of the living ([215]).

([212]) The translation " to " (for Hebrew *'et*), as suggested by LXX, can be supported by serious philological evidence (see Van Dijk, *Ezekiel's Prophecy* 42 f.).

([213]) For the past tense see above, pp. 33 f.; Van Dijk remarks that the second occurrence of this expression in this verse must be rendered " those who descended " and quotes some other participles expressing past actions: Jos 5,6; Jer 28,4; Ez 32,23; 39,10 (*ibid.* 42).

([214]) Considering the normal omission of the preposition *b^e* after *k^e* (Joüon, 133h), *kāḥorābôt* can be interpreted " as it were, in ruins ". Van Dijk (43 ff.) argues that *b^e* often does duty for *k^e* and vice versa: " *b^e* and *k^e* are collocated sometimes in exactly the same acceptation for poetic variety " (44). Moreover he proves that the *mem* of TM *mē^ʿôlām* must be explained as a *mem* encliticum: in all other cases the expression runs *ḥŏrābôt ʿôlām* (45).

([215]) With *BH* we vocalize *tāšubî*, but we do not take it as periphrastic; an allusion to the " land of no return " is very likely; possibly with a pun with preceding *yšb*. For " primeval ruins " see below, pp. 72 ff.

Moreover, in Ez 31,14 *yrd bwr* is accompanied by *mwt* and *'rṣ thtyt*; in 31,16 by *yrd š'wl* and *'rṣ thtyt*. The epithet " lowest " is then found with *bôr* itself in Lam 3,55 : " I called ... from the very lowest pit " [216].

Twice, not *bôr* but *b*^{e}*'ēr* is found with the same meaning. Sometimes emendation to *bôr* is proposed, but an explanation of the text is to be preferred. The word means " well of underground water " [217], i.e. a shaft reaching the water-level or an underground waterstore.

Ps 69,19 runs : " Let not the well close its mouth over me ". The expression is a current one ; see Gn 29,8 and 1 S 17,19. So the reading *b'r* is not suspect from that point of view [218].

1.9 šaḥat (Pit - Corruption)

Although disagreeing as to its root, most modern lexicographers propose " pit " as the only meaning of *šht*. An exception is Zorell, who translates : 1. " perditio " ; 2. " demersio, fovea " [219]. LXX apparently ignored the etymology and meaning of the word. Its translations are clearly *ad sensum* : *phthora* and composites, *lakkos* (cistern), *bothros* (pit), *thanatos, rhupos*. In Qumran the correct understanding of the term was preserved : we find it in the senses " pit " and " corruption " [220].

" The pit " can certainly refer to the nether world. The current expression *yrd 'l šht* [221] shows the word to be equivalent to *š'wl, bwr* and *'rṣ* [222], which appears moreover from the antithesis in Ps 49,10 : " When he could have lived jubilant for ever, and never have seen the Pit " (Dahood).

---

[216] *Plurale intensivum* : Ez 28,8.10 (Zimmerli, *Ezechiel* 664) ; Dahood on Ps 89,51 (*UHPh* 11), on Prv 11,30 (*id., Prov.* 25), etc.

[217] *KB* 105A.

[218] Living water stems directly from *t*^{e}*hôm* with its essentially double character (Wensinck, *Ocean* 60, 65). For the form of graves see H. Vincent, *Canaan* 210, 215, 226, 272 ; A. G. Barrois, *Manuel d'Archéologie biblique*, II (Paris 1953) 283-286, 295 ff. ; A. Jirku, *Die Ausgrabungen in Palestina und Syrien* (Halle [Saale] 1956) 69 f., 120 f., 188 f.

[219] *Lexicon s.v.* 836A. See now M. C. Astour, in *JNES* 27 (1968) 25.

[220] Cp. E. Lohse, *Die Texte aus Qumran* (München 1964) ; " Grube " in 1 QS 11,13 ; 1 QH 2,21 and CD 14,2 (*mwqšy* — 1 QH 3,12 (*mšbry* —) ; 3,18 (*dlty* —) ; 3,19 (// *š'wl 'bdwn*), etc. ; " Corruption " in 1 QS 4,12 ; 9,16.22, etc. ('*nšy* —) ; cp. H.-W. Kuhn, *Probeartikel Qumranwörterbuch* (Göttingen s.a.).

[221] Ps 30,10 ; 55,24 ; Jb 33,24, cp. v. 28.

[222] See I above, pp. 32 f. For Accadian *šuttu* see Tallqvist, *Namen der Totenwelt* 3.

Job 33 offers several clear examples. V. 18 reads : " ... to spare his soul from the Pit, His life from crossing the Channel " [223] ; and verse 22 : " His soul draws near the Pit, his life to the waters of death " (Pope) [224]. In the latter two texts parallelism leaves little doubt as to the postulated meaning.

Some texts suggest that this name passed from the grave to Sheol ; Jb 17,14 reads : " Say to the Pit, ' You are my father ', To the maggot, ' My mother and sister ' ... " (Pope). And Is 38,17 mentions the *šaḥat bᵉli*, the " pit of destruction, of corruption ", which obviously refers to the fate of the body in the tomb. Here the frontiers between grave and nether world cannot be drawn.

Sometimes the understanding of the word *šḥt* offers difficulties ; the texts will be reviewed here.

Ps 16,10 reads : " You will not put me in Sheol, nor allow your devoted one to see the Pit " (Dahood). In view of the examples quoted before in this paragraph, it is obvious that *šḥt*, here balanced by Sheol, serves as a local name [225]. It seems that a correct appreciation of TM here is often hampered by the LXX translation and its use in the NT. These depend on the interpretation of *'zb* as " to leave " and a rather subtle view on the second colon, which is made to say that the psalmist will see the " Pit ", but not " Corruption ", as he will rise. It is doubtful if all this can be read into the Hebrew text. The recognition of *'zb*, " to put ", sheds new light on the verse [226]. It is forthwith evident, then, that the second colon must be understood as expressing the same conviction : the psalmist trusts that God will preserve him from death [227]. The NT recognizes an allusion to the resurrection of the Lord in the defective LXX translation (as shown before, the LXX did not understand *šḥt*) and makes use of it to give a scriptural basis to that primordial fact. It is not the only example of its kind in the NT.

Job 9,31, a verse occurring in a passage where Job desperately confesses the impurity of man before God, reads : " Then you will plunge me into *šḥt* ". Horst comments : " Da die Grube nicht ohne weiteres schlammig ist, empfiehlt es sich, im Anschluss am G... *ba-*

---

[223] Cp. 33,30 and below, pp. 148 f.

[224] For " waters " cp. above, p. 65.

[225] As to the common opinion that Sheol and Pit stand for deathly peril here, Coppens rightly remarks : " Nothing suggests that the psalmist is in danger of illness " (*Onsterfelijkheidsgeloof* 16).

[226] Dahood, " The Root *'zb* II in Job ", *JBL* 78 (1959) 303-309, esp. 308, n. 16.

[227] Dahood, 90 f. ; *r'h šḥt* is equivalent to *r'h mwt* in Ps 89,49.

šuḥâ, Unrat, zu lesen " (²²⁸). This confidence in LXX is hardly justified. Others take refuge in emending to sᵉḥî (Lam 3,45) or to śuḥōt, by-form of sûḥâ (Is 5,25). The latter is a solution, postulated *ad rem*; and of both Pope remarks that there is no evidence that they denote liquid filth. His own argument for understanding šḥt as " filth ", however, is curious. It can be summarized in this way: as šḥt stands for the nether world, and the nether world is a muddy and filthy place, šḥt itself also means " liquid filth " (²²⁹). That is hardly philological logic. The present writer would prefer to take the Qumran evidence as a starting point. These texts prove the existence of šḥt = " corruption " in Hebrew, and consequently the possibility of this meaning in the OT cannot be discarded on basis of the fact (*dato non concesso*) that it would be a hapax. As biblical Hebrew certainly does not preserve the complete Hebrew vocabulary, a hapax legomenon is by no means surprising, especially not in Job, as evidence shows. Moreover it cannot be disputed that the Hebrew root šḥt can be related to the noun, meaning " corruption " concretely " corrupted matter, filth ". On this basis Pope's translation " filth " can be accepted.

Ps 55,24 mentions b'r šḥt, commonly translated " the lowest pit ". J. van der Ploeg, no doubt in view of the Qumran evidence, renders the phrase as " the pit of dissolution " (²³⁰). The word b'r, " well of underground water " (²³¹) is rather embarrassing. Gunkel makes the characteristic remark that in fairy tales the entrance to the nether world is often found in a well: Frau Holle (²³²). All the same, the interpretation of šḥt remains difficult. " The well of the Pit " is a rather wooden phrase (²³³). In our opinion one cannot reasonably reject the translation of van der Ploeg.

(²²⁸) Fr. Horst, *Hiob* (BK 16/1-4; Neukirchen 1960-1963) 141.
(²²⁹) Pope, *Job* 72 ff. See Pope, " The Word šaḥat in Job 9,31 ", *JBL* 83 (1964) 269-278.
(²³⁰) *De Psalmen* (Roermond 1963) 128: " De put der ontbinding ". Cp. Ps 40,3. The idea of dissolution points to the grave.
(²³¹) *KB* 105A.
(²³²) Gunkel, *Psalmen*⁴ 121. Cf. *Die Märchen der Brüder Grimm* (Leipzig 1924) I, 121-124.
(²³³) Fr. Baethgen reads " Der Brunnen welcher das Grab ist " (*Genitivus appositionis*; *Die Psalmen* [Göttingen 1904] 164). With many others he thinks bōr is to be read. His proposal cannot be discarded.

1.10   Ruin (maššû'â ; ḥorbâ)

In the fifth canto of his *Inferno*, lines 34-36, Dante describes Hell in this way :

> Quando giungon davanti a la ruina,
> quivi la strida, il compianto, il lamento ;
> bestemmian quivi la virtù divina.

> When they arrived before the ruin,
> where they screamed, lamented, moaned,
> and cursed Almighty God ... .

Here we are reminded of Ps 73,18b :

hippaltām l^emaššû'ôt, " You hurled them into Decay " (234).

The root *š'h* has been studied by J. T. Milik (235) ; the verbal form means " to fall ", " to fall into decay ", etc. Milik does not mention the noun in question, but parallelism (" In Perdition you transplanted them ") makes clear that it stands for a place of decay and desolation ; indeed, *GB* translates " Trümmer " (236). Ez 26,20, a text entirely dominated by Sheol, contains the words : " I will make you dwell in the nether world, among the primeval ruins ".

The word *'lm* is not rarely applied to the netherworld sphere : see *mētê 'ôlām* and *'am 'ôlām* (237).

The expression " ruins of old " hardly refers to persons ; see Is 58,12 and 61,4 (238).

Ps 9,7 might contain a reference to the same conception of Sheol ; with due reserve the following translation is proposed here : " The enemies — may they be consumed in perpetual ruins " (*ḥŏrābôt lāneṣaḥ*). The absence of a preposition before " ruins " is a difficulty in any interpretation, but in the proposed rendering it seems evident enough to be omitted (239). The perfect is parsed as a precative (240).

---

(234) For Ugaritic evidence see above, [p. 7. In Accadian, the nether world can be called *karmu* and *ḥarbu*, each of which means " ruin " (Tallqvist, *Namen der Totenwelt* 17,22 f.). This may apply to *ḥrb* in Jb 15,22 ; see Ps 9,7.

(235) In *Bib* 38 (1957) 249.

(236) *GB* 466B.

(237) *BDB*, 762A *sub* lb. Compare Accadian *uru ul-la*, " eternal city " (!) (Tallqvist, *Namen der Totenwelt* 16).

(238) *Contra*: Zimmerli, *Ezechiel* 607.

(239) Cp. Joüon, 133a. The omission may have been induced by the length of the colon. See also Ps 68,7 (*ṣḥyḥḥ*), etc.

(240) Cp. Dahood, *Psalms* 23.

After the unveiled reference to Sheol in Ps 73,18 an allusion to the nether world can be regarded as obvious :

> How are they delivered to Destruction (*šammâ*) all of a
> sudden ;
> come to an end, consumed by Terrors !
> (Ps 73,19).

Suggestive *ballāhôt* reminds one of the King of Terrors in Jb 18,14 ([241]).

In connection with Jb 18,14, N. M. Sarna has shown that the word *blhh* is always accompanied by the idea of destruction ([242]). From a quick survey of all occurrences it will appear that this thesis can be substantiated ; the word is generally found in texts dealing with the lot of the wicked, where their punishment by death and in Sheol are described, and could very aptly be rendered as " infernal terrors ".

Is 17,14 : The context announces an eschatological punishment for Israel's enemies. In vv. 12 f. we find the familiar images of mighty waters and harvest ; v. 14 describes the end of the adversaries in the thick of night :

> At evening time, behold, terror !
> Before the morning, they are no more !

([241]) It is not unlikely that the verb *ḥrb* also means " to be desolate, waste " without necessarily implying the idea of destruction ; this is a reasonable supposition where the stress apparently is on solitude and forlornness as in Is 51,3, cp. 48,21 (the noun meaning " deserts ") ; Jr 7,34 ; 25,11 ; 44,22 ; Zeph 2,14 and the proper name Horeb. This aspect might be predominant in the vexing verse Jb 3,14 which, in this interpretation, would quite properly refer to the burial which rich persons can afford :

> Kings and counsellors of the earth,
> who built themselves forlorn abodes.

Or : " abodes of destruction " ; this would refer to the devastating process to which corpses in the grave are subject. The abode of the evil spirits is called *bītu nadū*, " dilapidated house ", in Accadian (Tallqvist, *Namen der Totenwelt* 17). As that name is equivalent to *ḫarbu* (the word in Jb 3,14) in that language, the Hebrew formula may have a similar connotation. Cp. Jb 15,28 f. : " And he will dwell in ruined cities ; houses in which nobody should live will be his, which prove destined to remain heaps. He will not be rich nor his wealth endure, nor his possessions reach the nether world ... ". As man generally does not live in more cities and houses than one, it is tempting to consider the plurals as intensive, suggesting the City and House of Sheol. The " nether world " in v. 29 shows that this idea is not farfetched.

([242]) In *JBL* 82 (1963) 315-318.

> This is the portion of those who despoil us,
> and the lot of those who plunder us.

" Terror " here is the herald of approaching Death, which snatches the enemies away in the darkness of night time ; the end is indicated by characteristic 'ênnennû. It is explicitly said that this is the lot of the enemies.

Ez 26,21 : a prophecy announcing the fall of Tyre. After an undisguised appearance of Sheol in v. 20, we read : " I will make thee terror (KJ ; RSV : I will bring you to a dreadful end) and you shall be no more ... ". The RSV translation is significant ([243]) and so is the typical 'ênēk.

Ez 27,36, the end of the satirical funeral dirge on Tyre, is practically identical with 26,21 : " You have come to a dreadful end and shall be no more for ever ! " (RSV)

Jb 18,11.14. Bildad's description of the portion of the wicked is particularly instructive : he is in darkness (vv. 5 f.), his feet trip and are thrown in the net (vv. 7 ff.). The text proceeds :

> Round about TERRORS affright him,
> and harry him at every step.
> Let the Hungry One face him,
> with Death stationed at his side ([244]).
> His skin is gnawed by disease ;
> Death's first-born feeds on his limbs.
> He is snatched away from his comfortable tent
> And haled before the King of TERRORS. (Pope)

This text shows that the infernal terrors originate from Death himself : this panic is a certain symptom of his sway and announces the coming of his Kingdom.

In ch. 24 Job pictures the obscure practices of the wicked, who become photophobic as the Evil One himself : " Morning to them is darkness (ṣlmwt) ; Well they know the TERRORS of darkness " (Jb 24,17 ; Pope).

In Jb 27 we read :

13   This is the wicked's portion from God

([243]) The form ballāhôt may be explained as a singular as in Phoenician (Van Dijk, *Ezekiel's Prophecy* 22, with Harris, *Grammar* 58 f.).

([244]) For this verse see Dahood, *Psalms* 237 and above, p. 109 ; the other verses are Pope's.

The tyrant's inheritance from Shaddai ...:

19 Rich he lies down and the Victor gathers him;
    God fixes his eyes and he is no more ('ênnennû).
20 TERRORS overwhelm him by day,
    By night the tempest carries him off [245].

This man is never safe; in very daytime he is overwhelmed by the forces of darkness.

In ch. 30, finally, Job's lament describes the deplorable lot which is his:

15 TERRORS are turned on me,
    dispelling my dignity like the wind.
    Like a cloud gone my prosperity [246] ...
19 God casts me into the mire,
    I become dust and ashes.
23 I know that you will return me to Death,
    To the meetinghouse of all the living. (Pope)

It is not necessary to study the occurrences of the verb *bhl* here. Jb 22,10 f. be quoted by way of example:

    Therefore snares surround you,
    and sudden dread DISMAYS you,
    Darkness where you cannot see,
    The streaming water covers you.

Again some conspicuous members of the company are present: snares (*paḥ*), sudden dread (*paḥad pit*ᵉ*'ôm*), darkness (*ḥōšek*), waters (*mayîm*): the *Wortfeld* of Death is unmistakable.

In conclusion, we may say that " infernal terrors " are closely related to the presence of Death: they are a manifestation of his devastating and surprising influence in evil circumstances. This fact corresponds to descriptions of danger as found in individual laments, and indeed *blhwt* was found both in this literary type and in cognate genres (texts describing the miserable lot of the wicked or wishing them a fate as expressed in the IL). So the translation " infernal terrors " is justified.

---

[245] The translation of v. 19 is proposed by A. Blommerde.
[246] The same image for transitoriness in Jb 7,8 f.

1.11 Dûmâ (Fortress - Silence)

This word in Ez 27,32b has been shown to mean " fortress " by M. Dahood ([247]). It is related to Accadian *dimtu* and to the Mari local name, vocalized Dumtan. In Ugaritic it is written *dmt* (1002 : 43) and interpreted as a " kind of building? " by Gordon ([248]), but by Aistleitner (after Virolleaud) as " Burg " ([249]). This rendering can safely be labelled certain for Ez 27. The traditional emendation to *nidmâ* does not recommend itself by the very fact that it does violence to the structure of the lament. For not only is " der Gegensatz von Einst und Jetzt ... scharf herausgearbeitet " ([250]), but also the expressiveness of this composition depends on these two being clearly separated : 32b-33 (past) and 34-36 (present ; cp. 28,11-16a. 16b-19). In other words : destruction comes untimely in verse 27. Most likely the local name in Jos 25,52 has the same meaning, and if the identification with ed-Dōme by Albright (see *KB* 205 *B*) is correct, the same place might be intended in Is 21,11, as Udumu lies in the Se'ir mountains in Southern Judea ([251]).

It is a well-known fact that Sheol in ancient Semitic civilization was conceived of as a prison, a fortified city, a fortress ([252]). Two possible occurrences of *dûmâ* with this meaning will be proposed here. Ps 94,17 reads :

> If the Lord had not been my helper,
> my soul would have dwelt in *dûmâ*.

The common " land of silence " (RSV) seems a somewhat loose rendering of a word that indicates a condition rather than a place, which latter, however, is required by the verb *škn*. The translation, of course, is based on the traditional conception of Sheol as a *locus silentii* which is likely enough. But as " Fortress " is a local indication and at the same time squares excellently with ancient views on the nether world, it seems preferable.

The same reasoning holds true for Ps 115,17 :

> The dead do not praise the Lord
> nor do any that went down to the Fortress.

([247]) " HULex ", *Bib* 45 (1964) 83 f.
([248]) *UT* Gloss. 679.
([249]) *WUS* 763.
([250]) Jahnow, *Leichenlied* 212.
([251]) Abel, *Géogr.* I, 372 ; II, 49 ; carte 1). H. van Dijk argues that *dûmâ* is an apt name for Petra ; see Ps 60,11 ; 108,11 ; Ob 3 (*Ezekiel's Prophecy* 85 f.).
([252]) See pp. 152 ff. below.

Here we can refer to *yrd bwr*, *'rṣ*. In the present writer's opinion, however, this meaning might be very well merely predominant; the fatal meaning the word conveys may derive from its proximity to *dmm*, which means both " to wail, mourn ", and " to be silent " ([253]). The loss of these overtones is precisely the damage translation inevitably brings about ([254]).

In Egypt also there is an oppressive silence in the nether world: the Beyond is referred to as " the town of silence, the domain of rest " ([255]).

1.12   House (bêt)

" The ideas of the grave and of Sheol cannot be separated .... The dead are at the same time in the grave and in Sheol, not in two different places " ([256]). Consequently it is often very hard, if not impossible, to decide whether a text applies to Sheol or to the grave: thus formulated, the question more often than not hardly makes sense. " Indem der Tote den sichtbaren Raum des Grabes betritt, wird er auch Bewohner des Totenreiches und ist er dessen Existenzbedingungen unterworfen " ([257]). This should be kept in mind when one studies the word *byt* as a name of the grave. A clear example of this usage is found in Is 14,18:

> All of them rest in glory,
> each in his tomb (" house ") ([258]).

A remarkable occurrence was discovered in Gn 15,2:

> Lord Yahweh, what could you give me, if I pass away childless and if the one who pours out libations on my grave (" house ") is Eliezer ... ? ([259])

([253]) Cp. M. Dahood " HULex ", *Bib* 45 (1964) 402 f.

([254]) Cp. C. H. Dodd " The Translation of the Bible, Some Questions of Principle ", *Bible Translator* 14 (1960) 5 f.

([255]) Zandee, 93 A. 11. c.

([256]) Pedersen, *Israel* I/II, 462.

([257]) Barth, *Errettung* 84.

([258]) For Assyrian *bîtu*, " room, tomb ", see *CAD* II, 282A; compare *bīt mūti*, " house of death ", which is an equivalent of *arallū*, " nether world " (Tallqvist, *Namen der Totenwelt* 7); also *bīt etē*, " house of darkness ", and *bīt ipri*, " house of dust " (Tallqvist, *Namen der Totenwelt* 37 [cf. 34 ff.]). For Hebrew usage cf. *BDB* 1098B *sub* d. *Kābôd* as used here strongly recalls *yqr* (below); here the grave is really merged into Sheol (Pedersen, *loc. cit.*). In Egypt also the grave is called a " house " (Zandee, 103).

([259]) F. Vattioni, " Ancora su BEN-MEŠEQ di GEN. 15,2 ", in *Rivista*

It is not surprising that this name for the grave was also transferred
to the nether world; in fact this process is illustrated by Is 14,18,
quoted above. *Bêt* undoubtedly has this meaning in Jb 17,13:

> If I look for Sheol as my " house ";
> if I spread my couch in the Darkness ...

The grave is a " home " for successive generations of a family; this
house spans an endless period of time, it is a *byt ʿlm*.   Qoh 12,5 reads:
" ... man is about to go to his eternal home ".   As shown by Joüon,
the same compound is found in Palmyrene, Phoenician, Aramaic, and
Syrian, where it is balanced by *bt mqbrt'* and the like.   A Palmyrian
text mentions *yqr bt ʿlm'*, " monument (of honour), eternal house " ([260]).
Joüon remarks that the modification " eternal " bears upon the tomb
in its quality as a family grave ([261]).

The latter element is expressly put forward in Ps 49,12:

> Inside their eternal home (*bottêmô lᵉʿôlām*) ([262]),
> their dwelling place (*miškan*) for all generations.

(Here another name of the grave appears: *miškān*, also found in Is
22,16 and in Qumran) ([263]).   In the same Psalm *yqr*, quoted above,
occurs with a strong Sheol connotation (v. 13 etc.): " For man in the
mansion will sleep indeed ".

In fact sleep is a well-known activity of Sheol's inhabitants;
Sheol returns explicitly in vv. 15 f. ([264]).

" Viewed from the world of light, all the deceased form a common realm " ([265]).   The evolution of the use and meanings of *byt*
finally comes to an end in *byt mwʿd*; here all the graves are melted
together in one vast reality as appears in Jb 30,23:

---

degli studi orientali 40 (1965) 9-12, suggested " libatore " for *bn mšq*: see Dahood, *UHPh* 65.   That this was the son's duty may be seen in *UT* 2 Aq I:
28 f.

([260]) *CIS* II t. 3; t. 4192, p. 297 f.

([261]) P. Joüon, " Glanes palmyzéniennes ", *Syria* 19 (1938) 99-103.

([262]) The expression *bt ʿlm* is not yet apparently a fixed compound here;
the connection between *byt* and *ʿlm* is rather loose, for instead of a construct
chain with the possessive suffix added to the nomen rectum we have a prepo-
sitional construction, the suffix being attached to the first noun.

([263]) See Milik, *DJD* III 248.

([264]) For the translation: Dahood, *Psalms* 299.   The psalm describes the
condition after death of pious and wicked people alike, rather than the way
they die: Mulder, *Theol. Jesaja Apok.* 101 f.

([265]) Pedersen, *Israel* I/II, 460.

I know that you will return me to Death,
to the meetinghouse of all living. (Pope)

The name " House of Reunion " underlines the common fate of all
living; all men will " return " to the womb they came from ([266]).

([266]) For this idea see below, pp. 85 ff., 122 ff.

CHAPTER 2 : THE MILIEU

2.1 Destruction

2.1.1 Abaddon (Place of Destruction)

Although grammatically an abstract noun meaning " devastation, destruction " (¹), this word is always used concretely for " place of destruction ", i.e. the nether world. Sometimes we are reminded of Ugaritic *mt wšr* (Death-and-Rot) as in Proverbs 15,11 :

> Sheol and Abaddon lie open for the Lord,
> how much more the hearts of men !

Here it is pointed out how unfathomable the infernal depths are for man, though for the Lord they are transparent as a flat country on a sunny day.

In Jb 28,22 the question of Wisdom's elusive residence is treated with reference to the impenetrable depths of the nether world :

> Abaddon and Death say :
> " With our ears we heard a rumour of it ".

The general law of death is given expression in this proverb : " Sheol and Abaddon are never satisfied " (Prv 27,20).

Of course the question now arises as to the relation between Abaddon and its partners, Sheol and Death. We will therefore study the texts in which Abaddon is not found in pairs with an equivalent, but is illustrated by a related term in parallelism :

qbr : Is thy steadfast love declared in the grave,
     thy faithfulness in Abaddon ? (Ps 88,12)
sheol : Sheol is naked before God,
     and Abaddon has no covering (Jb 26,6).

Finally the term is found in isolation in Jb 31,12, where it denotes the far extreme of the universe : " ... a fire which consumes unto Abad-

---

(¹) Joüon, 88 M b.

don ". Nowhere in these texts does Abaddon appear as a department of the nether world distinct from Sheol, as in later rabbinism ([2]); in fact, it is parallel with Sheol, even with the grave, without any indication of climactic use. So we are justified in comparing the combinations in the first three texts with *mt wšr* (Death-and-Rot) in Ugaritic texts, reading the intervening *waw* as an " appositional " one ([3]).

The exact import of Abaddon in distinction to " Sheol " may be derived from its root *'bd* and its formation, indicating an abstract. On this basis Sutcliffe may very well be right when he says that the word is to be understood as " power of destruction ", as suggested by its Greek translation in Rev 9,11 " Apollyon " ([4]). In the OT it is indisputably used in a local sense in several cases. The idea of *'bd*, " to perish, to be destroyed ", suggests that the word was originally applied to the grave, where the human corpse perishes, i.e. is dissolved. An echo of this situation is heard in Ps 88,12, where Abaddon is balanced by " the grave ". So this name of the nether world seems to be one of the many transpositions from the grave to Sheol.

2.1.2 *rega'* (Death)

In the translation of M. Dahood, Ps 30,6 reads:

> For death is in his anger,
> life eternal in his favor.

Here *rg'* is rendered by " death ". The justification of this translation is as follows: " The prevailing antithetic parallelism of this poem indicates that *rega'* must connote the opposite of *ḥayyîm* ' life eternal ' " ([5]). This is further confirmed by *rg'*, which in Jb 26,12 is translated as " to annihilate "; it is parallel with *mḥṣ*, and in *UT* 67 : I : 1 f. *mḥṣ* again is balanced by *kly*, Hebrew *klh*. Finally, LXX understood the verb as " to destroy ", as affirmed by Seeligmann and Driver ([6]).

A quick glance in the major lexica shows that there is little general consensus as to *rg'*. *BDB* distinguish three roots *rg'*, *GB* two, while *KB* reduces all meanings to one root.

([2]) Strack–Billerbeck IV/2,1091.
([3]) W. F. Albright, in *BASOR* 164 (1961) 36.
([4]) Sutcliffe, *The Old Testament and Future Life* 43.
([5]) Dahood, *Psalms* 182; the interpretation of *ḥayîm* is not discussed here.
([6]) I. L. Seeligmann, " Voraussetzungen der Midraschexegese " (*VTS* 1 [1953] 150-181) 169, n. 2; G. R. Driver, " Problems in the Hebrew Text of Job " (*VTS* 3 [1955] 72-93) 74 f.

6

This confusion is also reflected in studies on the subject. For Seeligmann and Driver, the meaning is " to annihilate ", for Goldman, " to stir up " ([7]). According to Delekat, the oldest meaning is " sich zusammenziehen " ([8]).

Gunkel's translation : " to still, to quench " is adopted by Pope ([9]). Their arguments are convincing. Gunkel points to Ps 89,10 :

> Thou dost rule the raging of the sea,
> when its waves rise, thou stillest (*šbḥ*) them.

Opponents of the theory might now refer to Ps 89,11 (IL) :

> Thou didst crush Rahab like a carcass,
> thou didst scatter thy enemies ....

The solution of this problem is simple enough : in cosmogonic myths the primeval monster is pierced, etc., the chaotic waters are stilled. Now it seems that *rgʿ* is used to denote the latter. The theme is also referred to in Ps 65,8 (*šbḥ*) :

> who dost still the roaring of the seas,
> the roaring of their waves ... ([10]).

For Jb 26,12 (*rgʿ*) Gunkel pointed to LXX *katepausen* ([11]) ; Pope translates as follows :

> By his power he quelled the Sea,
> By his cunning he smote Rahab.

And as to *rgʿ*, " to quell ", he writes : " This is the sense required by the proper understanding of the context. In both the Mesopotamiam version of the battle between Marduk and Tiamat and in the Ugaritic version of Baal's battle with Prince Sea, the quietus is put on the sea " ; and further : " Admittedly in Is 51,15 and Jer 31,35 the verb *rgʿ* seems at first glance to have the sense of ' stir up ', but perusal of the context makes it clear that the message of comfort to Israel is

---

([7]) M. D. Goldman, *Australian Biblical Review* 2 (1952) 49.
([8]) L. Delekat, " Zum hebräischen Wörterbuch " (*VT* 14 [1964] 7-66) 59-66.
([9]) H. Gunkel, *Schöpfung und Chaos* 36 f., 91-111 ; L. Kopf, " Arabische Etymologien und Parallelen " (*VT* 8 [1958] 161-215) 202 (: *GB rgʿ* II. 1) ; Pope, *Job* 166.
([10]) Cp. Ps 46,4.
([11]) H. Gunkel, *Schöpfung und Chaos* 36 f.

drawn from the appeal to Yahweh's creative power and his defeat and control of the boisterous sea " ([12]).

So the present writer thinks that the argument for the translation " to destroy " cannot be maintained.

In this way it has become doubtful, if the translation " death " or " perdition " for *rg'* can be accepted. We think that most often " suddenly " or " in a moment " will do; this evokes specific bad associations. As D. Daube has shown, characteristic notions are apt to recur in texts with, or in close proximity to, the word " suddenly ". The technical sense " death, perdition ", however, seems based on a doubtful interpretation of the root.

2.1.3 *ḥalaq* (Perdition)

Till recently, Hebrew lexicography distinguished two roots *ḥlq*: I = " to make smooth "; II = " to divide " ([14]). But, as shown above ([15]), the existence of the root *ḥlq*, " to perish ", is now a firmly established fact in Hebrew lexicography.

Two derivative nouns are relevant here. The first is *ḥălāqâ*, occurring in Ps 73,18 :

> Indeed, in Perdition you transplanted them,
> You hurled them into Destruction ([16]).

This interpretation is recommended by the context, describing the unhappy end of the sinners; by the idiom " to transplant ", to be studied below ([17]) and by the parallelism with " Destruction ", another name for the nether world.

As *ḥlq* III is synonymous with *'bd*, this new name may be compared with Abaddon. No doubt these names stem from the grave, because of the devastating process corpses in a tomb are subject to. To stay in Sheol is tantamount to destruction and therefore a horrible prospect, because in Israel the reality of death was not disguised by the idea of a rebirth.

As to *ḥălaqlaqqâ*, its formation is a *qeṭalṭal*, denoting an intensification, " teils eine gesteigerte Energie des Handelns oder Verhaltens,

---

([12]) Pope, *Job* 166.
([13]) D. Daube, *The Sudden in the Scriptures* 9-11; for Daube *rg'* means " to agitate ", etc.
([14]) *KB* 305B.
([15]) See above, pp. 11 f.
([16]) Dahood, " HULex ", *Bib* 45 (1964) 408.
([17]) Cf. pp. 171 f.

teils eine grössere Stätigkeit des Verhaltens oder Zustandes " ([18]). Consequently the word in question connotes the utter perdition, the irrevocable ruin proper to Sheol. The noun occurs in Jr 23,12:

> And so their way shall be like Perdition (ḥălaqlaqqâ) to them; they shall be thrust into Darkness and fall into it ([19]).

This interpretation is a solid one. The literary genre is the same as in Ps 73, the lot of the wicked being under discussion; moreover the parallel Darkness and the verbs *dḥḥ – npl* belong to the same sphere of ideas ([20]). The prophet wishes his enemies an infernal life.

Another occurrence is found in Ps 35,6, an individual lament; the immediate context again deals with the fate of the wicked:

> Let their destiny be Darkness and Destruction,
> with the Angel of Yahweh pursuing them ([21]).

The affinity of this text with Jr 23,12 is remarkable; in either case it is the *drk* (" way, destination ") which will become infernally dark; Darkness and Destruction are combined and finally there are the verbs *dḥḥ – rdp* in Ps 35,5 f. and *dḥḥ* in Jr 23,12. It is rather clear that the thought of pernicious Sheol as the destination of the wicked fits perfectly into these contexts.

The *Wortfeld* is characteristic of the literary genre (cp. Ps 9,18). In Is 38,11 the word *ḥdl* seems to be another name for Sheol; it probably derives from the grave.

2.1.4   *dimyōn* (Cessation)

In Ps 17,11 the phrase *lin ᵉṭôt bā'āreṣ* is hard to understand, as commentaries show. A new proposal was recently offered by M. Dahood ([22]). He joins *dmynw* (v. 12a) to *'rṣ* and derives it from the verb *dmh*, " to cease " ([23]), occurring in Ps 49,13 and Is 6,5, and translates " Land of Perdition ".

This derivation may be considered safe: it is the normal form

---

([18]) *GK* 84b, a + n;
([19]) Dahood, *Psalms* 211.
([20]) Cp. below, pp. 93 f.
([21]) Dahood, *Psalms* 208. Rin (in *BZ* 11 [1967] 186) reads: " Let their way be dark and destructive ".
([22]) *Psalms* 98.
([23]) *BDB* 198B.

of abstracts in Hebrew ([24]); similar words are *pidyôn* and *ripyôn*. Its pronominal suffix is explained as "a mild emphatic". The verb *nṭh* is translated "to pitch", with a reference to Jb 15,29, where it also applies to the nether world ([25]). In this sense, however, the verb is applied to inanimate objects only. The present writer thinks that the rendering "to bend down" ([26]) is equally possible; the preposition *be* is not rarely used with verbs of motion "when the movement *to* a place results in rest *in* it" ([27]).

We may add that other references to Sheol are not absent in vv. 11 f. ([28]): the proposed translation merits serious consideration, although it must be confessed that the explanation of the pronominal suffix is rather uncommon. The rendering runs:

> ... they fixed their eyes
> to pitch me into the very Land of Perdition.

2.2 Dust ('āpār)

As appears from "Ishtar's descent into the Nether World" ([29]), in the Babylonian view dust is the all-pervading matter in the abode of the dead. As to biblical "dust" (*'pr*), Cl. Tresmontant certifies: "La poussière est l'image même de la mort ... sacrement de deuil" ([30]).

According to lexicography, however, the situation is more complicated. *BDB*, under the first meaning of the word, mentions *sub* b: "material of the human body", and *sub* f: "earth of the grave" ([31]). We think that existing connections are not sufficiently brought to light in this way; an analysis of biblical material will show that seemingly disparate meanings of the word have an underground coherence.

In fact the result of joining two phrases from the Yahwistic story of Creation and Fall is more than suggestive:

> Then Yahweh God formed man of the dust (*'pr*) from the

([24]) Joüon, 88 Mc.

([25]) Cp. below, pp. 187 f.

([26]) *BDB* 640A sub 3.

([27]) Quotation from *BDB* 88B I.4.

([28]) For "tottering legs" see below, p. 94; for lions, p. 11 and p. 112.

([29]) *ANET* 107, 8-11; H. Gressmann, *Altorientalische Texte zum Alten Testament*, (2nd ed.; Berlin–Leipzig 1926) 206,8-11.

([30]) *Essai sur la pensée hébraique* (Lectio Divina 12; Paris 1953) 16 f. In view of extra-biblical evidence it seems better to render infernal *'pr* as "slime, mud", *ergo* "dank matter" (Gunkel *Psalmen*[4] 128).

([31]) 779B.

ground (*'dmh*), and breathed into his nose the breath of life. You are dust (*'pr*), and to the dust you shall return ([32]).

We are reminded of Jb 1,21, where, in his bereft state, Job exclaims:

Naked I came from my mother's womb,
and naked I will return to it ([33]).

The parallelism with Gn 3,19 is evident. We will study here the dust as the material of the human body and as the place man came from and will return to.

Eliphaz describes the humans as "those who dwell in houses of clay, whose (i.e., man's) foundation is in the dust" (Jb 4,19). In this quasi-Platonic sentence (cp. Wisd 9,15), man's house is his body, whose transiency is indicated both by the material he was made of: clay (*ḥmr*), and by his origin, dust.

Jb 10,9 alludes to the same fact:

Remember that you have made me like a vase;
and will you make me return to dust now? ([34])

Here the word rendered as "vase" (*ḥmr*) contains a clear reference to man's origin from clay. Dust and clay are not simply identical: clay is potter's material; in Nah 3,14 it is accompanied by *ṭîṭ*, the common Accadian term. Jb 33,6 expresses the same idea: "I, too,

---

([32]) Gn 2,7; 3,19; *'dmh* stems from a peasant's, *'pr* from a shepherd's tradition (G. von Rad, *Das erste Buch Mose* 76).

([33]) Jb 1,21. An echo of this symbolism, which is far from isolated, we found in Gertrud von le Fort's *Schweisstuch der Veronika* (Herderbuchgemeinde 1961) 74, where she writes about the Roman ruins that "diese schauerliche Dinge" seemed to be "in ihrer letzten Sichtbarkeit, bevor sie in den dunklen Schoss der Welt zurücktauchten".

([34]) With Dahood we translate *ḥmr* as "wine-bowl, vat". In this sense the word *ḥmr* is found in Ugarit, e.g. in *UT* 52:6: *šty bḥmr yn ay*, "Drink from the bowl any wine" (the use of the preposition *bᵉ* being the same in modern French: "boire dans un verre"), also *'nt*: I:16 f. In Hebrew the word occurs in Ps 75,9: "For the cup is in the hand of the Lord and the bowl is filled with wine ...". Also Dt 32,14c. As related in Jr 18,4.6, *ḥmr* is the material vessels are made from (Dahood, "HULex", *Bib* 45 [1964] 408 f.). It can be reasonably supposed that the same noun denotes both the material and the product made from it: by way of example we refer to *'ṣ*, "wood": "shaft of an axe", Dt 19,5; "idol" Jr 2,27; *brzl*, "iron": "iron instrument", Qoh 10,10; "chains", Ps 105,18; 107,10; *nḥšt*, "copper": "chains", Lam 3,7; Judges 16,21, etc.

was shaped from clay " ([36]). And as a pitying father Jahweh " re-
members that we are dust " (Ps 103,14) : our actions will be brittle
as our being is ; man is transitory, but the steadfast love of God is
everlasting.

The idea of " returning to the dust " implies that men had pre-
viously left it. The idea is found more often than the assertion that
man was formed from clay (Gen ; Jb) and in a wider area (Jb, Qoh,
Sir, Pss) ([37]). Jb 34,14 f. reads :

> If He would make his spirit return to himself,
> and gather to himself his breath,
> all flesh would perish together,
> and man would return to the dust.

The allusion to Gn 3,19 and 2,7 (*nišmâ*) is unmistakable here : God's
quickening breath is given to man ([38]) and it returns to Him when
man dies, so that the union of breath and dust (which is living man)
is dissolved. " Wenn Gott seinen Odem zurückzieht..., so fällt der
Mensch zurück in tote Stofflichkeit " ([39]). The novelty here is the
explicit statement that the human spirit returns to God ([40]). The
same idea is expressed in Qoh 12,7 :

> The dust returns to the earth as it was,
> and the spirit returns to God who gave it ([41]).

([35]) Cp. *KB* 857, *s.v. qṣr* ; GB 608 A, *s.v. ʿpr* ; Dhorme, *Job* 445. In Ac-
cadian the nether world can be called *bit ipri*, " house of dust " (Tallqvist,
Namen der Totenwelt 37). Hebrew *ṭîṭ* was found with Sheol connotation in
Ps 40,3.

([36]) Cp. *KB* 857 B ; Sir 33,10.

([37]) For sapiential elements in Gn 2 - 3 see L. Alonso Schökel, " Motivos
sapienciales y de alianza en Gn 2 - 3 ", *Bib* 43 (1962) 295-316.

([38]) See Jb 27,3 ; 32,8 ; 33,4. It is very hard to establish the authentic
text ; one will have to choose between *yāśim libbô* or *yāśîb rûḥô* : parallelism
favours the latter which, moreover, makes lines 14-15 a beautiful unity, con-
stituted by the inclusion with *šûb*.

([39]) von Rad, *Das erste Buch Mose* 62.

([40]) But see Ps 104,29. O. Loretz (*Qohelet und der alte Orient* [Freiburg–
Basel–Wien 1964] 51 f.) thinks this is a supplement by Qoh. It is hard to say,
however, what happens to the spirit according to the author of Gn 3, who may
have omitted any reference to the destination of the spirit simply because it
did not suit the penal character he wanted to see in human death. Logically
Qohelet's conception follows from Gn 2,7. Cp. Sir 40,11 (Hebr.).

([41]) Cp. Sir 41,10 ; 1 Macc 3,62. As to Qoh 3,21, Hertzberg thinks there
is no opposition to 12,7 : going to God is not identical with going upward.
(H. W. Hertzberg, *Der Prediger* [KAT 17/4 ; Gütersloh 1963] 215).

Of course this idea of a cyclic return was warmly greeted by Qohelet, who, in his introduction, expressed the same view [42].

In Ps 146,4 the thought of human origin is subtly suggested by the possessive suffix: " ... when man's breath departs, he returns to his earth ", i.e., to the earth he came from. We remark that the " returning " part of man is identified with the human person. The word " earth " here (*'dmh*) reminds us of Gn 2,7: man is formed of dust from the *'dmh* [43].

The statement is put in an all-encompassing perspective in Sir 40,11 :

> *kl m'rṣ 'l 'rṣ yšwb* :
> all (that came) from earth : to earth will it return.

No doubt *'rṣ* bears the connotation of chaos, nether world, strongly here. We have already quoted a similar case in Ps 44,26 :

> Our soul is bowed down in the dust ;
> our body cleaves to the *'rṣ*.

Finally, a confession of universal transiency is found in Ps 104,29 :

29 a) When Thou hidest thy face, they are dismayed,
    b) when Thou takest away their breath, they gasp (*gw'*)
    c) and return to their dust.
30 When Thou sendest forth thy breath, they are created ....

G. R. Driver objects to 29c, which he considers to be a gloss [44]. As the animals are still alive, he remarks, " dust " can hardly refer to the grave ; so it denotes the material they were made of. That, however, is a late idea in the Old Testament. Another difficulty is the fishes turning to dust, as implied by the present text ; moreover the preposition is wrong: *'l* denotes a place and therefore is out of the question ; it should be *l*e. Consequently 29c is suspected ; it is a gloss with *gw'*, wrongly understood as " dying " because *br'* in line 30 is interpreted as " re-creating ". So far Driver.

We think Driver creates false difficulties. Indeed *'l* has a local

---

[42] " Damit ist der Mensch wieder zu seinem Ursprung zurückgekehrt und der ewige Kreislauf geschlossen, von dem die Einleitung sprach " (Hertz-berg, *ibid*. 214 f.).

[43] This use of *'dmh* seems to confirm our conclusions on pp. 26 f. above (cf. Num 16,20 ff.).

[44] G. R. Driver, ' Resurrection of Marine and Terrestrial Creatures ", *JSS* 7 (1962) 12-22.

meaning, but Driver's interpretation of dust is not correct. The objection neglects the supple meaning of 'pr, which evokes " origin and end " and its local meaning grave cannot be rigidly separated from the nether world (below). Driver, however, restricts it to the grave, the local sense being predominant in view of the preposition ; he then concludes that the preposition is wrong because 'pr must mean dust ; and he finally claims that dust is wrong because of the fishes. It might be simpler to say that 'pr here denotes origin and end of living beings and that 29c makes sense. As to the idea being late, this can hardly be said to be proved by the fact that it mainly occurs in later texts.

This type of argument, which is often taken for granted in studies on our theme, proves very little : " dust " and similar mythical categories cannot reasonably be expected to appear earlier, as they presuppose some degree of reflection on death, which is not liable to occur in narrative texts. But we may say that, as soon as death is referred to in more than purely factual communications, this happens in a language of a strongly mythical colouring.

Finally : Driver sees in verse 30 an affirmation of the " resurrection " of animals if 29c is maintained ; would not this statement simply affirm the dependence of all living beings on God's creative presence ? The Old Testament very often describes serious illness and the like in terms of death and recovery as a return from Sheol ; it seems verses 29c/30 should be understood from that point of view.

Instead of 'pr, the hapax dk' occurs in   Ps 90,3 :

> You make man return to dust (dk')
> and say : " Return, O mortals " (45).

Dust is the abode of the dead in the Old Testament. Here 'pr clearly has a local meaning. In the preceding sections the word was shown to denote " human material " and origin and end of both man and animal. Recurrent " returning " appeared to be a connecting link between different nuances there. But the predominantly local meaning, too, is closely related to the preceding ones : this is shown by the commonly occurring prepositions 'l and 'l, both denoting a place (46). That again implies that in these expressions " returning " was taken

(45) It is significant that Ps 90,2 also contains two clear references to the origin of the world as a series of births : " Before mountains were born and you had brought forth earth and world ".

(46) 'l : Jb 10,9 ; Ps 104,29 ; Sir 40,11. 'l : Jb 34,4 ; Qoh 12,7, etc. Cp. Driver, in *JSS* 7 (1962) 13.

locally as well; so its sense there is not merely modal (" to become again ").

Dhorme remarks that Job's answers to his friends often are concluded with a reference to Sheol: his eyes, groping for light, again and again lose their way in that impenetrable darkness, a wall before which his words come to a standstill ([47]). At the end of his first speech, Job sighs:

> ... now I lie in the dust;
> and Thou wilt seek me, but I shall not be ([48]).

Dhorme comments: " Lying in the dust, that is not merely being laid in the earth, but also going to rest in Sheol " ([49]).

Parallelism shows " dust " to have the same connotation in Ps 119,25:

> My soul cleaveth to the dust:
> O give me life according to thy word. (RP)

Another text clearly shows the relation of 'ênennî (" I am not ") to Sheol:

> ... thy eyes are upon me, but I am no more.
> A cloud fades and vanishes:
> so he who goes down to Sheol does not come up any more ([50]).

These depressing thoughts are particularly frequent in Job, where the poet plays with all the stops of his organ:

> ... 'mw will lie down on the dust ([51]).
> ... they lie down alike upon the dust ([52]).
> My hope will descend into the hands of Sheol
> when we descend together upon the dust ([53]).

([47]) Jb 7,21; 10,21 f.; 14,10-22; 17,13-16; 21,32 (Dhorme, *Job* 100).

([48]) 7,21; preposition l^e. Similar idea in Ps 37,36.

([49]) " Se coucher dans la poussière, ce n'est pas seulement être mis en terre, mais encore aller reposer dans le Shéol " (100).

([50]) Jb 7,8 f.

([51]) 20,11; preposition 'l; probably 'm is a substantive, its meaning might be " force " (M. Dahood, cp. *Psalms* 112 f).

([52]) 21,26; 'l. See H. H. Ridderbos, " 'pr als Staub des Totenortes ", *OTS* 5 (1948) 174-178.

([53]) 17,16; cp. Dahood, *Job* 62 and note parallelism with Sheol.

Twice " dust " occurs in Ps 22 :

> Thou dost lay me down in the dust of death ...
> before Him shall bow down all who went down to the dust ([54]).

And Ps 30,10, alluding to a characteristic Sheol motive, reads : " ... will the dust praise Thee ? "

The fluid relations between grave and Sheol are manifest in these texts ; it is obvious that " dust " also is a category transposed from the grave to the home of the dead.   So, in a late text, the nether world can be described as " the country consisting of dust " ([55]).   This last section reveals the place whose identity remained hidden in the preceding ones.   Man's origin is in the nether world ; that is why he can be said to return to it when he dies.

The fixed expression " raising the poor from the dust " is inspired by Semitic mourning customs : setting down in the dust and covering oneself with it.   Its background may be found in the conception described in this section : the stricken person feels in the clutches of death ([56]) and mimes this by means of the dust, the well-known symbol of death.   " The mourning Hebrew rolls on the ground, and covers his head with dust and ashes.   This gesture would bring to remembrance the earth whence the human being has been taken and whither he must return..., the grave in which his body is buried, and Sheol, which, like a shadow, he must henceforth inhabit "([57]).

2.3 Land of Descent (yardēn)

A characteristic expression for the process of dying is *yrd š'wl*, to descend (in)to Sheol, a current formula with quite a few variations (see above, pp. 32 f.). A reference to this idiom was discovered by Dahood in Ps 42,7b :

> ... the land of descent (*yrdn*) and of nets,
> ... the mountains at the rim ([58]).

This interpretation will be studied below ([59]).

([54]) V. 16 (preposition *lᵉ*) ; v. 30 (par. *'rṣ*).

([55]) Dan 12,2 with O. Plöger, *Das Buch Daniel* (KAT 18 ; Gütersloh 1965) 169 f. For this meaning of *'dmh*, see *GB* 11 B, *sub* 3. The construction *'dmt-'pr* resembles Accadian *bit ipri*, " house of dust " (see Tallqvist, *Namen der Totenwelt* 37).

([56]) For Ugaritic evidence see *UT* 67 : VI : 11-23.

([57]) R. Martin-Achard, *From Death* 27.

([58]) Dahood, *Psalms* 254.

([59]) See pp. 145 f.

2.4 môṭ and dᵉḥî (Shifting Sand - Fatal Tottering)

2.4.1

The noun *mwṭ*, a derivate of the verb *mwṭ* meaning " to stumble ", is found in a significative parallelism in Ps 66,9 :

> Who has kept us among the living,
> *wᵉlō' nātan lammōt raglēnû.*

The suggestion is reinforced by the use of the verb in Ps 13,5 :

> Lest my Adversary should exult when I stumble.

As this Adversary is nobody else than Death ([60]), it is not unlikely indeed that " stumble " has the connotation here of " stumbling into the jaws of death " ([61]).   Apparently TM interprets the word in Ps 66,9 as a noun : it is pointed with a dagesh forte.   So we are justified in explaining *mwṭ* here as contrasting with " among the living " ; it must stand for a situation in which there is no stable footing (Ps 69,3) ([62]). Consequently this colon may be freely rendered : " and has not put our foot in the shifting sand " ([63]).

The use of the verb *mwṭ* shows some characteristic constant features, especially in *niphal*.   This is found with a *cosmic* sense, referring to creation being threatened by chaotic forces, in hymns (Ps 104,5 ; 1 C 16,30) and royal psalms (91,3 ; 96,10 ; cp. 82,5).   Striking is the frequent occurrence of the rather rare negative particle *bal* with this verb (see *BDB* 115A ([64])).   For that reason it would seem that this is the original *Sitz* in literature of *mwṭ*'s specific use.   The application of the verb to man is metaphorical and consequently secondary. Its *anthropological use* is also well profiled in niphal ; as in its cosmic application it denotes " a staggering " which means a being threatened of one's existence by evil powers, a shaking which ends in " falling ", in " lying, not rising " ; this " tottering " means : " to have no firm stand " (cp. Ps 69,3).   In fact it is used as an expression of confidence, encouragement in anxiety, always having a personal and emotional connotation.   Applied to man, we find it four times in the first person sg. yiqtol with a negation, which thrice is *bal* again ; it is an

---

([60]) See below, pp. 114 ff.
([61]) Dahood, *Psalms*, 78 f.
([62]) Cp. Barth, *Errettung* 109, 136.
([63]) " Quagmire ", Dahood, *ibid.* 79 ; see also Ps 121,3.
([64]) G. B. Gray, *Isaiah*, I (ICC ; Edinburg 1912) 261, maintains that "*bal* is confined to the later literature " which from his quotations appears to be poetical and does not altogether justify the easy generalization of Gray's statement :   in fact *bal* is already customary in Ugaritic literature (*UT* Gloss. 466).

expression of confidence in all these cases (Pss 10,6; 16,8; 30,7; with *lō'* in 62,7.3 [in opposition to *ṣûr*]; further 13,5). This is the primary use of *mwṭ* in its anthropological connotation; it is found in laments and ThPs, contexts where Death and Sheol are at home. The niphal is moreover found five times with a 3rd sg. and pl., always with a negation, which four times is *bal*.

As to qal the root is used in a *cosmic* sense of the earth (Is 24,19; Ps 60,4), of mountains and hills (Ps 46,3; Is 54,10), of kingdoms and towns (Ps 46,6 f.); there seems to be a slight preference for collective laments and ThPs here. *Anthropologically mwṭ's* qal is exclusively applied to (the feet of) the just, both times in an IL (Ps 38,17; 55,23).

All this squares well with the postulated sense of the noun *mwṭ*, whose fundamental interpretation seems confirmed by the analysis of the verb. Confessedly the local meaning is less certain.

2.4.2

The use of the verb *dḥh*, ' to thrust down ', shows some constant features suggesting that it belongs to the same *Wortfeld* [65]. Ps 5,11 reads:

> Make them perish, O God,
> let them fall because of their schemes;
> for their numerous crimes
> hurl them down [66].

This verse is found in an individual lament and clearly is a curse. The succession of ideas is noticeable: destruction – ruin – *dḥh*.

Ps 35,5-6 runs:

5 Let them be like chaff before the wind,
  with the Angel of Yahweh driving (*dḥh*) them;
6 Let their destiny be Darkness and Destruction,
  with the Angel of Yahweh pursuing them.

This also is a curse in an IL; the thought of Sheol is near: Darkness and Destruction are names for the nether world [67].

---

[65] Dahood, *Psalms* 36, 224.
[66] *Ibid.* 28 f.
[67] Dahood, *Psalms* 208, 211; cp. above, p. 84.

Ps 36,13 reads:

> See how the evildoers will fall !
> Hurled down,
> They will be unable to rise ([68]).

Again a curse in an individual lament; succession of ideas: fall – *dḥh* –no rising. The latter is set in a nether world context in Ps 140,11: " From the miry depths they shall not rise " (Dahood); the slimy abysses should not pass unnoticed here.

The *Unheilsorakel* in Jr 23,12 has strong affinities with Ps 35,5:

> And so their way shall be like Perdition to them;
> they shall be thrust into Darkness and fall into it ([69]).

In all these cases the connotation of *dḥh* is the same.

The noun *dḥy* appears in Ps 56,14:

> Thou hast delivered my soul from Death,
> yea, my feet from *dḥy*,
> to walk before God in the fields of life ([70]).

The verse is an element of thanksgiving in an individual lament. It can hardly be dissociated from
— Ps 66,9 quoted above (collective Thanksgiving)
— Ps 116,8 (ITh): Thou hast delivered my soul from Death,
                 my eyes from tears,
                 my feet from *dḥy*.
— Ps 140,5 (IL):   Preserve me from violent men,
                 who have planned to *dḥh* my feet.

We may as well point to other terms for tottering:

Ps 17,11 (Ps of Innocence):

> My legs tottered, they surrounded me,
> they fixed their eyes
> To pitch me into the very Land of Perdition ([71]).

The verb used is *nwʿ*, " to totter ".

([68]) *Psalms* 218, 224.
([69]) *Ibid.* 211; see also Ps 118,13.17 and Prv 14,32.
([70]) For " fields ... " cp. Dahood, *Psalms* 222 f.
([71]) *Ibid.* 92, 99; see pp. 83 f. above.

And Ps 35,15a (IL) with *ṣlᶜ* : " When I stumbled they gathered with glee " (⁷²).

We may conclude that *dḥy* stands for some kind of fatal waylaying, which examples as Ps 56,14 and 116,8 show to be intimately connected with Death; it is a situation which manifests the insidious power of Sheol and might be connected with the representation of Death as a hunter, who tries to capture men in his nets. It may tentatively be translated " (place of) fatal tottering ".

2.5   The Land of Forgetfulness ('ereṣ nᵉšîyâ)

Ps 88,13 reads :

> Are thy wonders known in Darkness,
> or thy saving help in the Land of Forgetfulness?

The identity of that land is unambiguously established by *qbr* and *'bdwn* in v. 12 and the parallel Darkness here. Below we will return to the exact meaning of " forgetfulness " (⁷³).

2.6   Darkness and Death (various terms)

a) Sometimes the nether world is called Darkness and thus identified with the element pervading it. Job 15,22, with an unmistakable allusion to the " land of no return " reads : " He despairs of a return from Darkness ". See also 1 S 2,9; Ps 88,13 ; 143,3 ; Jb 17,13 ; Jr 32,12. Similarly " night ", as used in Ps 139,11 may be a discreet reference to Sheol. An Egyptian lamentation evokes the stay in the beyond thus : " Your night is beautiful to all eternity " (⁷⁴).

The biblical text, however, is not without obscurity. M. Dahood translates it in this way :

> Even in Darkness the Seer watches me ;
> And in the Night the Sun is all around me (⁷⁵).

This interpretation happily removes some difficulties ; unfortunately the structure " If ... then " of vv. 8a.a'-b', 8b.a'-b' and 9-10 is dropped in this way. Besides, it may be doubted if all novelties of this new

---

(⁷²) *Ibid.* 208, 213 ; cp. Ps 107,12 (*kšl*).
(⁷³) See p. 188.
(⁷⁴) Zandee, A. 10. f, p. 91.
(⁷⁵) Cp. Dahood, *Psalms* 16, 228 and now J. Holman, *Psalm 139. Basic Exegesis* (diss. Rome 1968), *in loco*.

translation are sufficiently established (*'mr* = to see; light = sun = Yahweh); at any rate the suggestion of Yahweh's presence in Sheol is rather uncommon ([76]).

So it can be said that Darkness is the lot of the wicked:

> Terrors shall come upon him ([77])
> Total Darkness is in store for him;
> An unfanned flame shall consume him. (Jb 22,25 f.; Pope)

b) Jb 38,17 mentions both Darkness and Death in a local sense:

> Have Death's gates been revealed to you,
> Have you seen the gates of the deathly dark Resort? ([78])

See also Ps 6,6:

> For in Death there is no remembrance of thee;
> in Sheol who can give thee praise? ([79])

c) Is 45,18 f. reads:

(18)a	For thus says the LORD, who created the heavens (he is God !),
b	who formed the earth and made it (he established it;
c	he did not create it a chaos, he formed it to be inhabited !):
d	" I am the LORD, and there is no other.
(19)a	I did not speak in secret, in a land of darkness;
b	I did not say to the offspring of Jacob, ' Seek me in chaos '.
c	I the LORD speak the truth, I declare what is right ". (RSV)

The structure of this *Spruch* is clear. The hymnic expansions of the *Botenformel* (18a-c) are essential for the understanding of 18d-19c, the *Spruch* proper. In v. 18, b-c constitute the central part, as is stressed by the inclusion with *yṣr* which also determines the decisive element in the description: God made the world a cosmos, a well-ordered totality. In v. 19, a-b run parallel with 18b-c: *tōhû* and *'ereṣ* return as

---

([76]) See below, pp. 199 f., on Ps 139,8. Dahood writes (privately): " I would identify *lylh* in Jb 27,20: ' Terrors overtake like the Flood (*kᵉmō yām*); Night kidnaps him like the whirlwind '. Note double-duty preposition *kᵉmō* ".

([77]) Terrors = *'ēmîm*; cp. Ps 55,5; 88,16.

([78]) See below, p. 153, Tallqvist notes that Accadian *mītu* means both " Toten " and " Totenwelt " (*Namen der Totenwelt* 6).

([79]) For Darkness see below, pp. 140 ff. For Death, see pp. 160 ff. In the expression " gates of Death " the latter is a local name; see Jb 30,23; Prv 5,5; 7,27. Reference in *BDB* 560B *sub* 3; Dahood, *Psalms* 38. (Several instances mentioned by these authors we would rather call personifications).

keywords. There is a correspondence between God's creative activity and his words; the latter are public and clear, plain truth, spoken by the prophets. The nature of creation reveals the character of God's word, which has no connection with chaos. Apparently the prophet refers to prophecy: " God does not make himself deliberately obscure, so that men are driven to seek (... here a cultic term ...) him by superstitious or occult or orgiastic means " (80). The contents of the rejection in v 19 can be specified, however. The verb *drš* is used technically here, for " obtaining an oracle " (81): that confirms a supposition, aroused by the repeated allusions to chaos. We think that K. Marti is right when, for v. 19a-b, he proposes as a possible interpretation: " Man kann das finstere Land als die Unterwelt verstehen " (82). In other words, the text intends to condemn necromantic practices. A further analysis of the terms supports this conclusion.

V. 19a *sēter*, was recognized as a name for the nether world: the Hidden Place (83); as to *'rṣ ḥšk*, this occurs in Jb 10,21 in an undeniable reference to Sheol:

> ... before I go, never to return,
> to a land of darkness and gloom (*ṣlmwt*). (Pope)

As said above, darkness is the element pervading the nether world (84). In v. 19a.b TM reads: *bimᵉqôm 'rṣ ḥšk*; in RSV, as in most translations, the first word disappears. Now, however, we are able to render it; as the text refers to necromancy, the translation " grave ", established by M. Dahood, is almost obvious. Compare Ez 39,11: " I shall give to Gog a *mqwm* there, a grave in Israel " (85). So we propose to point *māqôm* in our case and to translate " a grave ". In view of the chaotic character of Sheol the word *tōhû* in v. 19b may be interpreted as referring to the same reality. It is also clear now, that the preposition *bᵉ*, explicit before *str* and *mqm*, and implicit before *'rṣ*, is better rendered as " from " in our languages.

In this way the following translation results:

> I do not speak from the Secret Place, from a grave, or the
> [country of darkness;
> I do not say to Jacob's offspring: " Seek me in chaos ".

(80) C. R. North, *Second Isaiah* (Oxford 1964) 159.
(81) *GB* 169 B 2a.
(82) *Das Buch Jesaja* (Tübingen 1900) 313.
(83) Cp. above, pp. 46 f.
(84) Cp. below, pp. 95 f.
(85) Cp. Dahood, *Job* 61 f. " HULex ", *Bib* 48 (1967) 430 f. Is 65,4 explicitly refers to necromancy as practised in graves.

7

In this connection Is 8,19 may be quoted:

> When they say to you: " Consult the mediums and the
>   [wizards
> who chirp and mutter ", should not a people consult their God ?
> Should they consult the dead on behalf of the living ?

The opposition here is the same as in 45,18 f. Compare also 29,4
where " earth, dust " strongly suggest Sheol:

> Then deep from the earth you shall speak,
> from low in the dust your words shall come;
> your voice shall come from the earth like the voice of a ghost,
> and your speech shall whisper out of the dust ([86]).

([86]) See above, pp. 29 f.

Chapter 3 : PERSONAL ASPECTS

3.1 Sir Death (môt)

Gertrud von le Fort describes her grandmother's attitude towards death in this way : " Sie sah ihn bewusst auf sich zuschreiten als eine schwermütige Gestalt mit dunklem, unergründlichem Blick. Sie empfing ihn verhüllten Hauptes, ehrfürchtig und volkommen schweigend " (¹) Here the reality of death is densified to an approaching melancholic figure ; he is called " Goodman Bones " in popular joking, which, however, reminds one of the boy, shrilly whistling in a dark street.

The same tendency is found undisguisedly in Ugaritic literature, e.g. in the Baal cycle, when Sir Death the Divine is the personal adversary of Baal. To give one example : after Baal's defeat, his sister Anat wants to reclaim him from Death ;

> she grasps Mot by the hem of his robe,
> holds him tight by the edge of his cloak ;
> then lifts she her voice and cries :
> " Thou, Mot, surrender my brother ! "
> But the godling Mot keeps retorting :
> " What is it that thou art asking from me, o Virgin Anat ? " (²)

This tendency to personalize death is so universal that it can be labelled " archetypal ", i.e. corresponding to an innate structure or tendency of the human psyche. Some might be inclined to call this use " merely poetical ", but this view certainly does not take the phenomenon, including poetry, seriously enough. For Israel's neighbours Death was an extremely real and concrete reality, a monstrous personal power waylaying fertility and life. Of course in Israel itself the divine Mot was dethroned by Jahwism, but " zu den am längsten beiseite geschobenen und darum von Jahwäglauben lange nicht durchgestaltenen kanaanäischen Elementen gehören die Vorstellungen von Tod und postmortalem Dasein " (³).

(¹) *Schweisstuch der Veronica* (Freiburg 1961) 238.
(²) *UT* 49 : II : 10-14 (transl. Gaster, *Thespis* 220 f.).
(³) Maag, *STU* 17. Prof. Maag most kindly sent me a copy of his val-

Consequently the experience of death was not fundamentally changed in Israel and in the light of this fact the many occasions where Death is personified acquire a pregnant meaning.

One can hardly wave this away with the remark that it is poetical play. This personification of Death, often reduced to hints and allusions, was most likely far from a petrified form of speech. One might say that, in Israel, there was an evolution from a mythological conception of Death to the belief in the Enemy : Satan, the Devil. This phenomenon suggests that the image of Death remained that of a personal power throughout Israel's history ([4]).

This personification is given expression both directly and indirectly : directly where death is described as a person, called the Enemy, King, the Hungry One ; indirectly, where his hands, feet and mouth, and his instruments are mentioned. Though not strictly belonging to this chapter, " indirect " personification will be partially treated here, both as a further background to the Names and to avoid unnecessary repetitions.

G. R. Driver points to the local name *ḥṣrmwt*, " settlement of Death " and the personal name *'zmwt*, apparently theophoric, used at the time of David ([5]). Noth, however, thinks *'zmwt* (spelled *'azmôt* with LXX) a plant's name ([6]), and against Driver may be remarked that theophoric names with *'z* always have the first person singular possessive suffix attached to it : *'uzzî-yâ*, etc. In favour of Driver's view CC 8,6 may be quoted : *'zh kmwt ahbh* ([7]). So the idea of strength was apparently connected with death. The present writer cannot settle this dispute.

As to Ps 48,15c, *'l-mwt*, Johnson's proposal " (our Leader) against

---

uable article. Too late I found M. J. Mulder's study : *Kanaänitische goden in het Oude Testament* (Den Haag 1965) (on Mot : 65-70 ; on Resep : 87 f.).

([4]) See below, pp. 160 ff.

([5]) *JSS* 7 (1965) 120 f. This proposal was made earlier by Cassuto (see Rin, in *VT* 9 [1959] 324), who contrasts Beth–El and the like.

([6]) *Personennamen* 231.

([7]) Cassuto defends the personal interpretation of Mot here (Rin, in *VT* 9 [1959] 324). *UT* 54 : II : 14 looks like a parallel : *w.yd* (12) *ilm.p. kmtm* (13) *'z.mid* (14) *in.nṭkp*. " The ... is here very strong, like death. There is no relief ". To me it seems clear that the context recommends Aistleitner's translation : " Die Hand der Götter (lastet) hier schwer " (*WUS* 1138) rather than Gordon's " The love of the gods is here very strong " (*UL* 117) ; see the discussion by Dahood, in *Bib* 39 (1958) 309 ; " UHLex ", *Bib* 48 (1967) 436.

Death " (8) is bettered by Krinetzki's interpretation " eternally " (9). The following arguments can be presented. The word means " eternally " in Ugaritic. *UT* 1008 : 11-21 reads : (11) *ytn.nn* (12) *l.b'ln.bn* (13) *kltn.wl* (14) *bnh.* *'d 'lm* (15) *šhr 'lmt* (16) *bnš bnšm* (17) *l.yqhnn.bd* (18) *b'ln.bn kltn* (19) *w.bd. bnh 'd* (20) *'lm. wunṭ* (21) *in bh :*

> He gives it to B'ln, son of Kltn and to his son for ever, till the dawn of eternities (*'lmt*). Nobody shall take it from (*sic*) the hands of B'ln son of Kltn and from the hands of his son for ever. No statute labor is imposed on it (10).

These occurrences of *'d 'lm* and *'lmt* return in Ps 48,9.15 where, besides, they constitute a structural element, *'d 'lm* appearing at the conclusion of the first stanza, *'lmt* at the end of the second (11).

It can hardly be denied that this proposal is more reasonable than Johnson's : in the latter the unexpected looming up of Death at the end of the Psalm has a rather weird effect. On the other hand v. 15 (*'lm w'd* ; *'lmwt*) looks rather overloaded now :

> Our eternal and everlasting God — he will guide us eternally. (Dahood)

A personal approach to Death may also be suspected in Ps 118,18 :

> He has not given me over to Death (12).

Although Hebrew *ntn l*ᵉ is often equivalent to Latin " *dare in* " with the accusative (13), it also stands for " *dare alicui* " and then a certain degree of personification is present : Jr 18,21 (*r'b*) ; Mi 6,14 (*hrb*) (14).

Personified Death may occur also in Ps 55,16 :

> *yaššîmāwet 'ālêmô :* Let Death come upon them.

The interpretation remains uncertain ; generally the first compound is read as two words. Where the verbal form is connected with *nš'*

---

(8) *Sacr. Kingship* 81 ; Mowinckel, *Psalms in Worship* I, 182.

(9) L. Krinetzki, *BZ* 4 (1960) 73, n. 14.

(10) For line 15, *UT Gloss.* 2399 ; line 16 : *ibid.* 486 ; line 20 : *unṭ* " Frondienst ", Aistleitner, *WUS* 325.

(11) Dahood, *Psalms* 293 f.

(12) Johnson, *Sacr. Kingship* 116 ; Dahood, " HULex ", *Bib* 44 (1963) 297.

(13) Is 34,2 ; 42,24 ; Mi 6,16.

(14) Cp. below, p. 163. Other possible examples are Ps 68,21 (Albright, *HUCA* 23 [1950-1951] 38 ; Johnson, *Sacr. Kingship* 73 f.), and Jb 30,23 (Pope, *Job* 196 ; I would prefer a spatial understanding here).

or *šw'* it may be remarked that the shift from ' to *h* is not uncommon: *sgh-sg'* (" to grow "); *nhq-n'q* (" to weep "); *ksh-ks'* (" full moon "); *nkh-nk'* (" to be scourged "), etc.

Three times in the OT a covenant with Death is mentioned: in these cases, of course, Death is personalized, a covenant being essentially a pact between two parties.

A similar relation may be hinted at in *UT* 67: II: 12, a message of Baal to Mot: *'bdk an wd 'lmk*, " Thy servant I am and thy perpetual bondman " ([15]). Now in Is 28,15 we read:

> We have made a covenant with Death,
> and with Sheol we have an agreement;
> when the scourging flood sweeps through ([16])
> it will not come to us,
> for we have made lies our refuge,
> and in falsehood we have taken shelter.

This " scoffing " (v. 14; v. 22) apparently means that the politicians consciously took the part of iniquity, i.e., a line of conduct not in harmony with the prophet's demand for confidence in Yahweh, thus turning away from the living God; they realize this and in a fatalistic sneer call their politics " a covenant with Death ". Apostasy from Yahweh will not escape punishment. In this way the prophet mockingly translates his contemporaries' conduct: in turning away from faith, justice, and righteousness (v. 17 f.), they turned to lies and falsehood (v. 15) and looked for shelter in Death, which, however, is naturally an untrustworthy partner: they will be trampled by him, they will be washed away (v. 16) ([17]).

This interpretation may be buttressed by Wisdom 1,16: " The impious have made a covenant ([18]) with death ". i.e., they ask for it because of their very impiety; by their iniquity " they deserve to become his prey "; and this is contrasted with justice, which is immortal (v. 15) and with the right order in creation which for death is unattainable (v. 14), the latter being no part of God's creation (v. 13).

In Sir 14,12 " the covenant ($\delta\iota\alpha\vartheta\acute{\eta}\kappa\eta$) of death " which is not revealed to man seems to refer to the " décret qui fixe la mort " (BJ 911), i.e., God's decision about man's hour of death remains a secret between the two partners, God and Death.

---

[15] See above, p. 9.
[16] Cp. *BDB* 1009A, 1002A; see Is 28,17; 8,5-8 and the like.
[17] The same suggestion with Rin, in *VT* 9 (1959) 324.
[18] συνθήκη

Sir Death knows human emotions : *šmḫ bn ilm mt,* " Divine Mot rejoiced " ([19]).   In Is 14,9 Sheol likewise is a person, a landlord ([20]) feverishly rousing his guests to welcome the king of Babylon into the abode of the dead :

> Sheol beneath is excited about you,
> awaiting your arrival....

Death is a treacherous adversary :

> Death has come up into our windows,
> he has entered our palaces ;
> cutting off the children from the streets
> banishing the young men from the squares ([21]).
> Thus says Yahweh :
> Dead bodies of men shall fall like dung upon the open field,
> like sheaves after the reaper, and none shall gather them
> (Jr 9,20 f.).

In this small poem, which " belongs to the most impressive utterances in the Old Testament about the all-checking power of death " ([22]), Death is described as a robber ([23]) and a strangler, kidnapping children from the very streets (a fact only too well known in our day), and as a reaper, the now old-fashioned skeleton with a scythe on his shoulder. Certainly this conception is archaic ; its relation to 51 : VI : 8 ff. is disputed ([24]).   So Death does not merely await his guests, he enters the Cosmos to fetch them.   His rapacity is proverbial in the OT :

([19]) *UT* 67 : II : 20.

([20]) In Greek the name πολυδέγμων (" *grosser Wirt* ") for Hades occurs ; cp. Roscher, *Lexicon Mythologie* 1783.   In the part of the Scandinavian nether world which is called Elvidner (" Misery ") there are said to be dwellings for the " guests " (Guerber, 180). The motif returns in Goethe's *Iphigenie auf Tauris.* III : 3, 1314 f. : " Kommt mit ! Kommt mit ! zu Plutos Thron. Als neue Gäste den Wirt zu grüssen " (*Werke*, V [Hamburg 1958] 43).

([21]) See Dahood, " HULex ", *Bib* 45 (1964) 401.

([22]) A. Weiser, *Der Prophet Jeremia* (ATD 20 ; 4th ed. ; Göttingen 1959) 89.

([23]) Cp. the Accadian demon " Seizer " (Widengren, *Accadian and Hebrew Psalms* 198). The same conception is usual in Egyptian : " Death comes. He robs the child that is in the embrace of its mother, as much as the man who is old ". (Zandee, 87, A. 9.e ; pp. 85-87).

([24]) Cassuto's identification with 51 : V does not recommend itself, though it is rather popular among scholars ; Gaster's strictures (*Thespis* 188) are to the point. From 51 : VII : 18 f. it appears that this " window " is to be understood in the same way as in Gn 7,11.

Three things are never satisfied,
four never say: " Enough ":
Sheol, the barren womb,
the earth ever thirsty for water,
and the fire which never says: " Enough " (25).

Likewise in Prv 1,12 where bloodthirsty sinners are plotting against the innocent, saying:

Like Sheol let us swallow them alive
and whole, like those who went down into the pit !

A consequence of Mot's being a person is his having a body with its customary limbs. In Ugaritic texts his lips and jaws, his throat and his stomach, his hands and his feet are explicitly mentioned.

UT 67 : I : 6 :   *lyrt*
        7 *bnpš. bn ilm. mt. bm*
        8 *hmrt. ydd. il. ǵzr*

Verily, I have gone down into the throat of divine Mot, into the gullet of the hero loved of El.

UT 67 : I : 19   *pimt bklat*
        20 *ydy ilḥm* (26)

Truly, I'll eat with both my hands.

UT 67 : II : 1 :   [*k lmt m*
        2 *lt't.lar*] *ṣ špt.lšmm*
        3 [*w*]*lšn.lkbkbm.y'rb*
        4 [*b'*]*l. bkbdh. bph yrd*
        5 *kḥrr.zt.ybl.arṣ.* ...

Even as Mot has jaws reaching the earth, lips to heaven, and a tongue to the stars, Baal will enter his stomach (and) go down into his mouth, as the olive, the product of the earth (27).

---

(25) Prov 30,16, *RSV*; as to the proposal by Dahood, *Prov.* 59, we remark that in this way the climactic pattern 3-4 is lost. Cp. Prv 27,20.

(26) Text according to Herdner, *Corpus* I, 33.

(27) Reconstruction of the text and translation with Driver, *CMAL* 104 f. " jaws " is not quite certain. To show how topical is the theme cp. " ... into the jaws of death — into the mouth of hell — rode the six hundred " (Tenny-

UT 51 : VIII : 15 :   *al*

    16 *tqrb.lbn.ilm*
    17 *mt.al.y'dbkm*
    18 *kimr.bph*
    19 *klli.bṯbrn*
    20 *qbh*

Come you not near to divine Mot;
Let him not make you like a sheep in his mouth,
you both be carried away like a kid in his jaws [28].

Mot's feet left traces in 51 : VIII : 26 f. :

lp'n mt hbr, " at the feet of Mot bow down. "

Biblical Death also disposes of a spacious muzzle [29].

Therefore Sheol opened wide his throat (*npš*),
and distended his mouth without measure :
and her nobility and her multitude go down,
her throng and he who exults in her (Is 5,14).

Here parallelism clearly tells in favour of the translation " thro at "
for *npš*, as in Ugaritic Texts ; RSV " appetite " is too pallid [30].

His greed is wide as Sheol's,
like Death he is never satisfied :
he gathers to himself all the nations,
he collects to himself all the peoples (Hab 2,5) [31].

In this text *npš* is balanced b y the idea of satiation ; so the rendering
" greed " seems imperative.   Ps 41,3 was studied in a previous con-

son) " ... that's the jaws of death — and it champs up a couple of promising
young geniuses ... " (Joyce Carey, *The Horse's Mouth* [Penguin Books 648]
371).

[28] Interpretation of Dahood, *CBQ* 17 (1955) 181-183. In this way Fra An-
gelico painted hell on his panel: *The Last Judgment* (St. Mark's Monastery,
Florence) : a black devil cramming his muzzle with corpses. " I am game for-
his [Moby Dick's] crooked jaw, and for the jaws of Death, too ", H. Melville,
Moby Dick or the Whale (New York 1936) 235 (ch. 36).

[29] Confessedly it is generally Sheol rather than Death himself which is
considered to possess a mouth, etc. On the other hand, when the '*rṣ* is said
to swallow people (Ex 15,12 ; Nu 16,30 ff. ; Ps 106,17), this suggests the affinity between Sheol and '*rṣ* = nether world. For Jb 36,16 : below, p. 119.

[30] See Dahood in *Bib* 44 (1963) 105 (review art. " Entmytologisierung "
by J. de Fraine, *q.v.*) ; Dahood, *Psalms* 215.

[31] This suggestion has already been made by Cassuto (Rin in *VT* 9
[1959] 324).

text; it reads: " do not put him into the throat of his Enemy " (cp. Ps 27,12). The mouth of Sheol returns in Ps 141,7. Perhaps we are dealing with a worn-out metaphor ([32]) here, as seems the case in the expression " the well's mouth " (Gn 29,2; Ps 69,16 etc.): " Their bones are scattered in the mouth of Sheol " ([33]).

Several times Death's hands are mentioned in the OT. First in *byd*: " by the agency / instrumentality " ([34]), exclusively used of human persons; so certainly Death is taken personally in these cases. Probably the meaning " hand " is not entirely faded here.

> It (my hope) will descend into the hands of Sheol,
> when we descend together upon the dust ([35]).

myd is used even of inanimate things: fire, net, sword; so our case is less strong for this expression. It is not unlikely, however, that there is a personification in these occurrences.

" From the hand of Sheol He will surely take me " (Ps 49,16). A strict interpretation of *yad* is recommended by the preceding verse where Mot is certainly present ([36]). A close parallel turned up in a Ugaritic letter, *UT* 2059 : 21 f. : *wklhm. bd/rb. tmtt. lqḥt* " And I snatched all of them from the hands of the Master of Death (i.e., Mot) " ([37]).

> Where is the man who will remain alive and shall not see
> Death, who will deliver his life from the hands of Sheol?
> (Ps 89,49)

([32]) For the terminology: Wellek–Warren, *Theory of Literature* 185.
([33]) For Ps 5,10, see below, p. 113.
([34]) *BDB* 391 A, cp. Jean–Hoftijzer, p. 104, 13 ff.
([35]) Jb 17,16, Dahood, *Job* 62. *Bydy* occurs also in Ps 141,6: " May their rulers be thrown down into the hands of the rock and hear how sweet his words are ". In this uncertain interpretation, " rock " is understood as " cave " (cp. Is 2,10 // 2,19; Jr 48,28); it stands for a place of burial in Is 22,16; so it might have become a name of Death (uncertain: below, pp. 205 ff.). The suffix -*y* in the second colon is interpreted as 3rd m. sg. (Dahood, *Psalms* 10 f.) and the colon understood as an allusion to the judgment the " judges " themselves will have to undergo in the beyond. The word *n'm* has the same euphemistic meaning in *UT* 67 : VI : 5 f. (quoted on pp. 10 f.). The words *mydy pḥ* (v. 9) are to be compared with *mydy ḥrb* in Jb 5,20: a mythical origin is not impossible (see p. 163; v. 7 is studied on pp. 39 f.).
([36]) Dahood, *Job* 62; cp. Pope, *Job* 122.
([37]) Dahood, *Psalms* 302. A different translation of *rb tmtt* with Dietrich–Loretz, in *BiOr* 23 (1966) 132B: " Mannschaftsführer ".

Death and Sheol again are personified in Hos 13,14:

> Shall I ransom them from the hands of Sheol?
> Shall I redeem them from Death?
> O Death, where are your plagues?
> O Sheol, where is your destruction? (RSV) [38]

Against the background, outlined in this chapter, it would be certainly superficial to say that this is mere poetical *Spielerei*. The same profound experience of the uncanny powers of Death inspired both the mythological and the poetical view; one feels this concentration of irresistible power as the influence of an invisible but very concrete person. The fact that Mot makes use of instruments such as nets and ropes also suggests a personal interpretation of Death [39].

Moreover we may point to Is 25,8: " Yahweh engorged Mot for ever " [40].

Finally it should not pass unnoticed that the personification of Death is less frequent in the OT than in Ugaritic; another difference consists in the OT personifying also his abode, which is not done in Ugarit. The latter might suggest that Death himself was after all felt to be less personal by the Israelites.

3.2   The Hungry One (rā'ēb)

The folkloristic conceptions of after-life, the experience of cruel wars, the relative monotony of daily life, and the primitive level of medicine relentlessly showed the inescapable power of death in Israel. We have already noted how Death was portrayed as a voracious monster and in that light it is not surprising to see that Death sometimes appears in biblical texts under the guise of Hunger or the Hungry One.

" Consumed by Hunger, warred upon by Reseph ". (Dt 32,24)

This interpretation of *m^ezê r'b ûl^eḥūmê rešep,* proposed by R. Gor-

---

[38] According to 2 K 23,13 the Mount of Olives was called " Mountain of the Destroyer ". Referring to Ex 12,23 J. Morgenstern (" The King-God among the Western Semites and the Ancient Meaning of Epiphanes ", *VT* 10 [1960] 138-197, especially 179-181) argues that the Destroyer " could have been only Mot or Sheol, the god of the netherworld, Death himself " (p. 180). The use of sacrificing a red heifer on the spot would suggest the same fact, and Zach 14,4-5 and Ez 37 show that this mountain was " thought to cover the entrance to the netherworld " (p. 180). For most of this, however, Morgenstern offers little evidence.

[39] See below, pp. 172 f.

[40] Below, p. 172; for CC 8,6 see above, p. 64.

dis, merits serious consideration ([41]). There is ample documentation now about Reseph, a god of the nether world, in a Ugaritic text described as *b'l ḫẓ ršp*, " Reseph, Lord of the Arrow " ([42]). His presence in this text is evoked by the preceding verse, where Yahweh proclaims : " I will shoot my whole arsenal of arrows against them ". At the same time this verse shows that Reseph in v. 24 must be leading a reduced existence : he is overshadowed by Yahweh. On the other hand his presence is suggested both by these " arrows " and by the verb *lḥm* ([43]). Finally, if Reseph has personal traits here, this is most likely the case with parallel *r'b* also.

Jr 18,21 reads : *tēn 'et-b^enêhem lr'b w^ehaggirēm 'al-y^edê-ḥereb* :

> Deliver their sons to Hunger,
> give them to the hands of the Sword.

Because of the verb *ntn* and the " hands of the sword " we may be glimpsing the Hunger (*abstractum pro concreto*) ([44]) or the Hungry One (*rā'ēb*) in this fierce curse of the prophet ([45]). Personification is predominant in v. 21c also :

> May their men be murdered by Death,
> their youths be slain by the Sword in battle.

([41]) R. Gordis, " The Asseverative Kaph in Ugaritic and Hebrew " (*JAOS* 63 [1943] 176-178) 178.

([42]) *UT* 1001 : 3, Dahood, " Ancient Semitic Deities " 83 f. ; Donner–Röllig *KAI* II, p. 24 ; Pope, *Job* 42 ; Maag, in Schmökel, *Kulturgesch.* 584. The expression *'rṣ ršpm* occurs in a Phoenician text (*KAI* I, text 15), but apparently it refers to a kind of building, possibly of a cultic nature, as *ršp* is the god of the nether world (Jean–Hoftijzer, 26 ; *KAI* II, p. 24). Meanwhile *ršp* is also associated with fire (*KAI* II, 51 ; Ps 78,48), which probably is identical with lightning (his weapon is the arrow : " Lord of the Arrow " ; Ps 76,4 ; his symbol is the vulture). For all these reasons *'rṣ ršpm* is not likely to mean " land of the flames ", i.e., the nether world (Jean–Hoftijzer, 284 : Meyer's proposal).

([43]) The translator is facing the dilemma : *lḥm* " to war upon ", or " to eat away " ? Hebrew, however, could express both senses in the same word. I think that " to war upon " is justified in view of Reseph's character, which is evoked by v. 23 ; this understanding implies the idea of destruction, present in " to eat away ". The expressions of v. 24b also evoke the sphere of the nether world : see above, pp. 164 f. A similar remark to that on Dt 32,34 may be made for Ps 78,48. By means of the verb *sgr* in hiphil (see below, p. 115 and pp. 155 f.), vv. 48-50 form a small unit ; there we find *sgr*, *ršp*, *mal'ăkê rā'îm*, *mwt / ḥyh*, *dbr* (see below, pp. 162 f. and 204). For v. 49, see below, p. 149.

([44]) Dahood, *Psalms* 32 f.

([45]) In spite of Accadian (*CAD* V 61 f.) and Ugaritic evidence (*WUS* 703) the interpretation of *ngr/grr* remains doubtful.

Ps 33,19 runs thus:

> Mark well: The eye of Yahweh
> is on those who fear him ...
> To rescue them from Death,
> to preserve their lives from the Hungry One. (Dahood)

Parallelism suggests that r'b is a designation of Death, in which case "Hunger" (concretely) or "the Hungry One" may be meant (cp. ad Jr 18,21). So it seems that this verse contains an allusion to the insatiable appetite of Death. The preposition b^e, balanced by *min*, is used for variety's sake and may be rendered "from". Although the usual translation ("to keep them alive in hunger") remains a sound one, the one proposed here seems better in keeping with Israelite view on death [46].

Jb 18,12 reads:

> Let the Hungry One meet him,
> Calamity wait at his side.

The second colon offers no difficulties, but the understanding of the first is troublesome. Pope reads "with his wealth he is famished" on the basis of a possible haplography of b^e; as to Fohrer's translation ("Hungrig nach ihn ist sein Verderben" 296 f.), which is substantially the same as Moffat's, Pope remarks: "It is difficult to find plausible emendation to give this sense" [47]. With due reserve another solution is proposed here: '*ōnô* is understood as participle qal of '*nh* III, "begegnen", "to meet", with affixed personal pronoun third person sg. As to the *suffixum coniunctum* instead of l^e with suffix, this is not uncommon with verbs of motion [48]; there is no precedent of '*nh* III in qal, which constitutes the weak point in this interpretation [49]. For the idea cp. Ps 91,10:

> No evil will meet ('*nh*, pual) you:
> no plague will approach thy tent.

---

[46] See Dahood, *Psalms* 203.
[47] *Id., Job* 125; Moffat: "Ruin is ravenous for him".
[48] M. Bogaert, "Les suffixes verbaux non accusatifs dans le sémitique nord-occidental et particulièrement en hébreu", *Bib* 45 (1964) 220-247, especially 231 ff. and 239 f.; Dahood, *UHPh ad* 6.21; for '*nh* III, see *GB* 53 A; *BDB* 58 B.
[49] See Dahood, *Psalms* 203, 237.

We conclude that not all examples of *r'b* as a personification are equally convincing. It should not be forgotten, however, that the texts treated here must be understood in the light of the preceding considerations about Death as a personal Being. Moreover in all cases we are dealing with poetry (especially with curses and threats) where the " overtones " are essential for the full effect of the texts. Poetry lives by grace of the pluridimensional character of human speech.

3.3 The Archenemy

In Ugaritic mythology, Mot appears as the enemy of Baal, the god of life and fertility, as a rapacious and insatiable monster, " *quaerens quem devoret* ". In Egyptian writings the conception of Death as an adversary is so clearly formulated, that a book on Egyptian after-life conceptions can be entitled " Death as an Enemy " ([50]). The principal demon, Apophis, is called simply " The Malicious One " ([51]) because he and his collegues do not leave humans in peace, neither on earth nor in the nether world. In Accadian laments a chief enemy is not found; the numerous and various hostile demons, however, often penetrate into human life, frequently disguised as human adversaries ([52]).

Against this background an appearance of Death as " Enemy " would not be surprising in the Old Testament.

3.3.1 The enemies and the Enemy ('*ôyēb* - *ṣar*)

First of all, then, it cannot be disputed that human adversaries and Death have much in common in the OT: there is a close resemblance between them. They generally appear on roughly the same stage: the *Unheilsprophetie*, the lament, and the corresponding thanksgiving psalm.

Ps 124, a collective ThPs, describes past dangers entirely with categories belonging to the *Wortfeld* of Death and Sheol: the verb " to swallow " (*bl'*), the infernal, destructive waters, crushing teeth, snares and nets ([53]).

([50]) J. Zandee (Leiden 1960).
([51]) *Ibid.* 217 ff.
([52]) Widengren, *Accad. and Hebr. Pss* 209, etc.; S. Moscati, *Geschichte u. Kultur der Semitischen Völker* (Urbanbücher; Stuttgart 1953) 56 ff.
  ([53]) These themes are treated elsewhere in this study, For *bl'*, " to swallow, to engorge ": Ps 35,25 (below); for waters, pp. 59 ff. above; Ps 18,17 f.; 32,6; 65,8; 69.2.15; 77,17; 106,11; 144,7; Jr 6,23; Is 8,7, etc. For Rahab = Egypt:

" If the Lord had not been on our side ", now may Israel say :
" if the Lord had not been on our side, when men rose against
                                                              [us,
Then they would have swallowed us up alive :
when their anger was kindled against us ;
Then the waters would have swept us away,
and the torrent gone over us (54) :
then the raging waters would have gone clean over us.
But praised be the Lord :
who hath not given us over for a prey unto their teeth.
We have escaped, as a bird out of the snare of the fowler :
the snare is broken, and we are delivered ". (RP)

The enemies also prepare a pit for their innocent victims (55) and they
are compared with lacerating lions : the way malefactors are thus
put on a level with the Evil One suggests that there is more than a
superficial correspondence between them.   Human enemies appear as
Death himself in visible shape : just as Death's sway becomes visible
in the ill-fated situation, so his personal activities show themselves
in the efforts of human adversaries.   " Übrigens liegt dem symbo-
lischen Denken die Gleichsetzung des menschlichen Feindes mit Dämon
und Tod durchaus nahe " (56).   Yahweh's presence means life and
happiness, his absence implies danger and death.   Adversity, therefore, implies that Yahweh averts his face from man ; consequently
destructive powers take over control.

The unhappy Israelite knows that the shadows of Death reach
him already ; he is entangled in the nets of Death and the waters of
Styx come up to his throat.   In other words : as all happiness comes
from the living God, so all misfortune ultimately originates from Death
himself.

Ps 87,4 ; Is 30,7 ; for Ez 29,1-16 and Is 27,1 see O. Kaiser, *Bedeutung des
Meeres* 149. (Ps 65,8 is parallel with 65,6, and *šbḥ* with *bṭḥ*, the latter being
used in its (probably original) sense of " to soothe, to still " and denoting a cosmogonic motif.   With the same sense it is found in Ps 22,10 by Dahood, *Prov.* 7,
n. 1 and *id.*, *Psalms* 139). For nets see below, pp. 172 ff. ; teeth also in Ps 3,8 ;
57,5 ; 58,7 ; cheek in Ps 3,8 ; throat in Ps 27,12 ; 35,25 ; 41,3 ; tongue (mostly
as " slander ") 64,4.
   (54) " Torrent " is quite naturally understood as referring to Styx.
   (55) Pit : Ps 7,16 ; 9,16, 35,7 f., etc. ; also *'ên maṣṣîl* in Ps 71,11 (see below,
p. 204).
   (56) Eliade, *Das Heilige* 30 ; " Die Feinde gehören zu den Mächten des
Chaos " (*ibid.* 29), therefore the enemies are often said " to return " to Sheol ;
they belong to it (Pedersen, *Israel* I/II, 466).

Rescue my life from their pits,
my face from the young lions....
...they open wide their mouth against me...
Lest they boast in their heart,
" Aha, our throat ! "
Lest they boast, " We have engorged him "
                                        (Ps 35,17.21.25 ; Dahood).

These accumulations of motives are not uncommon : see Ps 22.
13 f. 16 f. ; 10,7-10 ; 35,6-8.17.21.25 b ; 57,5.7 ([57]).
The identification of Death and human adversaries is striking
in Ps 73,9 where impious plutocrats are described in this way :

They set their mouth against the heavens,
and their tongue struts through the earth.

H. Ringgren correctly points to the similarity with *UT* 67 : II : 2 :

1   (Even as Mot has)
2   [jaws (reaching)] to the earth, lips to heaven
3   [and] a tongue to the stars.... ([58])

The context shows that here Mot is pictured ; the image expresses
his voracity, as appears from *UT* 52 : 27 f. ([59]). And Ringgren com-
ments : " Der Feind wird in mythischen Kategorien beschrieben.
Er steht wie die Gottlosen unseres Psalmes mit dem Tod und dem
Totenreich in Beziehung und er sammelt zu sich alle Völker .... Ihr
Treiben wird als ein Werk der Chaosmachten aufgefasst " ([60]).
But these allies and assistants of Death will finally arrive where
they belong ; Ps 73,18 reads :

([57]) Cp. below. Death and enemies are compared with lions in Ps 10,9 ;
17,12 ; 35,17 ; 7,3 ; 22,14.22 ; 57,5 ; 58,7 ; 91,13 ; Dan 6 ; 2 Tim 4, 17 ; 1 Petr
5,8 (cp. W. Michaelis *ThWNT* IV [Stuttgart 1943] 258 f., n. 21 : sarcophagi
having the shape of a lion ; also Jb 10,16 ; Hos 5,14 ; 13,7). The symbolism of
the lion is richer : it is associated with Ishtar (P. Grelot, in *RHR* 149 (1956)
29 ff.) : it is " eins der beliebtesten (Bildern) im Lobpreis der Qina " (Jahnow,
Leichenlied 229, cp. 147 f., 205). As to dogs, according to W. R. Smith the
divine hunters Heracles and Melqart, both associated with the nether world,
were accompanied by them (*Religion Semites*³ 292).
([58]) Driver, *CMAL* 105.
([59]) See above, p. 9.
([60]) H. Ringgren, " Einige Bemerkungen zum 73. Psalm " (*VT* 3 [1953]
265-272) 268.

> Surely in Destruction will you plant them;
> you will cast them into Ruins ! ([61])

Ps 5,10 also shows the fundamental identity between Enemy and enemies :

> For there is nothing firm in his mouth,
> his belly is an engulfing chasm;
> A grave wide-open is their throat,
> and with their tongue they bring death. (Dahood)

The language of this verse is strongly reminiscent of mythological descriptions of Mot, who was well known for his colossal throat, his insatiable appetite and his residence " Mudville ", where no firm ground is found ([62]). The evil tongue recalls *UT* 67 : II : 2 f. quoted above ([63]).

Concluding that in these cases we are facing demythologized imagery is, in the present writer's opinion, saying too little. The statement does not do justice to the fact that the *Wortkreisen* are equally applied to both the sphere of Death and to enemies : this justifies the conclusion that a partial identification of both realities takes place here. Maag expresses this phenomenon successfully where he writes about the enemies in apocalyptic literature : " Sie sind der soziologische Aspekt der schöpfungswidrige Mächte " ([64]). In the same way the enemies in Psalms are manifestations of the Archenemy and his lethal power : because they are part of him, are allied to him. This use finds a parallel in some modern languages where critical circumstances may be described as " an infernal situation " ([65]).

The man who is in straitened circumstances, is in Sheol; those who bring about this situation, are representing the King of Terrors and in this sense are demonic powers. So Kraus correctly comments on Ps 22,17 : " Aber es wird zu bedenken sein, dass diese ' Feinde ' in den Klageliedern stets von Gott scheidende, dämonische Machten repräsentieren " ([66]). For this he refers to Accadian incantations. In

---

([61]) For the first colon see above, p. 83 ; for the second, p. 72.

([62]) Cp. Dahood, *Psalms* 34 f. ; see Ps 27,12 ; 41,3 above, pp. 35 f.

([63]) Above, p. 112.

([64]) Maag, *Tod und Jenseits* 30 ; see the sudden transition in Ps 65,8 ; 144,7 ; 11,3 ; 82,5.

([65]) For " Sheol " meaning " diminished life " see index *S. U.* "need" (C. Barth, *Errettung*; id., *Einführung Pss* 52, *sub* 3).

([66]) *Psalmen* I, 180, cp. 42.

fact Widengren writes about these : " The enemies (of the king) are the demonic powers of life " ([67]).   Mowinckel also shows that political enemies of the king are sometimes called " evil demons " in Assyrian and Babylonian texts ([68]).   This does not necessarily imply, however, that the enemies are consciously acting as such, in other words, that they are sorcerers ([69]).   Because he threatens life, an enemy is *ipso facto* an ally of Death.

All these considerations justify the following concluding remarks : Enemies and Death belong together; the former are manifestations of the latter's threatening activity.   Death therefore is pre-eminently the Foe : the Archenemy.   In view of the close connection between the Enemy and the enemies a clear distinction between them will prove difficult.   Starting from a careful analysis of the texts an attempt will be made in the following paragraph.   A minimal result to be hoped for will be a better insight in the close relation between Death and human adversaries.

3.3.2   Death, the Enemy

The pious psalmist of Ps 13 is on the verge of despair.   The threatening shadows of Death are clouding his life and Darkness seems about to overwhelm him.   By calling him the " Enemy " the psalm sets Death in marked opposition to the living God.   Vv. 3-5 read :

> How long must my Foe rejoice over me ?
> Look at me, answer me, O Yahweh, my God !
> Enlighten my eyes, avert the sleep of death !
> Lest my Foe should boast, " I overcame him "
> Lest my Adversary should exult when I stumble ([70]).

In Ps 18,4 the proposed interpretation is almost obvious in view of following parallelism; the same remark is true for v. 17 f., where rescue out of the " waters " is identified with deliverance from the Enemy.   V. 4 f. reads :

> I called Yahweh, and was saved from my Foe.
> The snares of Death encompassed me....

([67]) *Accad. and Hebr. Pss* 209.
([68]) *Worship* I, 200.
([69]) *Id., Psalmenstudien* I, 96 f. Further, Gunkel–Begrich, *Einleitung Pss* 196-208 ; Barth, *Einführung Pss* 52 f.
([70]) Dahood, *Psalms* 77 ; " stumble ", TM : *mwṭ* ; see above, pp. 92 f.

For " Foe " TM reads a plural, which is interpreted here as a *plurale excellentiae*, Death being " the adversary *par excellence* " ([71]). He probably returns at the end of the Psalm where the three categories of enemies, mentioned before, are summed up; v. 49 reads:

> Who delivered me from my Foe,
> exalted me above my assailants
> rescued me from my calumniators ([72]).

In Ps 30,2 the proposed understanding is suggested by the connection with v. 4:

> I shall exalt you, O Yahweh,
> for you drew me up,
> Nor let my Foe rejoice over me.
> ... O Yahweh, you lifted me from Sheol,
> you restored me to life
> as I was descending to the pit (Dahood).

Ps 31,8 f. runs thus:

> When you saw my affliction,
> you took care of me against the Adversary ([73])
> You did not incarcerate me in the hand of the Enemy,
> but set my feet in a broad domain.

The verb *sgr* evokes the conception of Sheol as a prison; as we shall see below, the association is so strong in Psalms, that it generally does not make sense to ask whether literal imprisonment is meant or a difficult situation ([74]).

M. Dahood finds the Enemy also in Ps 42,10:

> I shall say: " O El, my Rock,
> why have you forgotten me?

([71]) Dahood, *Psalms* 105; in v. 18, TM reads singular, but it is important to notice that in vv. 4, 49 the plural entirely depends on Massoretic pointing.
([72]) Dahood, *Psalms* 104, 119.
([73]) Thus Dahood, *Psalms* 188, interpreting *ṣārôt* as a plurale excellentiae, with a reference to *UT* 68:9, where *ṣrt* stands for " enemy " in the singular. Parallelism, however, favours the traditional " You have taken heed of my adversities ", in which case the 1st pers. sg. possessive suffix is balanced by *napšî*.
([74]) Cp. below, pp. 154-156; the transition to plurals elsewhere in this Psalm is well accounted for in our interpretation.

> why must I go in gloom
> because of the harassment by the Foe,
> because of the Assassin within my bones ? ”
> My adversaries taunt me.....

He comments : “ When the Foe is identified, it becomes likely that
reṣaḥ, “ murder ”, may be another designation of the archenemy of
the psalmist ”.   And for the conception that Death resides in the body
of a sick person he points to a Ugaritic name of a goddess subduing
Death : “ Death on the one hand is shattered, Shataqat (lit. ‘ she who
makes depart ’), on the other, is victorious ” (*UT* 127 : 13 f.) (⁷⁵).

Ps 55,4 f. reads as follows :

4   I am distraught by the noise of the Enemy,
     because of the oppression of the wicked... (⁷⁶).
5   My heart is in anguish within me,
     the terrors (*’êmôt*) of death have fallen upon me (cp. RSV).

RP, interpreting “ terrors of death ” as a superlative form (⁷⁷), reads :
“ deadly fears ”.   As, however, in an individual lament, Death and
Sheol are always on the threshold, *māwet* may very well have its original vigour here ; moreover the phrase “ terrors ” faintly recalls the
“ King of Terrors ” (*blhh*) in Jb 18,14.   So we can safely give to “ death”
its full force in this verse ; the genitive may be both *genitivus objec-*

(⁷⁵) Dahood, *Psalms* 260 ; for Ps 41,3 see above, pp. 35 f. A Sumerian incantation reads : “ Dann wird sich der Schicksals-Dämon, der im Leibe des
Menschen ist, entfernen.... Der böse Totengeist, der böse Teufel möge hinausgehen ; der böse Gott ... möge hinausgehen... Herzkrankheit ... Leiden, Kopf-
krankheit ... mögen hinausgehen ” (Falkenstein–von Soden, 40 : 32 f., 42 ff.,
47 f. ; pp. 216 f.).   And in an Accadian prayer to Ishtar we read : “ Reiss den
bösen Späher ... der in mich fuhr, mich dauernd verfolgte ... am heutigen
Tage aus meinem Leibe heraus ” (*ibid*. B 63 : 14 ff., p. 336 ; cp. B 56 : 40 ff,
p. 323).
(⁷⁶) Hebrew : *rāšā‘*, the Evil One. In view of the available evidence it
does not seem likely that this was a name for Death in the OT. It may be
tempting to explain Is 11,4b in this way, interpreting *’rṣ* as “ nether world ”.
The opposition with the poor and meek, however, suggests that a human tyrant
and wicked is meant. The word *r‘* may stand for Death in Ps 140,12 (Let the
Evil One hunt down the violent man...).   Ps 84,11 also looks germane : “ Better
is one day in your courts than thousand in the grave ; I would rather be a door-
keeper in the house of my God, than dwell in the tent of the Evil One ” (Dahood, private communication ; the suggestion was made by D. N. Freedman).
(⁷⁷) Cp. D. Winton Thomas, in *VT* 3 (1953) 219 ff.

tivus and *subjectivus*. Consequently " enemy " in v. 4 not improbably denotes the same Death ; the transition to a plural in the second colon offers no difficulty because of the intimate connection existing between the Enemy and the enemies ([78]).

Not rarely the meaning of " the enemy " in Psalms is rather veiled. Here we should not pin our interpretation down to one definite category of enemies, but rather try to do justice to the variety of meanings suggested by a vague and general term. We are justified in supposing that this vagueness was not a casual one ([79]). As shown before in this chapter, the context often suggests an interpretation involving Death as the Archenemy.

Another example is Ps 61,4, which should be read in the light of the preceding verse :

3   From the edge of the nether world I called to you
     when my courage failed.
     Unto a lofty rock you led me from it.
4   O that you would be my refuge,
     a strong citadel against the Enemy ([80]).

When the psalmist is approaching Death, Yahweh alone can save him from his hands. The description is reminiscent of the miry depths of Sheol, of the quicksand where man's feet find no hold, and of the attacks of the powerful Foe.

In the description of Ps 10,9 ff. the figure of Death seems suddenly to loom from behind the " wicked " :

     He sits in ambush in open villages,
     in secret places he murders the innocent ;
     his eyes spy on the unfortunate.
     He lurks in secret, like a lion in his lair,
     he lurks to seize the afflicted ;
     he seizes the afflicted to drag him away.
     Into his net the oppressed man tumbles,
     while the unfortunate fall into his pit. (Dahood)

([78]) For the same reason the sudden *rāšāʿ* in Ps 17,13 might imply the thought of the Archenemy also.

([79]) For this cp. N. Füglister, *Das Psalmengebet* (München 1965) 116 ff. (" Offene Sprache ").

([80]) Cp. Dahood, *Psalms* 260 ; 19. For " strong citadel " may also be read " towered fortress ".

At least the " lion " and the " net " belong to the *Wortfeld* of Death ([81]) ; some other elements resemble Accadian descriptions of demons, among which we find the " Lurker " and the " Seizer " ([82]).

Ps 27,12 reads :

> Do not put me into the throat of my adversaries,
>> for false witnesses have testified against me....
> In the Victor do I trust,
>> to behold the beauty of Yahweh
>> in the land of life eternal. (Dahood)

Both Yahweh's title " Victor " and the term " land of life " imply a contrast with Death.   Moreover the phrase " do not put me into the throat of my adversaries " is identical with Ps 41,3b, where it applies to Death ([83]).   The plural " enemies " is exclusively due to the Massoretic pointing.   So we are justified in concluding that Death or at least a connotation of Death is to be found in *ṣry*.

Ps 143,3 is intimately related to Ps 7,6 :

> For the Enemy has pursued me,
> has smitten my life into the nether world,
> has made me sit in Darkness like those long dead.

Here the intensive plural *maḥăšakkîm*, which undeniably belongs to the nether world's *Wortfeld*, is parallel with *'rṣ* and so suggests the interpretation " nether world " and " Enemy ", i.e., Death.

([81]) Biblical occurrences of the " lion " are summed up on p. 112 above and on pp. 164 f. below ; we quote from an Accadian list of gods : " Alluḫappu (hunting-net) had the head of a lion ; the Death-god was provided with the head of a serpent-dragon (!) ; ... the evil Utukku had the head of a lion ; Nedu, the gatekeeper of the nether world had the head of a lion " (*ANET* 109 B). From a Sumerian incantation : " Samana, der mit den Löwenmaul..., der wilde Löwe Enlils, der Löwe Enkis, der den Hals abschneidet ; der Löwe Nininsannas mit dem bluttriefenden Maul ; der Löw der Götter, der das Maul aufsperrt.. " (Falkenstein–von Soden, t. 39, p. 214). An Accadian incantation mentions " Istar Löwin " (Falkenstein–von Soden, B 61 : 31, p. 330). Widengren comments : " My quotations indicate that these animals ought rather to be regarded as demons in animal guise.   It is of course difficult to say whether the same applies to the Israelite texts, as even human enemies may be depicted in demoniac colours " (*Accad. and Hebr. Pss* 242 f.). See also Kraus, *Psalmen* I, 180 on Pss 22,17, cited above.   In our opinion there are traces of several demons in the OT ; Death is one of them. See below, pp. 160 ff.

([82]) Widengren, *Accad. and Hebr. Pss* 198 f.

([83]) Dahood, *Psalms* 248 ff.

Job 36,16:

> He lured you out of the mouth of the Enemy,
> In unconfined expanse he set you ([84]).

Though the translation of 16b is uncertain, the contrast between ṣār and raḥab lō'-mûṣāq is obvious; but this does not require the common impersonal translation of ṣār. As ṣar = enemy properly means " Bedränger ", i.e., " somebody who oppresses, who closes in ", the personal interpretation by no means sacrifices the contrast. Moreover it maintains the strength of mippî ṣar, as it recognizes an allusion to the muzzle of Death here. Compare the way the beginning of Ps 107 summarizes the evils listed in the psalm: " Whom he has redeemed from the hand of the Enemy " (v. 2).

3.4 King of Terrors (melek ballāhôt)

> He is snatched from his comfortable tent,
> and haled before the King of Terrors (Jb 18,14) ([85]).

The context undoubtedly shows that this " King of Terrors " can be no other than Sir Death: he is explicitly mentioned in the preceding verse, where his Firstborn appears. In Hebrew the title runs melek ballāhôt. The latter term, meaning " dismay, horror " very often has an eschatological connotation; it is found together with winds and waters, traps and snares, disaster and destruction, ruins and mire ([86]). But for Is 17,14 it is always found in an intensive plural, which denotes its expressiveness. The verbal form taṣʿidēhû, rendered " haled " by Pope, is translated " they march him " by W. Moran, its subject being either an " indefinite plural " or " the denizens of the underworld " ([87]). Pope remarks: " The title may be taken to imply that Mot is ruler over a host of infernal spirits who seize the victim and hustle him into the presence of their king " ([88]).

([84]) Pope, *Job* 231 translated: " He lured you out of distress " and notes on p. 233: " Literally ' from the mouth of distress ' ".

([85]) Pope, *Job* 123.

([86]) Jb 18,11; 27,20; 30,15; Is 17,14 (sg.); Ez 26,21, etc.; Ps 73,19. Characteristic is Jb 24,17: " Well they know the terrors of darkness (ṣalmāwet) ".

([87]) Moran, " New Evidence on Canaanite taqtulū(na) ", *JCS* 5 (1951) 33-35; cf. *Bib* 45 (1964) 82, n. 1; *Fs. Albright* 71, n. 108. Moran rejects Sarna's interpretation of the prefixed t- as a m. sg. (put forward in *JBL* 82 [1963] 31; cp. Dahood, *Prov.* 5 f.).

([88]) *Job* 126.

In this way the author of Job gives us precious information here : the stay in Sheol is frightening for living man, not merely because of the lack of life and its fullness, but also in view of the torture he will have to face there. This title of Mot seems to disclose fragmentarily otherwise unknown traditions describing the horrors of the nether world. Biblical statements about the after-life generally tend to suppress this aspect of Sheol which is copiously depicted in Egyptian sources ([89]). So mention of Mot's title " King of Terrors ", or " Horrible King " suggests that Israel was acquainted with this view of the beyond ([90]).

3.5 Death the Shepherd (rô'ê)

In his commentary on Jb 18,14, Pope writes : " The God Mot is termed the shepherd of the denizens of the nether world in Ps 49,14, shepherd being an ancient royal title " ([91]). Ps 49,15 (RSV : 49,14) is a notorious crux, which need not be fully analysed here ; as to Death as a shepherd scholars generally agree. We quote the verse in Dahood's rendering :

> Like sheep they will be put into Sheol,
>   Death will be their shepherd ;
> When they descend into his gullet like a calf,
>   their limbs will be devoured by Sheol,
>   consumed by the Devourer.

As the translator himself confesses, not every detail is equally certain in this translation. Retaining TM consonantal tradition, he reads :

> kaṣṣe'ōn-li še'ōl šîtû
> māwet yir'ēm
> weyār'dû bemêšārîm lebāqār
> wesîrām leballôt še'ōl
> mezē bōlê lô ([92]).

([89]) See Zande, *passim*. See, however, pp. 190 ff. : Jb 18,14 gives direct expression to the frightfulness of a (premature) death ; torture in Sheol itself is generally identical with the fate of the corpse in the grave or, rarely, a mere prolongation of the miseries of this life. In Accadian, Nergal is named *lugal-ḫušuru*, " King of the horrible city ", and *ša irṣiti*, " King of the nether world " (Tallqvist, *Namen der Totenwelt* 11, 36).

([90]) Human reaction accordingly consists in " terrors of death " (Ps 55,5) ; See Romans 5,14.17.

([91]) Pope, *Job* 126.

([92]) Dahood, *Psalms* 300 f. In Accadian Tammuz is called *rē'ū irṣiti*,

The use of the preposition l^e with Sheol is fairly common; Dahood points to Ps 16,10. The qal passive is not so rare as is often assumed [93]. The idea is also found in *UT* 51 : VIII : 17 f., quoted before [94]. The conception of Death as a shepherd is also found in the Magical Papyrus Harris, as put forward by Albright; there it is a title of Horon, a god connected with the nether world. (His name probably means "The one of the pit" [95].) In *UT* 67 : VI : 6 "the land of grazing" belongs to the domain of Mot; this text was studied above [96].

yrd is a normal term to denote the transition to Sheol; *bqr* beautifully balances initial $ṣ^e$'on [97]. As to b^emêšārîm, Dahood writes: "a doubtful translation". He finds it in the same sense in Prv 23,31 f. and CC 7,10. For the imagery, see *UT* 67 : I : 6-8, quoted above [98]. The thought of v. 14b is in keeping with other descriptions of Sheol, derived from the grave. The last colon resembles Dt 32,24 m^ezê rāʿāb, " consumed by the Hungry One " [99]; the idea of " devouring " is not rarely connected with Sheol: it returns in Dt 32,24 : " devoured by Reseph " and perhaps in Ps 56,2 : " all day the Devourer oppresses me " [100] and is also found in Egyptian netherworld literature [101]. For our present purpose, however, the most relevant conclusion of these considerations is the discovery of another name of Sir Death: unnecessary to add that it is an ironical one [102].

" shepherd of the nether world ", and the Sun bears the same title (Tallqvist, Namen der Totenwelt 10 f., 13). These gods, however, are of a different nature in comparison with death.

[93] Cp. Gordon *UT* Gramm. 9 : 31 and Dahood, *UHPh* 9 : 13, 9 : 31.

[94] Cp. " The Hungry One ", pp. 107 ff. above.

[95] On Horon, see J. Gray, *The Krt-text in the Literature of Ras Shamra* (Leiden 1955), on Krt III : 55 ; Gaster, *Thespis* 155 f., note ; Dahood, " ULex " 89, where a bibliography is found.

[96] Pp. 10 f.

[97] For the preposition *BDB* 516 A-B, *sub* 5. j.

[98] See Dahood, *Psalms* 300 ; for *yrd b*, see Jb 17,16 ; b^emêšārîm means " according to justice " in Ps 9,9 ; 98,9.

[99] Above, pp. 107 ff.

[100] *lḥm* as in Dt 32,24 ; the proposal was made by Widengren, *Accad. and Hebr.* 112 f., cp. 201, but it remains a doubtful one.

[101] Zandee, 158. In Hos 13,14 H. W. Wolff translates ' Dornen ' and " Stachel " and remarks that these are normally the instruments of a herdsman. If this is correct, this verse contains an allusion to Death as a Shepherd (*Hosea* 297).

[102] With different methods and results our verse was treated by R. Pautrel, " La mort est leur pasteur ", *Recherches de Science religieuse* 54 (1966) 530-536. Personally, I now prefer to translate : " They descend to the Herdsman

3.6 Terra Mater (various terms)

Comparative Religion has gathered abundant documentation about Mother Earth in different civilizations ([103]). The connection with agriculture is obvious ; earth is the " fertile womb " and when man is buried, he is laid to rest in his mother's womb. In Egypt, India, and Greece the dead were laid on green foliage, interred in ploughed land and covered with sowings ([104]). This custom eloquently attests the fact that death was conceived of as an entry to new life. The " monistic " conception of death in Egypt indeed understood the future state as identical with potential life, even with the highest form of life : the deceased is a divine being ([105]). Vegetative gods stay in the nether world ([106]) ; this place remains a fertile womb ([107]). And of Osiris it is said that " the mother of this god was at the same time his grave, because life rises from the grave " ([108]). In this light the custom of burying people in a squatting position, i.e., with their knees pulled up, is quite natural ; this is the last posture of a child in its mother's womb ([109]). Death is a return to chaos, the situation of disorder preceding creation : creating means : " separating ", bringing order, assigning to everything its proper place ([110]). The Israelites, however, did not yield to the temptation to obscure the inexorability of death as the Egyptians did. For the Israelite death is the end.

> Naked I came from my mother's womb,
> and naked shall I return there (Jb 1,21) ([111])

Commentaries often appear embarrassed at this text. Driver writes : " To infer from ' thither ' that ' my mother's womb ' means the womb

---

($b\check{e}q\bar{e}r$, cf. Am 7,14) as they deserve ; their figure will be devoured in Sheol where its dwelling is ". For " dwelling ", see J. v. d. Ploeg, " Notes sur le Psaume XLIX " [OTS 13 (1963) 137-172] 155. For bqr cp. Ez 34,11 f.

([103]) The evidence in summarized by Eliade, *Das Heilige* 81-85.
([104]) Kristensen, *Leven uit den dood* 228 f.
([105]) *Ibid.* 30 f., 54. According to the monistic view, " Death is considered the necessary condition for eternal life. Without death no victory over death ". For the dualistic view death is the enemy of life (Zandee, 1 ff.).
([106]) Kristensen, *Leven uit den dood* 239.
([107]) Van der Leeuw, *Phänomenologie* 363.
([108]) Kristensen, *op. cit.* 130.
([109]) Vincent, *Canaan* 269.
([110]) Cp. the remarks of F. M. Th. Böhl, *Het Gilgamesj Epos* (Amsterdam 1941) 118 f. ; Eliade, *Traité d'histoire des religions* 24-31.
([111]) Pope, *Job* 3.

of the earth is mistaken " ([112]); Job merely refers to the thin, unsubstantial life after death which does not differ much from " the absence
of life that precedes birth ".   The text inspires Ricciotti to the improbable statement that the idea of a return to Sheol " serait contraire
à toute la tradition hébraique à outretombe " ([113]).   He proves this
by referring to the custom of interring the dead in an embryonal
posture.   Fohrer's comment is more complicated.   " Ebensowenig
kann ausdrücklich die Unterwelt gemeint sein, denn der Mensch kommt
nicht von dort auf die Welt " ([114]); even the limited biblical evidence,
however, suffices to show that this is wrong.

According to Fohrer the stress is on the nakedness; *šam* serves
as a metrical complement of the line and as a counterpart of the
" womb ".   He acknowledges, however, that the thought of the nether
world is resounding " a little bit " also, because the grave is in the
earth and the dust is taken from there.   This exegesis avoids the
issue.

We think all these authors are victims of a special kind of " logical
thinking ".   Our introduction of this paragraph shows how natural
and evident these things are for men who are not alienated from nature
and perhaps even from biblical thinking : Ps 139,13.15 reads :

> Yea, Thou hast created my kidneys,
> woven in my mother's womb.
> My bones were not hidden from thee
> when I was made in secret
> spun deep in the earth ([115]).

Here there cannot be the slightest doubt about the equation of the
mother's womb and the depths of the nether world.   So there appears
to be a proper logic in this way of thinking.   Indeed man can be said
to return to the nether world, for he came from there.   It is quite

---

([112]) S. R. Driver – G. B. Gray, *Job* 19 f.

([113]) G. Ricciotti, " Et nu j'y retournerai ", *ZAW* 67 (1955) 249-251.

([114]) G. Fohrer, *Das Buch Hiob* 93. " Die menschliche Mutter wiederholt
nur den uranfänglichen Akt der Geburt des Lebens aus dem Schoss der Erde "
(Eliade, *Das Heilige* 83).   The equation finds its most startling expression in
Jb 30,23 : " I know that you will return me to Death " (Pope, *Job* 192, 96).

([115]) With the LXX the second colon may be translated this way : " protected me from my mother's womb ".   Although this interpretation is sound
both lexicographically (Zor 553A *skk* 2) and syntactically (see above, p. 48,
n. 124j, the present writer prefers the translation given above (see general argument of the psalm and the parallelism 13a/13b and 13b/15c).   Apparently '*rṣ*
in 15c stands for the nether world.

useless to weaken either of the two expressions. Representations, to us simply inconsistent, are coexisting peacefully in primitive thought ([116]).

The idea underlying Jb 1,21 finds its clearest expression in Sir 40,1:

> Great travail is created for every man,
> and an heavy yoke is upon the sons of Adam
> from the day that they go out from their
>   mother's womb
> till the day that they return to the
>   mother of all things. (KJ)

The Isaiah Apocalypse expresses the novelty of the Israelites' resurrection in this same archaic speech when it says:

> The underworld will give birth to the shadows (25,19).

E. S. Mulder's comment is to the point: " The earth is represented here as a bearing mother who bears shadows " ([117]).

The close relation of this idea with that of Sheol is visible in Jon 2,3: " From the womb of Sheol I cried out for help ".

Finally, Jb 38,8 shows its cosmic dimensions:

> Who shut the sea within doors,
> When it came gushing from the womb...? (Pope)

In view of this motif Hos 13,13 f. is interesting: the prophet mentions the possibility that the womb becomes Sheol before birth, because life does not loose itself from darkness ([118]). This thought is probably based on the association of the mother's womb and the Earth (womb-grave):

> The pangs of childbirth came for him (Ephraim),
> but he is an unwise son;
> for now he does not present himself
> at the mouth of the womb.
> Shall I ransom them from the hand of Sheol?
> Shall I redeem them from Death?

([116]) Van der Leeuw, *Primitieve Mensch en de Religie* 39.

([117]) " Die aarde word hier as barende moeder voorgestel wat skimme baar " (E. S. Mulder, *Theol. Jesaja Apok.* 51).

([118]) H. W. Wolff *in loco*: " Der Gedanke (kann) mitschwingen dass der Mutterleib Grab und Totenort zu werden droht ", *Dodekapropheton* 1, *Hosea*, 297. The reference to Jr 20,17 is to the point.

3.7 Belial (Swallower)

First, different proposals for an etymology of this word will be listed here. They can be classified in two groups: one dividing the word into *bly* and a verbal form, another analysing in the root *blʿ* and an *-l* ending.

A.1 Gesenius derives *-yaʿal* from the root *yʿl*, whose hiphil in biblical Hebrew means " to be useful ". Consequently, Belial means " Unnützes, Nützloses " ([119]).

A.2 Cross and Freedman take Jb 7,9 as a basis for their interpretation; this verse reads: " He who goes down to Sheol does not come up " (*lō' yaʿălê*). So Belial means: " (a place from which) none arises " ([120]). In fact this seems a new form of de Lagarde's definition: " welcher nicht hinauflässt " ([121]). In this case hiphil is understood. These authors refer to 2 S 22,5 where *mwt* is balanced by Belial.

B.1 G. R. Driver distinguishes between *blʿ* I, " swallowed ", and *blʿ* II " slandered " (derived from the Arabic). Afterwards *blʿ* is rendered " confused "; by means of the final *-l* it is made a substantive " confusion ". According to this scholar *-l* formation is well attested: see *gbʿl*, *krml*, *ʿrpl*. For the double *-y-* two guesses are made ([122]).

B.2 Guillaume connects *blʿ* with Arabic *blġ*, so that Belial means " damage " and the like ([123]).

B.3 D. Winton Thomas refers to Arabic *baliya*, to swallow; Belial originally signified " swallower " ([124]).

Critique:

A.1: Driver remarks that in this (and de Lagarde's) case one would expect Hebrew hiphil and not qal. This can hardly be denied for Hebrew as far as we know it.

A.2: Strictly speaking *bᵉlî* does not mean " none " but " not ". But because the third person singular might be understood impersonally, this objection is not insurmountable. Driver's stricture that

---

([119]) *GB* 100b; for typographical reasons *bᵉlîyaʿal* will be written Belial here.

([120]) *JBL* 72 (1953) 22, n. 6.

([121]) Quoted by *GB* 100 B.

([122]) *ZAW* 52 (1934) 52 f.

([123]) *JNES* 13 (1962) 320 f.

([124]) In J. N. Birdsall and R. W. Thomson, editors, *Biblical and Patristic Studies in Memory of Robert Pierce Casey* (Freiburg 1963) 11-19.

one would look for *ya'ăleh* is hardly cogent, as the final *-h* is often dropped with these verbs ([125]). Philologically this interpretation seems a sound one.

B. The weak point in these solutions is the supposed final *-l* which necessarily remains hypothetical, as the phenomenon is rarely attested in Hebrew ([126]).

B.1 It is not clear, why *bl'* is rendered " confused "; the *-y-* is not explained.

B.2 The weakness of these arabizing etymologies is the numerous (and not rarely contrary) meanings of words and verbs in this language, in spite of the original consonants being well preserved (e.g., distinction between *ḥ* and *ḫ*; ' and *ġ*). Ugaritic, however, proves more trustworthy because it combines the latter quality with a close semantic affinity with Hebrew.

B.3 We shall see that current usage in biblical Hebrew favours the etymologies offered under Belial here rather than group A. This argument, however, cannot be conclusive : a word may have undergone a semantic shift in its history, e.g., a specific meaning may become more general. A consequence of this is the relative unimportance of the etymology for establishing the proper meaning and full import of a word in a later phase of its existence ([127]). D. W. Thomas's proposal merits consideration as it finds some support in biblical texts. Hebrew *bl'* is found 20 times in qal; 6 times its subject is *'rṣ* or *'dmh* with Sheol-connotation ([128]); once Sheol ([129]), once *mṣwlh* ([130]), once a sea monster ([131]); once Nebuchadrezzar compared with *tannîn* ([132]); once Israel's enemies in a context strongly reminiscent of Sheol ([133]). This quick survey shows that there is serious reason to postulate both

---

([125]) See Joüon 17 f. : *GK* 75 k.

([126]) " In some cases (... possibly Hebr *karmel*, cf. *kerem*) we may have to identify independent patterns with suffix *-l*, even though of rare occurrence ", S. Moscati, ... *An Introduction to the Comparative Grammar of Semitic Languages* (Wiesbaden 1964) 12. 21, p. 82. Recently more examples of this phenomenon were brought forward by S. and Sh. Rin in *BZ* 7 (1967) 192 ; Belial is not referred to there.

([127]) Barr, *Semantics* 107, 109.

([128]) Ex 15,12 ; Nu 16,30.32.34 ; Nu 26,10 ; Dt 11,6.

([129]) Prv 1,12.

([130]) Ps 69,16.

([131]) Jon 1,17.

([132]) Jr 51,34.

([133]) Ps 124,3 cp. 4 f. : *mayîm* ; *naḥ^elâ*.

in poetry and prose, an intimate relation between *bl'* and the nether world : *bl'* is a verb with an ominous connotation ([134]).

The next step will be an investigation of current biblical usage ; the last section will occupy itself with the further development of Belial's meaning.

V. Maag wrote a clear and accurate article on the meaning of Belial in biblical usage ; it will be sufficient to give a summary of pertinent points here ([135]). The word Belial, occurring 27 times in the OT (out of which 21 times as a genitive), applies to the nether world only thrice.   The analysis of the remaining 24 occurrences shows that " belīja'al ist, was die Schutzdämme gedeihlichen Daseins negiert, was grundsätzlich auflösend, destruktiv, chaotisch wirkt : belīja'al ist, was *urböse* ist " ([136]). It is a religious conception : it comprises all that is contrary to God and the fundamental regulations concerning social life. Belial affects the " framework " of a life filled with happiness, it attacks its protections and gives way to chaos and confusion. According to Maag, its origin is to be looked for in the Canaanite culture, more specifically in Kingship, where cosmic, political, civil, and ethic structures were united. This, however, is mere speculation without any positive evidence.

In this way its application to the nether world is fully understandable ; in fact, the fundamental meaning of Belial is a perfect description of the very essence of Sheol. We already noticed before how intimate are the relations between chaos and nether world in the OT. Belial is explicitly applied to Sheol in Ps 18,6 which is practically identical with 2 S 22,5, though the two text should not be harmonized. Ps 18,6 reads :

> The cords of Death encompassed me,
> the torrents of perdition (Belial)
> > assailed me,
> the cords of Sheol entangled me,
> the snares of Death confronted me (RSV).

The parallelism Death–Sheol–Belial is significant ; in view of common biblical usage Belial is probably not a proper name of Sheol, but rather an epithet.

([134]) Cp. other occurrences as Gn 41,7.24. In Egypt also " to devour " belongs to the *Wortfeld* of the nether world, but there it is torture after death ; Zandee, 158 ff.

([135]) V. Maag, " Belija'al im Alten Testament ", *ThZ* 21 (1965) 287-299.

([136]) *Ibid.* 295.

Maag recognizes the same connotation in Ps 41,9 :

A deadly thing (d^{e}bar b^{e}lîya'al) has fastened upon him;
he will not rise again from where he lies.

Here, as in all other cases, Belial implies a personal, "affektbezo-
gen" attitude of the speaker towards the reality, thus characterized ([137]); this was also true for the verb *bl'*: it is not unlikely that the
two were associated with each other. As to Ps 41,9, the second part
of this verse indeed reminds one of Sheol: the phrase "not to rise
again" is connected with other expressions belonging to the *Wortfeld*
of the nether world ([138]).

It need not be argued here that Belial, in later development,
became a proper name for personified evil, the Devil. This is the
result of an organic evolution: on the one hand Sheol is often personified in the OT and on the other it is intimately connected with
a chaos, which is the negation of life.

[137] *Ibid.* 289.
[138] Cp. the verb *mwṭ*, to waver, etc. (above, pp. 92 f.).

PART II. IMPLICATIONS AND EXPLICATIONS

CHAPTER 1: LOCATION AND SCENERY OF SHEOL

1.1 Underworld; Underworld and Grave

A. It is a well-known fact that, in the IL and ThPs, the psalmists often claim to be in Sheol when, in our view, they are still alive; and to be delivered from the abode of the dead, while to our way of thinking they have not been there at all. Chr. Barth's book: *Die Errettung vom Tode in den individuellen Klage- und Danklieder des Alten Testaments* is an important contribution to the solution of the problem.

Barth starts his study with an examination of the meaning of " life " in the OT, and it appears that it contains more than the absence of physical death. " Life " is to have the possibility to be and to become oneself; it implies time and activity, communion with like-minded people, food, freedom, certainty, health, happiness, joy. In short, " life " is human existence on earth worth being lived [1].

Death is the lack of this fulness, of the opportunities for development; in other words, impotence, illness, calamity, restraint belong to the essence of death [2]. In the words of A. R. Johnson: " Just as death in the strictest sense of the term is the weakest form of life, so any weakness in life is a form of death " [3]. Any reduction of

---

[1] Barth, *Errettung* 53-66; see the parallelism in Ps 119,107: " I am afflicted above measure, give me life, O Lord, according to thy word ".

[2] " To be healed " is identical with " to be restored to life ": Ps 30,3 f. reads: " I cried to you, and you healed me. O Yahweh, you lifted me from Sheol, you restored me to life " (Dahood).

[3] " Jonah 2,3-10. A Study in Cultic Phantasy ", in H. H. Rowley (editor), *Studies in OT Prophecy* 82-102, esp. 90. It is only fair to quote also the father of the theory, J. Pedersen: " If afflicted by misfortune, illness ... then one has little life, but all the more death. He who is ill or otherwise in distress may say that he is dead, and when he recovers, he is pulled out of death ", *Israel* I/II, 153 f. A modern youngster describes boredom as " a kind of temporarily being dead " ... (*De Tijd*, July 1, 1966; p. 6).

human fulness of life is equal to a being delivered to the power of death and, consequently, to an arrival in his domain, Sheol. Death manifests itself in any form of misery, and the character of the domain of death corresponds with these expressions of his sway : prison, land of forgetfulness, Abaddon, etc.

Locations of Sheol are primarily to be understood as descriptions. Attempts at a reconstruction of the antique world-picture are foredoomed to failure. " Das Totenreich ist überall da, wo der Tod seine Herrschaft ausübt. Genauer und zugleich umfassender lässt sich das Totenreich nicht lokalisieren " (⁴). Sheol's being called " deep " is first of all to be interpreted as an expression of the distance between the domain of death and the land of the living : anybody who is in Sheol is removed and alienated from God and the human community, and therefore from life. As many other descriptions of Sheol, this one, too, is taken from the grave ; the only difference between the tomb and the beyond is the latter's universality. A question as to the priority of Sheol or the grave, however, creates a false problem.

Special manifestations of Sheol are the grave, the desert, and the ocean ; there is partial identity between them and Sheol : this is linked up with the Israelite's mental pattern of thinking in totalities (⁵).

All this does not imply that Barth denies the difference between this form of reduced life and complete physical death. The distinction is clearly made by the psalmists themselves in IL – ITh : the afflicted man never identifies himself with a dead person ; he is still able to pray to God ; there is still the possibility of a return, a recovery ; he speaks of having become " like those who descend into Sheol " and of having arrived " near the domain of death ". The poor psalmist is in deadly peril, in the neighbourhood of Sheol : for him this is real experience of death itself. This appears from the ThPs, where the intolerable situation is identified with the reality of death, without any reserve. Once delivered, the psalmist takes heart to call a spade a spade, a thing he did not venture to say when he was in need (⁶).

N. W. Porteous very properly praised Barth's study as " an important contribution to the elucidation of the meaning of ' life ' and ' death ' in the Old Testament " (⁷). Indeed, the investigation into the impact of these two ideas proves to be a very happy one.

(⁴) Barth, *Errettung* 38 ; these ideas are developed on pp. 77-89.
(⁵) See J. Pedersen, *Israel* I/II, 99-133, especially 110 ff.
(⁶) *Ibid.* 114-118 ; 145. But see our remarks above on p. 21, n. 3.
(⁷) In H. H. Rowley, *Eleven Years of Biblical Bibliography* (Indian Hills 1957) 148.

In spite of this the present writer thinks that some modifications are called for.

B. *a*) It may be doubted if there are sufficient arguments to attack the traditional oriental world-picture in the way Barth does ; in our opinion it has left plenty of traces in the OT ([8]). We will quote some examples here showing that the oriental world has a cellar with a pronounced oceanic character.

Gn 2,6 : the primordial river in the earth ([9]). Gn 7,11 : the fountains of the great deep (under the earth) and the windows of the heavens (above). Ex 20,4 (Dt 5,8) : " You shall not make yourself a graven image ... of anything ... that is in the water under the earth ". And Ps 24,2 runs : " The earth is Yahweh's ... for he based it upon the seas, established it upon the ocean currents. "

Dahood comments : " The pillars upon which the earth rests have been sunk into the subterranean ocean " ([10]). Jon 2 : the prophet is in the heart of the sea, at the foundations of the mountains. The latter are in the nether world ([11]). Indeed, the nether region manifests itself in the ocean ; at the same time, however, it appears that Jonah can only think of Sheol as being under the *earth.*

Jb 38,8 reads : " Who shut in the sea with doors, when it burst forth from the womb ? "

The reference to the underworld is unmistakable here ([12]). On the basis of these indications the flat denial of a subterranean ocean can be labelled rather temerarious ([13]). The aversion from a subterranean location for Sheol may be inspired by the conception that Sheol was thought to be present in the desert. Martin-Achard writes : " Sheol is connected with the wilderness, the country hostile to man, the lifeless land where demons and the spirits of dead men prowl ... where briers and thorns grow ... a region of death for whoever ventures there " ([14]).

([8]) Cl. Schedl, *Geschichte des AT*, I (2nd ed. ; Innsbruck 1965) 244 ; Johnson, " Jonah " 88 ; Reymond, " L' eau " 167 ; the objections raised by Sutcliffe (*The O. T. and Future Life*, 46 f.) against this conception arise from a technical conception which is not biblical and are therefore invalid.

([9]) See above, p. 25.

([10]) *Psalms* 150 f.

([11]) Pedersen, *Israel* I/II, 463.

([12]) See also Jb 26,5 ; 38,16 f.

([13]) Above, pp. 69 ff.

([14]) *From Death ...* 44 ; Pedersen, *Israel* I/II, 470 ; Barth, *Errettung* 86 ; Reymond, " L' eau " 213.

This fact is put on record by several historians of religion ([15]). By way of biblical evidence texts such as Jr 2,6.31; Jb 12,24 f.; Dt 8,15 are quoted, and indeed they suggest that man in the barren desert feels within reach of death, that chaotic forces are reigning there.

But in the present writer's opinion this evidence is far from exhaustive. Sheol is conceived of as an utter chaos: this is expressed in the names it has in common with anti-cosmic waters. Primitive thought, however, also knows a " dry chaos " (Gn 2,4b-6). The cosmos consists in the territory a people or tribe is occupying; outside of it there is a strange, chaotic space, where demons and the spirits of the dead are roaming. Occupation and reclamation are repetitions of creation, as is chaos then turned into cosmos ([16]). This conception of the uninhabited desert land is also reflected in the Bible. As Wensinck remarks, the word *tōhû* (elsewhere for " wet chaos ") is applied to the desert in Dt 8,15; Jb 6,18; Ps 107,40 ([17]).

Our analysis of the term *šdmwt* suggests the same conclusion: uncultivated land is connected with death ([18]). Where devastation of cities or countries is portrayed as a relapse in to barren conditions, we are confronted again with an expression of the same thinking. " Die Feinde gehören zu den Mächten des Chaos. Jede Zerstörung einer Stadt ist ein Rückfall ins Chaos " ([19]). Sometimes in an indi-

---

([15]) Eliade, *Images* 47; *Mythe* 26; van der Leeuw, *Phänomenologie* 359 ff.; Barth, *Errettung* 79, 86.

([16]) Eliade, *Das Heilige* 18 f.

([17]) Wensinck, *Ocean* 53.

([18]) See above; for Azazel cp. Barth, *Errettung* 87; S. H. Cooke connects this custom with the Tammuzian liturgy where expiation is obtained by means of a substitute, " *a puḫu* for Ereshkigal ", *Babylonian and Assyrian Religion* (Oxford 1962) 36. " The concept of the desert is closely connected in Sumero-Accadian and in Hebrew, especially so far as the idea of the Nether World is concerned " (A. Haldar, *The Notion of the Desert in Sumero-Accadian and West-Semitic Religions* [Uppsala-Leipzig 1950]) 12). See also Tallqvist, *Namen der Totenwelt* 17-22 (*edin* and *ṣeru*, both meaning " desert ").

([19]) Eliade, *Das Heilige* 29. A more explicit reference to the desert as infernal may be found in Ps 68,7, where God is said to set prisoners free, *'ak sôrărîm šākᵉnû ṣᵉḥîhâ*. M. Dahood proposes to render this as " but the stubborn were entombed in the Wasteland " remarking that the latter word is translated with " in graves " by LXX. For his interpretation of *škn*, see above, p. 32 (in Ps 7,6). Although this is a real possibility, it does not impose itself and it is questionable if LXX really understood the word *ṣᵉḥîhâ*: in view of its sense in Ez 24,7 etc. (adjective; " smooth ", of a rock) they may have taken " grave " for the proper meaning of the term. But on any supposition LXX

vidual lament the psalmist identifies himself with barren and burnt
land: Ps 63,2; 143,6.   These allusions no doubt are to the thirst of
the nether world ([20]), a consequence of the desert conditions prevailing
there.

On the other hand, the desert is never clearly and explicitly identified with the abode of the dead in the OT.   Our provisory conclusion,
also prompted by the fact that Sheol is often and explicitly identified
with a watery territory, is that allusions to the nether world as a desert
and dry place must be interpreted qualitatively (i.e., as referring to
a complex of conditions) rather than locally.

B. *b*) We have some doubts as to the correctness of the spatiality,
as put forward by Barth; on the one hand it is too wide, as it does
not do justice to the uniqueness of the abode of the dead; on the
other it is too restricted because it leaves no room for other categories
(illness, prison, etc.), which have no fixed spatial ties but nevertheless
are expressions of death's sway.   It seems imperative to distinguish
between death's province comprising both local realities as ocean and
desert, and other realities as prison, illness, and wild beasts — and
the abode of the dead proper, which is situated deep in the earth.
Sheol then is the complete reign of Death, the abode of the dead from
which nobody returns; it is partially identical with the grave and
with the primeval ocean also.   " Sheol is the entirety into which all
graves are merged....   The " Ur "-grave we might call Sheol; it belongs deep down under the earth, but it manifests itself in every single
grave.   Where there is grave, there is Sheol; and where there is Sheol,
there is grave " ([21]).   Sepulchral gifts and the cult of the dead sufficiently shows this coherence between the grave and Sheol and at the
same time the difference from desert, ocean, and the like.   Sheol
proper is deep in the earth: see the name '*rṣ* used also for chaos in
a strict cosmological sense (a chaos with pronounced oceanic attributes) ([22]); we can refer to the verbs *yrd* and '*lh*; to the expressions
with *tḥt* ([23]).

appear to have understood the tendency of the colon: in many primitive cultures the desert is a present chaos, pertaining to the domain of Death, so that
fully human life is impossible there. Even if we prefer the more moderate
interpretation, " but the stubborn dwell in barren country ", the quotation
of the verse is relevant in this context.

([20]) See also below, pp. 191 ff.

([21]) Pedersen, *Israel* 462. See Heidel, 173-191.

([22]) With an anthropological sense it is also found in individual laments:
Ps 7; 141; 143.

([23]) See Barth, *Errettung* 81.

Moreover it is clear that heaven and hell are the two extremes of the biblical universe : Ps 95,4, describing the universe in a polar expression, reads :

In his hand are the unfathomable depths of the nether world, his are the summits of the mountains.

Similarly Ps 139,8 :

If I climb up into heaven thou art there : if I make Sheol my bed thou art there also.

Is 7,11 : the king is offered a boundless choice :

Ask a sign of Yahweh your God ; let it be deep as Sheol or high as heaven.

Is 44,23 runs :

Sing, O heavens, for the Lord has done it, shout, O depths of the nether world.

Am 9,2 :

Though they dig into Sheol ... though they climb up to heaven ...

Prov 25,3 :

The heavens for height, the nether world for depth. (Dahood)

In Sir 24,5 Wisdom affirms :

I alone compassed the circuit of heaven, and walked in the bottom of the deep. (KJ)

So we find the underworld as the deepest extremity of the universe in different literary genres ; moreover both in its cosmological (Ps 95,4 ; Is 44,23, etc.) and anthropological sense (Ps 139,8 ; Is 7,11, etc.) [24]. Moreover we might point to the tripartite division of the universe. It occurs in *UT* '*nt* III : 19-22, quoted elsewhere [25], and is, with due reserve, proposed for Ps 77,19 :

[24] See above, pp. 44 ff.
[25] Cp. above, p. 59.

> The peal of your thunder came from the vault of heaven,
> your shafts of lightning lit up the world,
> the nether world trembled and shook ([26]).

It might also occur in Jr 10,12:

> It is he who made the nether world by his power,
> who established the world by his wisdom,
> and by his understanding stretched out the heavens ([27]).

See Phil 2,11: " every knee, in heaven, on earth and under the earth "
(cf. Rev 5,3).

The evidence is overwhelming: the abode of the dead is under
the earth ([28]). Of course this world picture is not a result of scientific
research; it is rather of a mythical nature, " eine Glaubenssache und
also ein Geheimnis " ([29]). This distinction, however, is a modern one.

B. c) The foregoing conclusion must have its consequences for
the axiom: " Whoever is in need, is in Sheol ": it is quite evidently
an overstatement. The identification between " need " and " Sheol "
is partial indeed. First of all it seems necessary to point out that
this use of nether-world phrase is at home in the IL and ThPs; no
doubt there are secondary traces in other genres, but it has been remarked, correctly it seems, that the utterance " I am in Sheol " as
an expression of distress is never found in the second person in biblical
literature.

As to the more hesitating utterances (" I am nearly ...; like
those " ...) one might ask whether these are understatements or not ([29]).
On the basis of Barth's evidence it would be tempting to consider the
radical formulas as exaggerations, the understatement being hardly

---

([26]) Dahood, *Psalms* 109; cp. Ps 18,8; cf. above, p. 45.

([27]) Proposal of M. Dahood. The sequence yields a beautiful verse, but
I hesitate, as the creation of the nether world is a *contradictio in terminis* in
the OT and is consequently never affirmed there (cp. Is 45,18c).

([28]) In Egyptian Pyramid Texts the nether world is sometimes called " coun-
ter-heaven " (Zandee, 237, B. 20.1). In the same texts " Nun, the primeval
ocean, is thought of as the realm of the dead. This conception is very close
to that of a nether world, as the primeval ocean extends under the disk of the
earth " (*ibid.* 94, A.11.d). Because Sheol is located where also chaotic waters
are thought to be, names and descriptions of Sheol in terms of waters also contain a reference to the situation of the Beyond.

([29]) Barth, *Errettung* 81.

in keeping with the Israelite character : curses found in individual
laments show sufficiently the vehemence of its feelings.

But such a position is untenable in view of the results of ethno-
logical research. This fact was noticed by W. Baumgartner as early
as 1933 when he wrote : " Es fehlt nicht bloss die genaue Unterschei-
dung des Todes von seinem Bruder, dem Schlaf; auch Scheintod, Ohn-
macht ... gelten schlechthin als Tod. Ebenso Krankheit .... Das wirkt
sich bis in die Sprache des alttestamentlichen und babylonischen Spra-
chen hinein, wenn sie das Verfallen in schwere Krankheit als ein Ster-
ben, ein Betreten der Unterwelt schildern ; es ist dies mehr als nur
die Uebertreibung orientalischer Leidenschaftlichkeit ; wirklicher Volks-
glaube steht dahinter " ([31]).

For Egypt the fact is attested by Zandee, who writes : " Whoever
is in miserable circumstances on earth, is dead, even though he still
lives. Piankhi calls the inhabitants of a town which he is besieging :
You who live in death " ([32]).

Traces of the same conception are also found in Ugarit : in *UT*
68 : 1 we read : " My hand is broken. I am dead " ([33]).

So Barth is fundamentally right. It must be recognized that
his very careful formulations are an impressive effort to do justice
to biblical evidence ; his balanced exposition is admirable. Indeed,
these texts are best understood as expressing a real but partial experience of death ; the person in need stands half-way between life
and death. This also appears from text as Ps 18,5 f. :

> The breakers of Death encompassed me ;
> the torrents of Belial overwhelmed me.
> The cords of Sheol surrounded me,
> the traps of Death confronted me. (Dahood)

Schmidt commented : " ... mythische Worte für die dunklen Wasser,

---

([30]) " Der Tod wird oft in ein und demselben Klagelied als Gefahr und
als vollendeter Tatsache bezeichnet (vgl. Ps 88,4 und 7 f. ; 69,15 f. und 2 f. ;
143,7b und 3 !). Die beiden Darstellungsformen können sich also nicht auf
verschiedene Situationen beziehen ; sie reden auf verschiedene Weise von *einer*
Bedrängnis " (*ibid.* 145 ; italics are Barth's).

([31]) *Zeitschrift für Missionskunde und Religions-Wissenschaft* 48 (1933) 194,
sub 2 (= *Zum AT und seiner Umwelt*, [Leiden 1959] 125 ; reference in Maag,
" Tod u. Jens. " 35 f. n. 33).

([32]) P. 14, n. 3.

([33]) The text is not quite certain ; also *UT* 68 : 32 ; 67 : I : 5.

durch die man hindurch muss, wenn man in das Totenreich hernieder-steigt " ([34]).

Most likely the allusion is to Styx, and the cords are thought of as dragging their victim into Sheol. This applies also to Ps 69,3; 116,3; and 55,5. So the psalmist feels himself in the clutches of Death already, in a situation dominated by the Arch-enemy; but he is not irretrievably lost ([35]).

For the present writer it remains questionable, however, whether Barth fully appreciates the reserve, the restrictions of many formula-tions. According to Barth, a real but ' partial ' stay in Sheol is ex-pressed; but as it is not obvious what a partial stay there involves, we would prefer to introduce a distinction; the psalmist is in the domain of Death, but no means in the domain of the dead.

The latter excludes the possibility of a return, from the former, man can be saved by Yahweh's mighty hand. Consequently we should prefer to speak of " the presence of the powerful Foe ", of a " situation controlled by Death ", of " the supreme sway of the Evil One ". With Johnson: " To fall ill is experience the disintegrating power of death " ([36]). For, as remarked before, many descriptions of Sheol should be taken qualitatively (i.e. as symbols of a fatal situa-tion) rather than locally.

B. d) As we have seen, Barth rejects the traditional localization of Sheol.

It therefore comes as a surprise, that, analysing the way deliver-ance from death is described, the same author stresses the spatial con-notation of the verbs in question. " In Todesnot geraten heisst für die Menschen des Alten Orients: in die Tiefe stürzen " ([37]). He con-sequently proclaims that life and death are thought of as opposite areas, " gegensätzte Räume ". Of course there two points of view are connected. If every kind of misery implies the presence of Sheol, or rather, a stay in Sheol, then this condition can be described with spatial terms, borrowed from the nether world.

We agree with Barth when he stresses that any kind of diminished life was experienced as a real presence of death. But when he rejects the question which is the original: the grave or Sheol, he comes into

([34]) H. Schmidt, *Psalmen* 28.

([35]) " Wenn der alttestamentliche Mensch sagt, Jahwä habe ihn in die ' sch^eol gelegt ' ..., so .. redet (er) von einer realen Zuständlichkeit ", Maag, " Tod u. Jens. " 25.

([36]) Johnson, " Jonah " 100. See also Maag, " Tod u. Jens. " 23-25; Martin-Achard, *From Death...* 43.

([37]) *Errettung* 124, see pp. 124-132.

conflict with common logic.   It seems evident that terms like " grave "
and " ocean " were in the first place employed to denote these perceptible realities and only subsequently the intangible reality of the
nether world.   Man does not dispose of any other language than
symbolism to describe the discoveries of his intuition.   When the
terms under discussion denote Sheol, Barth says, the qualitative aspect
(i.e., the idea of distance) prevails [38] : this is in fact another proof
of the secondary character of the terminology.   He practically affirms
this view where he writes : " Dass die gleichlautenden Namen und
Bezeichnungen des Totenreiches aus der Anschauung des Grabes stam-
men, kann nicht in Ernst bezweifelt werden " [39].   The present writer
would propose to explain the phenomenon in this way :

— Deadly peril is esperienced as real death, diminished life as life
  finished, partial death as total death ;
— Atqui, death implies a stay in Sheol, a well-determined region ;
— Ergo, a situation of partial death may be described as a local stay
  in the nether world, in other words : a condition of misery may
  be depicted in local terms.

This squares perfectly with our statement about the location of Sheol ;
in the case of illness and misery being pictured in terms properly denoting a netherworld situation, we are dealing with a secondary and
figurative use of the terms involved.

    This is practically acknowledged by Barth himself, who uses the
phrase : " Der Not des einzelnen ist nicht nur ein Zustand, sondern
zugleich ein Aufenthalt in der Sphäre der Bedrängnis .... Im übrigen
ist wohl an ein Herausführen aus der Situation und Sphäre der Bedrängnis gedacht " [40].

    As a matter of fact the evidence collected by C. Barth shows that
the spatial connotation in verbs expressing deliverance has greatly
faded :

— in about 50% of the occurrences these verbs are used absolutely,
  i.e. without explicit reference to the *locus a quo* [41].
— Moreover Barth himself confesses that the local connotation of
  several verbs (*yš‘*, *mlṭ*, *plṭ*, *rwm*, *śgb*, etc.) is virtually extinct.

A striking example of the secondary, technical character of this use

[38] *Ibid.* 84.
[39] *Ibid.* 83.   See our remarks below, pp. 180 f.
[40] *Errettung* 126.
[41] *Ibid.* 141.

is found in *šûb*, denoting deliverance from death : Sheol being the place of no return, compare Jb 33,30 ([42]).

The use of the nether-world terminology, though implying a real experience of death and consequently being more than mere poetical ornamentation, must, as far as the peculiar use in IL and ITh¹ is concerned, be considered as secondary and technical. This accounts for the peculiar use of terms connoting spatiality ; in our categories this may be classed also as a " spherical " conception of Sheol ([43]). In the process of evolution this use constitutes an intermediary stage between the original employment of terms and a more ethically coloured one, found by N. Lohfink in Proverbs 1 - 9. He writes : " Hier wird der Gedanke des Zusammenhangs zwischen Torheit und Tod syste-matisch durchgeführt, dazu wird der drohende Tod nicht nur als ver-früher Tod gesehen, sondern stärker als früher auch als Sphäre des Todes, die auch den biologisch noch lebende Sünder schon um-schliesst " ([44]). NT categories of life and death suggest that the develop-ment, traced briefly here, continued on into the New Testament. It is questionable if this fact is always given sufficient attention.

B. *e*) A final remark about the relation between grave and Sheol. We think the theory about the partial identity between the two far preferable to the bilocation Maag proposes : Ez 32,17 ff. clearly shows that the individual grave is " merged into Sheol " (Pedersen), which is found in the depth ([45]).

Barth dismisses the question as to the priority of the grave or Sheol ; but this refusal to establish which representation is older is *a priori* and does not square with the evidence ([46]). Barth recognizes that the element of Depth passed from the grave into Sheol and that descriptions of Sheol apply to the grave in every detail ([47]). It is only logical then to conclude that these descriptions were transmitted

---

([42]) *Errettung* 131 f.

([43]) Cp. N. Lohfink, " Der Mensch vor dem Tod ", in *Das Siegeslied am Schilfmeer* (Frankfurt am Main 1964) 198-243, esp. 207.

([44]) *Ibid.* 204 ; it would seem that this view is related to the " mystic " conception of life, found by von Rad in some psalms with a cultic background (Ps 27,4.13 ; 63,3-6 ; 65,5 ; 36,8-10 etc.) (" ' Gerechtigkeit ' und ' Leben ' in den Psalmen " 428-436). The same conception prevails in the Fourth Gospel ; see 8,51 ; 5,24 f. ; 6,47-54 ; 11,25.

([45]) Maag, " Tod und Jens. " 20 ff. ; J. Pedersen, *Israel* 2/II, 462 ; cp. the remarks by Zimmerli, *Ezechiel* 783 f., who does not find Barth's theory in Ez 32,17 ff.

([46]) *Errettung* 84.

([47]) *Ibid.* 83 f.

from the tangible and well-known phenomenon of the " grave " to the unfathomable nether world. The " grave " must be the older conception. Therefore authors like Stade, Schwally, Procksch, Heiler, and others are quite right in assuming an evolution from the grave to Sheol ; though this evolution cannot be ascertained in the Bible itself (it must be older), certainly biblical speech is in favour of it ([48]).

Jan de Vries maintains the same development for German religions : originally the dead person is tied to the place where he died ; the unity of the family remains, there is no thought of a universal domain of the Dead. In the long run the tombs are combined to a subterranean kingdom of the dead, where the goddess Hell governs ([49]). Logically posterior is the experience of Death himself in any threatening situation, which conception justifies the expressions investigated in this chapter.

1.2 Scenery

Hebrew Sheol is a collection and reflection of deadly perils, dangerous regions, and dark situations on earth : the scenery consists of treacherous marshes, threatening seas, impetuous rivers, and engulfing deeps. We need not repeat all these phenomena, most of which were mentioned above. Three themes will be treated here : darkness, " the mountains at the rim ", the Styx.

1.2.1 Darkness

1.2.1.1 *ṣalmāwet*

" De origine veteres paene omnes in eo consentiunt, vocem compositam esse ex *ṣēl* et *māwet*.... Ita quoque Rabbini vetustissimi, licet

---

([48]) B. Stade, *Geschichte des Volkes Israel* I, 418 (sees a reflection of the older view in Jr 31,15 ; Is 65,4) ; Schwally, *Das Leben nach dem Tode* 54-63 ; Procksch, *Die Theologie des Alten Testaments* 499 : " Älter als die mythologische Vorstellung ist im AT die des Grabes. Beide ist natürgemäss miteinander verflochten und vermischt worden, will aber seinem Inhalt nach auseinandergehalten werden " ; he thinks that the idea of Sheol was adopted from the Phoenicians in the time of Solomon (498) ; Heiler, *Erscheinungsformen und Wesen der Religion* 520. Our reasoning applies also to descriptions of Sheol as a prison, a hospital, a walled town, etc. Cp. the semantic development of *bôr*. Gunkel's radical rejection of a relation between *bôr šaḥat* and the grave cannot be accepted (*Psalmen*⁴ 121 ; 54) ; his suggestion that the expression " to dig a pit for NN " stems from sympathetic magic is plausible.

([49]) In G. van der Leeuw, *De Godsdiensten der Wereld* II (Amsterdam 1941) 134 ; cp. for Egypt : S. G. F. Brandon, " Life after Death. IV. The After-Life in Ancient Egyptian Faith and Practice " (*ET* 76 [1964-1965] 217-220) 218B.

alia opinio, de qua revocatur ad rad. *ṣlm*, iis non ignota sit " ([50]).
Modern lexicographers, however, do not share Gesenius' enthusiasm ;
they are divided :

A. Some scholars derive the word from the root *ṣlm*, to be dark ([51]).
    The form *ṣlmwt* is then parsed as

    A.a   an intensive plural ;
    A.b   an abstract noun, vocalised *ṣalmût* ([52]).

B. Others stick to the traditional interpretation, which starts from
    the division *ṣl-mwt*.
    B.a   " Tenebrae mortis " (i.e., qualis in mortuorum sede, in orco
                [est...) ([53]).
    B.b   *-mwt* is a superlative ending ; *ṣlmwt* means : utter dark-
                [ness ([54]).

Critique :
    A. The root *ṣlm* with this meaning is unusual in biblical
           [Hebrew.
    B. Objections raised against this interpretation are these ([55]) :

        a) " Shadow " is always a favourable element in the
             Bible.
             Answer : This is an *a priori* argument : the very end-
             ing *-mwt* might serve to bring about the contrary
             meaning.
        b) *ṣlmwt* is only exceptionally applied to Sheol : Jb
             10,21 and 38,17 ([56]).
             Answer : This conception of Death's domain is too
             restricted ([57]).
        c) D. Winton Thomas : the word has no relation what-
             soever to the darkness in Sheol.
             Answer : this scholar quite surprisingly does not ex-
             plain the origin of *-mwt* as a superlative form. Natu-

---

([50]) W. Gesenius, *Thesaurus Lingua Hebraicae* III, 1 (2nd ed. ; Leipzig,
1842) 1169 A.
  ([51]) See *GB* 684 B.
  ([52]) So Dhorme, *Job* 24.
  ([53]) Gesenius, *loc. cit.*
  ([54]) D. Winton Thomas, " *Ṣalmāwet* in the Old Testament ", *JSS* 7 (1962)
191-200.
  ([55]) Cp. Driver–Gray, *Job* 18.
  ([56]) Add with Gesenius : Jb 28,3 ; 12,22.
  ([57]) See above, p. 47.

rally, *-mwt* stands for a superlative in an unfavourable sense and as such must be contrasted with '*ēl* as a superlative form ([58]).   In this way the origin of this use becomes clear : *-mwt* is the evil *par excellence*. Correctly Gesenius ([59]): " ... tenebrae mortis ... i.e. tenebrae densissimae.   Proprie de caligine orci et locorum subterranearum....   Dein de tenebris quibuscumque ".

Conclusion : the etymology put forward under B. cannot be excluded (cp. *šdmwt*).   In later development the word stands for a department in Sheol ([60]).

1.2.1.2   Darkness in general

Light is a symbol for life ; darkness a symbol for death ([61]), and as such is found in poetical texts.   " Das Licht ist die erste Schöpfung ; ohne Licht kein Leben und keine Ordnung.   Vor dem Licht war die Welt dunkel, leblos, wirr ; Finsternis und Chaos sind grauenvoll ; grauenvoll ist auch die Scheol, die kein Licht hat ; das Licht ist gut und heilsam " ([62]).   It will be sufficient to quote a few relevant texts ; parallelism is to be noted.

ṣlmwt :

Jb 10,21 f. :
> .. a land of darkness (*ḥšk*) and gloom (*ṣlmwt*),
> a land of utter darkness (*'pth-'pl*),
> of gloom (*ṣlmwt*) without order ([63])
> which shines like darkness. (Pope)

Jb 12,22 :
> (God) reveals from darkness mysteries,
> brings forth dense darkness to light ([64]).

([58]) D. Winton Thomas, in *VT* 3 (1953) 219 ff. and Dahood, *Psalms* 220.
([59]) See above, p. 141, n. 50.
([60]) Strack–Billerbeck IV/2, 1091.
([61]) Pedersen, *Israel* I/II 464 ; Barth, *Errettung* 67, 79, 80, 33 f. ; see Dahood, *Psalms* 90 f., 222 f.   In Accadian the name *bīt etē*, " house of darkness ", describes the nether world (Tallqvist, *Namen der Totenwelt* 37).
([62]) Gunkel, in Gn 1,2 (*Genesis* 105).
([63]) Note the chaotic element.
([64]) Pope, *Job* 86.   " It seems clear that the verse refers to God's control of darkness and the nether world.. " (Pope, 91).

Jb 28,3 puts the same fact on record as to the depths of the earth in a purely cosmic sense:

> Man puts an end to darkness,
> every recess he searches.
> Through dark and gloomy rock
> he sinks a shaft far from habitation. (Pope)

Jb 38,16 f. passes from the nether world in the cosmological sense to its anthropological dimension (Sheol is in the depth indeed):

> 16 Have you entered the springs of the sea,
> walked in the recesses of the deep?
> 17 Have Death's Gates been revealed to you,
> Have you seen the Dark Portals?
> 18 Have you seen the nether world's expanse? ([65]).

Ḥōšek

Jb 18,18 reads, in a clear opposition:

> Driven from light into darkness,
> chased out of the world.

Jb 17,13:

> If I await Sheol as my home,
> spread my couch in darkness....

Jb 15,22, with a reference to the " land of no return ";

> He despairs of return from darkness.

Jb 19,8 again contains an allusion to Sheol:

> He (God) has blocked my way so I cannot pass,
> He puts darkness upon my path.

Ps 107, with its significant triplet desert–prison–sea:

> Some sat in darkness and in deep shadow (*ṣlmwt*):
> being fast bound in fetters of iron (v. 10; RP).

Ps 35,6:

> Let their destiny be Darkness and Destruction ([66])

Ps 88,7 reads:

> Thou hast put me in the depths of the Pit,
> in the regions dark and deep.

Ps 88,13 reads:

> Are thy wonders known in the darkness,
> or thy saving help in the land of forgetfulness?

([65]) As in all quotations, according to Pope, *Job*; v. 18 differs from his translation (see above, p. 50).

([66]) Dahood, *Psalms* 208; above, p. 84.

Ps 143,3 runs :

> For the enemy has pursued me ;
> he has smitten my life into the nether world ;
> he has made me sit in darkness like those long dead.

Is 5,30 :

> If one look to the land,
> behold, darkness and distress ;
> and the light is darkened by its clouds ([67]).

Jr 2,31 :

> Have I been a wilderness to Israel,
> or a land of thick darkness ? ([68])

Again the parallelism is significant ; darkness is balanced by an impressive number of netherworld names, as may be seen in the texts quoted in this section.

Jr 23,12 was already quoted above ; it reads :

> And so their way shall be like Perdition to them ;
> they shall be thrust into Darkness and fall into it ([69]).

Lam 3,2 runs :

> He has driven me and brought me into darkness
> without any light (see v. 6).

Its meaning cannot be doubtful in a lament ; the afflicted man feels locked up in Sheol.

1 S 2,9, in the canticle of Hannah, we hear :

> The wicked shall be cut off in Darkness (RSV) ([70]).

1.2.2 Mountains

The two mountains bordering the nether world appear in Jb 17,2: " Surely the two nether-world mounds are with me ... " ([71]).

Another reference to this phenomenon was found by Dahood in the crucial text Ps 42,7 f. :

([67]) Cp. v. 29 ; the lion and the characteristic 'ên maṣṣîl. Darkness belongs to the *decor* of the Day of Yahweh : Am 5,18.20 ; Jl 10,21 ; Zep 1,15, etc. ; Mt 24,29 ; 27,45, etc.

([68]) See the lion in v. 30 ; cp. 2,6.

([69]) See above, pp. 83 f.

([70]) Verb *yiddāmû* ; see *yiddᵉmû lišᵉ'ôl* in Ps 31,18. It seems that these two texts can hardly be isolated from each other ; if the same verb, meaning " to hurl " occurs in Ex 15,16 also, we would have to assume an enclitic *mem* in three cases with the same verb. It then seems preferable to consider *-m* as belonging to the root (cp. Dahood, *Psalms* 190) ; see also Wisd 17.

([71]) Above, pp. 54 f.

*'ezkār*ᵉ*kā*
mē'eres yardēn wᵉhermônîm mēhar misᵉᶜār
tᵉhôm 'el tᵉhôm qôrē' lᵉqôl sinnôrêkā

Recently two scholars tried their hand at this text; Tournay accepted Kruse's suggestion to explain the first *min* as *min* comparationis and to delete the second as dittography ([72]). No attention was given to the surprising *'rs yrdn*, an unique combination; moreover *yrdn* always has an article but for Jb 40,23 where it has the generic sense " river " (see parallelism). As to the exceptional plural form of Hermon (only found here and in Sir 24,13), it is interpreted as intensive or extensive by Kruse, but this use with a geographical name is both unique and unlikely. Those who maintain the second *min*, or rather the form *msʾr*, are unable to offer a solution ([73]). One may venture to say that a fresh approach proved imperative; it was made by Dahood ([74]). We will give his exposition here.

— *'rs yrdn*: " the land of descent ". For *yrd* = " to go into Sheol " see above ([75]).

As to the ending *-n*, Joüon mentions final *-ān* for abstracta ([76]); in this case one would expect the vocalization *-ôn*, but for this we have an analogous case in *māgēn* (for *māgōn*) ([77]). The motive is quite normal in individual laments (Barth), and occurs in texts as Jon 2,3; Ps 88,5-7, etc.

— *tᵉhôm* confirms this interpretation: it belongs to the same *Wortfeld*. Moreover v. 8 contains a clear allusion to the Double Deep, as remarked by Patton ([78]). See I QH 3,17.

— *hermônîm*: this word is explained as a by-form of *hrm*, " net ", occurring in Ez 26,5.14; Hab 1,15; Qoh 7,26 ([79]).

([72]) H. Kruse, " Two Hidden Comparatives: Observations on Hebrew Style I. Psalm 42,7-8 ", *JSS* 5 (1960) 338-343; R. Tournay, in Bulletin, *RB* 71 (1964) 623 f.

([73]) So *BDB* 859 A.

([74]) *Psalms* 258 f.

([75]) Cf. above, pp. 32 f.

([76]) Joüon, 88 M b.

([77]) Dahood, *Psalms* 16; M. Kessler, " The Shield of Abraham? ", *VT* 14 (1964) 494-497.

([78]) Dahood, *Psalms*. 259, quoting J. H. Patton, *Canaanite Parallels in the Book of Psalms* 46.

([79]) See below, pp. 172 ff.

Other examples of this phenomenon: Hebr. *mḥsr* and Ugar. *mḥsrn*; Hebr. *bṣqln* and Ugar. *bṣql*; Ugar. *drb* and Hebr. *drbn* ([80]).

The motive is found in other texts as well. One might compare an Egyptian Coffin Text, where the sentence "You hurry along the valley of the net" indicates escape from death ([81]).

— *hrm ṣ'r* :   Dahood reads *hārē-m* (dual or plural with enclytic *mem* in a construct chain ([82]) -*ṣ'r* and refers to *UT* 51 : VIII : 4-8 (quoted above, ch 2, p. 6) for the latter, putting *hrm ṣ'r* on a par with *tlm ġṣr*. Because of further affinities between the two texts this is a tempting proposal, but as Ugar. *ġṣr* develops into Hebr. *'ṣr* the supposed metathesis remains hypothetical. An alternative solution, which also is uncertain, is the translation " *cruciatus* " proposed by Zorell for Sir 31,19 ([83]). The idea fits well into the picture, but the combination with " mountain " is less common.

The result thus obtained reads :

42,7   My soul is very sad
        because I remember you,
        From the land of descent and of nets ([84])
        from the mountains at the rim;
            (or: from the mountains of torment)
   8   Where deep calls to deep,
        at the peal of your thunderbolts;
        And all your breakers and your billows
        pass over me.

([80]) Dahood, *Psalms* 258.
([81]) Zandee, 231, B. 19.e.
([82]) See H. Hummel, " Enclitic *mem* in Early North-West Semitic ", *JBL* 76 (1957) 85-107.
([83]) Zor 698 A.; (neohebraice, aram. piel " cruciavit ").
([84]) " From " could very well be rendered by " in " in our languages; see see Ps 28,7b *miššîrî 'ăhôdennû*, " in my song will I praise Him " RP (RSV: with... cp. Ps 69,31 : *bᵉšîr*); also 2 S 18,10 (Vulgate), " vidi Absalom pendere de quercu " (Hebr. *bᵉ*), RSV " in an oak ". See N. H. Sarna, " The Interchange of the Prepositions *beth* and *min* in Biblical Hebrew " *JBL* 78 (1959) 310-315. Preposition *min* not rarely stands for our " in ": Dahood, *Psalms* 105 f.; van Dijk, *Ezekiel's Prophecy* 87.

The translation recommends itself by the perfect succession of ideas, v. 8a and 8b referring to well-known characteristics of the nether world ([85]).

1.2.3   The River

> God, reads Job 33,16 ff., opens men's ears,
>   terrifies them with warning
> 17 to deter man from evil,
>   to keep man from pride,
> 18 to spare his soul from the Pit,
>   his life *mēʿăbōr baššālaḥ.*

At this point let us examine if the Hebrew expression is equivalent to Dante's " trapassar lo rio " (*Inf.* III 124).

A.   According to M. Tsevat, *šlḥ* means " to pour out " in *UT* 51 : I : 26-27: *yṣq.ksp.yšlḥ.hrṣ* ..., " he pours out silver, he lets gold flow " ([86]). Most specialists, however, seem to reject this interpretation; Gordon's glossary translates *šlḥ* II " to cast, to beat out (a metal) " ([87]). About *yṣq* Gordon writes: " to pour out, Hebrew *yṣq* has the same nuances as in Ug.; e.g., to cast (metal) " ([88]). So quite unexpectedly *yṣq* saves Tsevat's interpretation of *šlḥ*; as the former, the latter also means: " to pour out " and " to cast (metal) ". We shall return to this connection.

For *šlḥ* meaning " to pour out ", Dhorme pointed to Ps 104,10: *hamᵉšallēaḥ maʿyānîm bannᵉḥālîm* ([89]). Evidently KJ translates very woodenly: " He sends the springs into the valleys ". And some thirty years after Dhorme's comment, RP presents exactly the same rendering. We should translate: " You let the springs flow into the valleys. "

The piel of *šlḥ* is also found in Jb 20,23: *yᵉšallaḥ bô ḥărôn ʾappô*. Of course the translation " He shall send on him his fierce anger " is a reasonable one. We would like to recall the expressions *špk ḥmh* (e.g., Ps 79,6) and *špk zʿm* (e.g., Ps 69,25) and *špk ḥrwn ʾpw* (Zeph 3,8; Lam 4,11). This suggests that *šlḥ* in these cases also stands for " to pour out ":

> He shall pour out on him his fierce anger (Jb 20,23).
> He poured out upon them the furiousness of his

([85]) For 8b see above, p. 65.
([86]) " The Canaanite God *šalaḥ* ", *VT* 4 (1954) 41-49.
([87]) *UT* Gloss. 2420; cp. Dahood, *Psalms* 100, 309.
([88]) *UT* Gloss. 1141.
([89]) Dhorme, *Job* 452 f.

wrath, anger, displeasure, and trouble
(ḥrwn 'pw 'brh wz'm wṣrh) (Ps 78,49).

You pour out your fury (Ex 15,7 : ḥrwn) (⁹⁰).

Indeed the distance between " to send, to set free " and " to let flow, to pour out " is insignificant, and because of this semantic affinity it is not justifiable to assume two roots šlḥ.   For this, see Job 12,15 :

If he withholds ('ṣr) the waters, there is drought,
if he lets them go (šlḥ), they engulf the land.

And Ez 31,4 : the waters nourished it ...
                  making its rivers run (hôlîk) ...
                  letting its streams flow (šlḥ) ... (⁹¹).

There is an immediate connection between " pouring out " and the casting of metals.   In some languages the former word is used to describe both processes : Dutch " gieten " (bells, statues ...), German " giessen ".   This depends on techniques, which have remained essentially the same since their invention.   The verb " to cast " is defined by Webster : " II.10... to give a particular form to (liquid metal or other material) by pouring it into a mold and letting it harden " (⁹²).   In view of these logical transitions of meaning we are justified in concluding that there is one root

šlḥ, meaning :   — to send, etc.
                          — to pour out
                          — to cast (metals) (⁹³).

    B. Quite likely the substantive šlḥ in Ugaritic has a meaning, connected with the verb in the sense " to flow ".
    In an enumeration of evils in Krt 16-21 we find as agents : kṯr, zbln, ršp, ǵlm ym, and šlḥ as culmination-point.   As at least kṯr, ršp,

---

(⁹⁰) With most substantives for " anger " špk is more frequent. Cp. Milton, *PL* I : 219 f. : .. " but on himself / treble confusion, wrath and vengeance poured ". See the corresponding expression in Jb 21,20 : " Let him *drink* of the wrath of Shaddai ".

(⁹¹) This also offers a natural solution for Neh 4,17 : " We did not put off our clothes ; everybody let his water go (šillᵉḥû ; mayîm [sc. *raglâw*] " : BDB 565B *sub* 3).

(⁹²) *Webster's New International Dictionary of the English Language* (Springfield, Mass. 1953) 417 C.

(⁹³) See now also the remark of Dietrich–Loretz, *BiOr* 32 (1966) 132 B.

and *ym* are names of gods, Leibel proposes to translate *šlḥ* as "river (of the dead)" and in view of the preceding *ym* and this expression being the culmen of a climactic "numeral ladder" this proposal must be judged at least probable. Leibel leans on Tsevat, who backs up Dhorme's interpretation of *šlḥ* in Jb 33,18: "canal, conduit, torrent" which was established with a reference to Assyrian *šiliḫtu* [94]. Tsevat collected the evidence about the nether world god *šlḥ*; he cites the name Methu-šalaḥ (Gn 5,21) which in a parallel (and also archaic) tradition occurs as *Metûšā'ēl* in Gn 4,18. Mutu- in theophoric names must be very ancient: *GB* refers to Amarna *mtb'l* [95], a name also found in Ugaritic [96].

Moreover it seems that the relative *ša* does not belong to the pattern of Accadian theophoric names; J. Lewy proposes to read *metû-š'ol*. If all this is correct, *šlḥ* is equivalent to *š'l*. Supposing the latter name to be Accadian, the present writer wants to point to the fact that the word Sheol is extremely rare in that language (see above, p. 21). From that point of view Lewy's suggestion is not beyond doubt [97].

Further, Tsevat quotes the Phoenician name *'šršlḥ*, which he explains as a syncretistic combination of Osiris and *šlḥ* But according to Harris [98] the name itself is uncertain; moreover its composition is rather uncommon. More convincing is the name *'b-šlḥ*. In Middle Hebrew Tsevat finds (*śdh*) *byt hb'l* (irrigated by rain) and (*śdh*) *byt hšlḥyn* (artificially irrigated). The quality of *b'l* suggests that the contrasting *šlḥyn* also derives from a mythical name; according to Tsevat, it was originally a plural of *šlḥ* [99]. But why this plural next to the singular *b'l*?

The same author studies Dt 21,1-9: the procedure to be observed when a corpse has been found and the murderer cannot be traced. He thinks that this ceremony harks to an old custom, a sacrifice to the god of the nether-world river who is visibly present on earth in the perennial river (which is required, v. 2). The Accadian code of law knew the river ordeal, in which the river orcus was to pass judg-

---

[94] D. Leibel, "*'br bšlḥ*", *Tarbiz* 38 (1964) 225-227; M. Tsevat, "The Canaanite God Šälaḥ", *VT* 4 (1954) 41-49. *ši-li-iḫ-ti ša nar bāni-ti*: the mouth (branch) of the Baniti canal.

[95] *GB* 474 B.

[96] *UT* Gloss. 1569.

[97] Pope, who adopts Tsevat's theory, significantly omits the identification of the two names (*Job* 218).

[98] *Grammar* 83; Donner–Röllig offers no name with *'šr*: text 47: 2 (see *KAI* II 64) shows the Phoenician names *'sršmr* and *'bd'sr*.

[99] The plural *-yn* is found in ancient spelling: Cross–Freedman, *EHOrth* 25.

ment where human judges failed. The Canaanite name for *Yam*, " Judge River ", justifies the assumption of a similar use in that country. In this way the necessity of a perennial river (which may be far distant from the place of the murder), the condition that land and beast are untouched are well explained ([100]).

C. The preceding section prepared the return to Jb 33,18. The meaning " canal " is undisputed for Neh 3,15 and there is no doubt as to the verb *šlḥ* meaning " to pour out ", which fact is corroborated by both *šelaḥ* and *šiloaḥ*. Moreover " la trista riviera d'Acheronte " (*Inf.* III : 78) is a constant element in nether-world mythology ([101]), reflected also in biblical use : " the torrents of Belial " in 2 S 22,5, etc.

So Pope's translation is fully justified :
> ... to spare his soul from the Pit,
> his life from crossing the Channel ([102]).

The same idea returns in Jb 36,12 :
> If they obey not, they cross the Channel
> And they die for lack of knowledge ([103]).

([100]) For these reasons and because of the way of slaughtering, von Rad thinks the rite is no sacrifice, but he seems to argue from the standpoint of the Israelite priests, whose presence is of later date as he himself acknowledges, *Das fünfte Buch Mose, Deuteronomium* (ATD 8 ; Göttingen 1964) 97 f. The ceremony is understood as a sacrifice to the god by Bahya ben Asher (14th century) ; Mišna forbids sacrifices at the border of rivers because it could seem a sacrifice to *śr' dym'*. For the Accadian " river of Judgement " cf. Tallqvist, *Namen der Totenwelt* 24.

([101]) For Egypt see Zandee, 167, B. 7. h. For Accadian *ḫubur* see Tallqvist, *Namen der Totenwelt* 33. The Scandinavian nether world, Niflheim, is situated under the earth, beyond the river Gjöll. The bridge spanning it is suspended from a hair and guarded by the monster Mödgud (Guerber, 178).

([102]) Pope, *Job* 215 ; Fohrer, *Das Buch Hiob* 454 ; " in den Spies zu rennen " ; unfortunately because of this translation (which is peculiar to that case) he is obliged to delete it in 36,12.

([103]) " L'expression *bibᵉli daᶜat*, par manque de science, donne la raison de la mort " (Dhorme, *Job* 495). The verb *gwᶜ* normally means " to breathe one's last " (21,14) ; *dᶜt* (see 35,16) has a religious connotation as in 21,14 (*GB* 395 B) ; the structure of the bicolon is A-B-B'-A' (B-B' referring to the fact and A-A' to its cause). A similar idea may be found in Is 5,13 : " My people go into exile for want of knowledge " (*mibbᵉli dāᶜat*) ; there is no doubt, however, that the context (see v. 14) refers to Sheol. For its lack of convincing arguments we hesitate to accept the beautiful translation " They die in the Land of Unknowing ". Fohrer follows Budde : " Sie wissen nicht, wie " (an allusion to the suddenness of death ; *Das Buch Hiob* 131, on 4,21).

In CC 4,13 *šlḥ* is problematic; the figurative speech of this text hinders its correct interpretation. Robert–Tournay and Gerleman translate " rejeton ", and " Schösslinge, Triebe " respectively ([104]). KB 976B (with Haupt and Staerk) derives his interpretation " womb " from *šlḥ*.

Dhorme, who judges the preceding conception too realistic, proposes " canal ", i.e. of the garden ([105]); this squares well with the Fountain in the immediate context, which returns in v. 15. Moreover we know now that the meaning is not uncommon for *šlḥ*, while its meaning " sprout, shoot " would be unique. Dhorme's interpretation is thus preferable.

---

[104] A. Robert – R. Tournay, *Le Cantique des Cantiques* (Paris 1963) 181, 443 ; G. Gerleman, *Ruth und das Hohe Lied* (BK 18 ; Neukirchen 1965) 159 f.
[105] *JPOS* 3 (1923) 45-48, quoted by Tournay, *Le Cantique*.

CHAPTER 2: STRUCTURAL ELEMENTS

2.1 City

The conception of the nether world as a " città dolente " (*Inf.* III: 1) was not unknown in the Canaanite milieu. This appears from *UT* 51: VIII: 8-14:

> Be counted among those who went down into the nether world.
> Then, indeed, set face
> (Toward El's son Mot),
> Midst his city ' Slushy '.
> Ruin is the throne where he sits,
> Infernal filth his inheritance ([1]).

It seems only natural to assume that this view left its traces in the OT. Some maintain: " Die Vorstellung vom Totenreich als eine Stadt ist in der Bibel nicht bekannt " ([2]). We think it correct that Sheol is never explicitly called a city in the OT, though *'yr mtym* in Jb 24,12 may tempt one to believe the contrary. With Pope, however, we think *mtym* parallel with *ḫllym* and subject of *yn'qw*:

> From the city the dying groan,
> The throats of the wounded cry.

The conception of the nether-world city is found with certainty where " the gates of Sheol " appear ([3]). Although one might argue that this might as well refer to Sheol as a prison, it is to be noted that the OT never speaks of the *š'r* of a gaol. In Ps 9,14 f., moreover, the contrast is suggestive:

> Raise me up from the gates of Death

([1]) Pope, *Job* 72. Compare Accadian *Urugal*, " great city ", and *uru ul-la*, " eternal city " (Tallqvist, *Namen der Totenwelt* 7; 16).

([2]) H. Haag – A. van den Born, *Bibellexikon* 1635 A.

([3]) Series of gates are found in Mesopotamia (*ANET* 106-108) and in Egypt (Zandee, 114 ff.).

> That I may recount all your praises
> from the gates of daughter Sion.... (Dahood)

Man knows that there is no hope for one who enters these gates : " Lasciate ogni speranza, voi ch'entrate " (*Inf.* III, 6).   The same emotion overwhelmed the Israelite :

> ... they drew near to the gates of Death.
> Then they cried to Yahweh in their trouble (Ps 107,18).

Jb 38,17 :

> Have Death's gates been revealed to you,
> have you seen the Gates of the deathly dark Resort ?

Is 38,10 reads :

> I am consigned to the gates of Sheol.

Here the " gates " stand as *a pars pro toto* for " city " (⁴).

Wisd 16,13 runs :

> For thou hast power of life and death :
> thou leadest to the gates of hell, and bringest up again. (KJ)

See also Sir 51,9 (⁵).

(⁴) See *BDB* 1045 B *sub* b.

(⁵) Above p. 43. Also Mt 16,18 ; Rev 1,18. For comparative material Gaster, *Thespis* 199 n. Albright finds the epithet " city " for the nether world in the name Milk-qart, God of Tyre and equivalent to Hercules (*ARI* 81 ; *FSAC* 307) ; this is adopted by Maag, in Schmökel, *Kulturgesch.* 583 and " Tod u. Jens. " 19 f. [identification with the Jerusalem Schalim-Mäläk, Milkom and Kemosch, all of them manifestations of the astral 'Aschtar, uniting the symbolisms of welfare and victory with that of dominion of death and nether world, his cult being celebrated in the Ben-Hinnom Valley where children were sacrificed to him. This would explain " dass die Totenwelt solange sie vom Jahwäglauben nicht in den Heilshorizont von Jahwäs Walten eingegliedert werden konnte, dem alttestamentlichen Mensch ein aussergöttlicher Bereich war " (*ibid.* 20) ; this theory is rather speculative]. Pope thinks that Mlkqrt is El, living under the earth (*El* 27 ; see Pope in Haussig, *Wörterbuch der Mythologie* 297 f.).   The theory is rejected by Johnson, *Sacr. Kingship* 37, n. 3 ; Donner–Röllig, *KAI* II, 53 write : " nichts sicheres zu sagen ", which is a realistic statement, with a touch of minimalism ; see also Du Mesnil du Buisson, in an article on the Pantheon of Tyre : *RHR* 164 (1963) 154 ; and R. Tournay, " Le Psaume LXXII,16 et le réveil de Melqart ", in *École des Langues Orientales de l'Institut Catholique de Paris : Mémorial du Cinquantenaire* 1914-1964 (Paris 1964) 97-104.

According to Jon 2,7, these gates are provided with bars:

> I went down to the nether world whose bars
> closed upon me for ever.

" Chiuser le porte que' nostri avversari... " (*Inf.* VIII,115).

Curiously enough in *UT* 1001: rev. 8 the phrase *brḥ 'rṣ* occurs. Unfortunately the obscure context does not enable us to establish its precise meaning: it is either " bars of the nether world ", or " bars of the city " as in Phoenician usage ([6]).

In an Egyptian Book of the Dead the deceased asks the gatekeepers of the nether world to be let through: " Open your roads, open your bolts to me " ([7]). Where in the OT " bar(s) " is used in the sense of " bolt, lock " it is applied to cities and castles, unless it is employed in a metaphorical sense. According to *BDB* ([8]) in older usage " bar " occurs in the singular, as " the great bar across the gate ":

> All these were fortified cities with ([9]) high
> walls, gates, and bars... (Dt 3,5).

> A brother helped is like a strong city,
> but quarrelling is like the bar of a castle (Prv 18,19).

Later, the plural is used:

> He strengthens the bars of your gates (Ps 147,13; cp. Neh 3,
>   [*passim*).

2.2 Prison

" A dungeon horrible " — Milton, *Paradise Lost* I: 61.

Life, as the Israelite understands it, implies freedom of movement and is symbolized by light. The nether world, therefore, is a prison, where " darkness visible " reigns, where one's feet find no hold (cp. Jr 38,6).

Allusions to the nether world as a prison are extremely frequent in Egyptian literature. Zandee writes: " When death sets in the body stiffens. Man cannot move any more and go where he wants. This is the cause of considering death as a being fettered or an imprison-

([6]) Dahood, " HULex ", *Bib* 44 (1963) 297.
([7]) Zandee, 131, B.2.a.
([8]) *BDB* 138A, *sub* 2.
([9]) For " with " see above, p. 40, Ps 143,3.

ment " ([10]). In this light several allusions to Sheol in the OT can
be understood and recognized. It is not surprising to find most of
them in laments.

Lam 3,6 f. reads :

> He has made me dwell in darkness
> with the dead of long ago.
> 7 He has walled me about (*gdr*) so that I cannot escape ;
> he has put heavy chains upon me ;
> 9 he has blocked (*gdr*) my ways with hewn stones ....

The formula of v. 7a returns in Ps 88,9 :

> I am shut in so that I cannot escape.

Its verb *kl'* is found in the same sense in Jr 32,2 and in the substantive *kele'*, prison. The relatively rare verb *gdr* (seven times in the
OT) returns in Jb 19,8 which belongs to the same *Vorstellungenwelt* :

> He has blocked my way so that I cannot pass ;
> He puts darkness upon my path.

The reference to the prison is explicit in Ps 107 :

> 10 Some sat in darkness and in deep shadow ;
> being fast bound in fetters of iron.
> 16 He hath broken the gates of bronze,
> and smitten the bars of iron asunder. (RP)

As noted by Kroll, in v. 16 a nether-world motive appears ([11]): the
" broken doors " belong to the process of the *Descensuskampf*. Combined with the allusions in v. 10, this makes it very likely that the
theme of this section was chosen because of its affinities with Sheol.
We do not agree with Kroll, however, in his tendency to dismiss these
references as " Pathosformeln " without objective background.

We find another hint to Sheol as a gaol in the verb *sgr* in Ps 31,9 :

> You did not incarcerate me (*sgr*) in the hand of the Foe.

([10]) Zandee, 78 ; cp. A.7 ; cp. B.2, 125 ff. In Accadian, *bīt me-šur* means
" prison " (as in 1 P 3,19 ; Rev 2,10 (?) ; 20,7) ; Manungal, the goddess of the
nether world, is named *ša ṣibitte*, " goddess of imprisonment " and *ṣabbutitu*,
" she who seizes " ; snatching, detaining, and warding are characteristic activities of gods of the nether world (Tallqvist, *Namen der Totenwelt* 37 f.).

([11]) J. Kroll, *Gott u. Hölle* 343 f.

Another occurrence of *sgr* may be brought to light in Jb 12,14:

> If he (God) imprison, there is no release. (Pope)

This colon contains a reference to the theme found in Lam 3,7 and Ps 88,9a. Parallelism suggests the same interpretation for Ps 69,34 (IL):

> Yahweh hears the needy,
> and he does not despise his own that are in bonds.

Because of the allusion to the stereotyped statement that there is no praise of God in Sheol, Ps 142,8 also must contain a reference to the nether world:

> Bring me out of prison,
> that I may give thanks to thy name.

Anybody in whatever kind of need can say this prayer; see the title of the psalm: "A Maskil of David, when he was in the cave" ([12]).

2.3 Rooms; beds

Sheol is a house with a forbidding interior; it is a prison, a hospita of a lugubrious kind. There are rooms in this dwelling-place:

> The ways to Sheol lead to her (the harlot's) house,
> going down to the chambers of Death (Prv 7,27) ([13]).

Compare the *ḥdry š'wl*, the Rooms of Sheol in I QH 10,34. This conception is another consequence of the relation between the grave and the nether world, as found in Is 14,18 and Ez 32,25. Indeed Maag writes about the graves in the Ghassul-period: "Das Grab war eine kleine, sorgfältig mit Steinen ausgelegte Kammer" ([14]). This is also reflected in texts, where *ḥdr* is applied to the grave. So this inscription *ḥdr bt 'lm qbr* ([15]); a new-Punic inscription from Cherchel: .. "das

---

([12]) See also Jb 40,13 (studied above on p. 46): Wisd 17,2.15. See Jb 36,8. Note the parallelism in Ps 79,11; 102,21.

([13]) Interpreting *bêtâ* as an accusativus directionis.

([14]) In Schmökel, *Kulturgesch.* 455.

([15]) *CIS* I: 124 (Lidzbarski, *Handbuch* I, 139 [Weimar 1898–Hildesheim 1962]. According to Donner–Röllig (*KAI* II, 94) in Phoenician and Punic *ḥdr* means "Gruft"; and as to t. 83 *rbt b'lt hḥdrt* they remark that *ḥdr* there is a designation of the nether world (*ibid*). Hebrew *ḥdr* stands for a "dark room" (*KB* 278B): in Prv 18,8 it designs "the innermost parts" (of the belly).

(Grab)gemach mit seiner Urne " ([16]) and the ἀέναος θάλαμος in a Greek inscription ([17]).

And in this house there are beds; here also the evidence suggests that this view derives from burial customs:

> They buried him in a tomb.... They laid him
> on a bier (*mškb*) which had been filled with
> various kinds of spices (2 C 16,14; RSV).

This idea is transferred to the nether world in Ez 32,25:

> They have made her (Elam) a bed (*mškb*)
> among the slain, with ([18]) all their
> multitudes, their graves round about her.

From the preceding verse it appears that Elam is in the nether world. The same connection with the grave is obvious in Is 14,11:

> Your eminence is brought down to Sheol,
> the sound of your harps;
> a bed of maggots is spread beneath you,
> and worms are your covering.

Compare Jb 21,26:

> Together they lie on the dust,
> and worms crawl over them.

As in Jb 14,13, etc., Sheol serves as the traditional hiding place in Ps 139,8b:

> If I make Sheol my bed, you are there also.

House and bed are explicitly put together in Jb 17,13:

> If I await Sheol as my house,
> spread my couch in Darkness...

ḥpšy

Ps 88,6a, *bᵉmētîm ḥopšî* may be discussed here. The expression reminds one of *bt ḥpṯt*, a Ugaritic name for the nether world:

([16]) *KAI* I, 161:3; cp. III, 150 f.
([17]) *CIA* III, 1336 (Quoted by Lidzbarski).
([18]) According to van Dijk the *bᵉ* is merely emphatic (*Ezekiel's Prophecy* 83).

UT 51 : VIII :   7   *wrd.bthptt*
                    8   *arṣ.tspr.by*
                    9   *rdm arṣ.*

Moreover Ps 88,5a : *neḥšabtî ʿim-yôrᵉdê bôr* is equivalent to *tspr byrdm arṣ* (" be counted among those who go down to the nether world ") in the Ugaritic text.

Unfortunately the interpretation of *UT* 51 : VIII : 7 ff. is uncertain ; the text only serves to make the discussion more laborious.

The disagreement of Ugaritic scholars begins with the analysis of *bthptt*.

1. a) Gaster divides *bthptt* into the preposition *bᵉ* and the noun *thptt*, meaning ' filth, corruption ', which may be compared with *ḥḥ arṣ*, the filth of the nether world ([19]).   Grelot also quotes Arabic *ḫabaṯa*, which has the same meaning ([20]).

b) Van Selms accepts the same division, which he defends with a reference to the great accuracy *UT* 51 shows in the use of punctuation marks : it should be noticed that there is no word divider between *bt* and *ḥptt* ([21]).   He explains *thptt* as a feminine substantive with prefixed *t-* from the root *ḥpt*, " to be free " : *thptt* is " tax-free land ".   As the grave is a piece of land, proper to the dead and received from the earth-gods, it can obtain that name as well ([22]).   The latter argument is rather speculative ; and as to the division of the compound, we think that the evidence is overstrained here.   Anyway Herdner in the *Corpus* gives *bt ḥptt* in the text, mentioning the other interpretation as a possibility in a footnote.

2. Most scholars read *bt ḥptt*.

a) Albright, discussing the word *ḫbt*, points to Arabic *ḫbt*, " to be base, vile ", which became Canaanite *ḥpt*.   Pope supposes this interpretation, which is practically identical with Gaster's given above, in translating the expression under discussion as " infirmary " ([23]) or " charnel house " ([24]).

([19]) " The Canaanite Poem of Keret " (Review), *JQR* 37 [1946-1947] 285-293) 292.

([20]) J. Grelot, " *ḫofši* (Ps. LXXXVIII 6) " (*VT* 14 [1964] 256-63) 261 ; Pope, " The Word *šaḥat* in Job 9,31 " (*JBL* 83 [1964] 269-278) 277.

([21]) Cp. Herdner, *Corpus* 30.

([22]) *Marriage* 131 f.

([23]) *El* 65 ; cp. 2 K 15,5.

([24]) In Haussig : *Wörterbuch der Mythologie* 300 f. ; Pope *Job* 73 ; in *ARI* 198, n. 5, Albright reads : " Guesthouse (?) of the nether world ".

b) Driver points to Arabic *ḫpṯ* II, " to be unproductive " (²⁵);
Grelot adds *ḫabaṯa* (above *sub* la).

c) Grelot also suggests another possibility : a root *ḥbš*, inUgaritic
and other languages meaning " to bind, to imprison " (²⁶). In this
case, however, there would be no connection with Ugaritic *btḫpṯṯ*.

d) Gray proposes a *ḫpṯ*, " to separate ". It is used for mercen-
aries set free for military service ; the meaning " peasant landholder "
for *ḥpš* in Hebrew may be a development of the former. Often in
history meritorious soldiers were rewarded with pieces of land ; see
1 S 17,25 (²⁷).

3. *GB* 251A connects the word in Ps 88,6 with *ḥōpeš*, occurring
in Ez 27,20 and translated " Reitdecken ", which translation is substantially adopted by Zimmerli (²⁸). In this light, the term in Ps
88 would mean " cover ", *ergo* " couch ".

Taking *ḥpšy* as presented under 3, we translate the verse under
discussion as follows :

    A   Among the dead
    B   is my couch ;
    C   among the slain,
    B′   buried (²⁹)
    A′   in the grave.

This translation recommends itself by its clear sense and perfect structure. The term " slain ", denoting a particularly shameful end (³⁰),
vigorously expresses the miserable condition of the psalmist. In C
the preposition *kᵉmô* has the force of " in, among " ; its use in this
sense, after *bᵉ* in A, is normal (³¹).

(²⁵) Driver, *CMAL* 140A, n. 8.
(²⁶) Grelot, in *VT* 14 (1964) 258-263.
(²⁷) *Legacy* 100, n. 6 ; see 169 f., n. 7 ; *KB* 323A.
(²⁸) *Ezechiel* 631 ; reference to Accadian *ḫipšu*, " Stoff ". See also Zor
260 B.
(²⁹) For *škb*, " to lie down in death ", see *BDB* 1012, *sub* 4 b + c. Jb
3,13 : " For now I would be lying quiet ; I would be asleep and at rest ... " ;
Jb 7,21 : " ... that I might now lie in the dust " (cp. 21,16) ; Jb 14,12 : " And
man lies down and never rises ; they wake not till heavens decay ; they rouse
not from their sleep " (Pope). For *mškb* see above, p. 157.
(³⁰) See below, p. 101.
(³¹) See van Dijk, *Ezechiel's Prophecy* 43 ff. Dahood writes me that he
will propose a slightly different analysis in *Psalms II*. See now his article " A
New Metrical Pattern in Biblical Poetry " (*CBQ* 29 [1967] 574-79] 577 f. :
" In Death is my cot / like the slaughtered / My couch is in the Grave ". See
also " HULex ", *Bib* 48 (1967) 434.

T. H. Gaster writes that in studying Old Testament demonology, the following fundamental consideration should be kept in mind: demons, in the sense of malign spiritual beings, " often survive as figures of speech long after they have ceased to be figures of belief. Accordingly, the mention of a demon's name in a scriptural text is no automatic testimony to living belief in him ". And he adds that, as demons often have the names of illnesses, a distinction between the two is often difficult to make ([1]). It must be recognized that this is a careful statement, but we think that there is sufficient evidence to go beyond this stage.

3.1 Death

In view of the evidence collected in part I of this study ([2]) we are justified in concluding that in the OT the personification is more than a petrified form of speech. We agree with Barth where he says that death is not a mere poetical hypostasis of the mortal's end, but that the mythical way it is described shows it to be a personal power. He writes: " Ihnen (sc., den Psalmisten) erscheint ' der Tod ' als eine von Gott geschiedene, seiner Regierung entgegengestetzte und darum in absolutem Sinn feindliche Macht, die an Furchtbarkeit alle menschlichen Widersacher übertrifft " ([3]). To show the personal character of Death, he refers to biblical descriptions, which are strongly reminiscent of ancient Near Eastern mythology: the expressions portraying misfortune in terms of Sheol, the formulas picturing Death's reign, his power, and the deliverance from him as a military process ([4]), and his subjection to Yahweh. Maag writes correctly: " In dieser Zwielichtigkeit der Jahwäferne hatte sich dieser Gott ... als König der $sch^{e}ol$ noch in der volkstümliche Vorstellung zu halten vermocht. Nicht nur waltet nach Ps 18,5 in der Unterwelt eine Macht, die voller

---

([1]) *IDB* I, 818B.
([2]) Cfr. above, Part I, ch. 3.
([3]) *Einführung Pss* 57.
([4]) Ps 17,13 f. ; 35,1 ff. ; 55,24 ; 68,1 ff. ; 18 ; 144 (Barth, 59 ; these references imply some identification of enemies and Death).

Abscheu als *Belīja'al* bezeichnet wird. Vielmehr weiss Job 18,14 sogar, dass es sich um einen regelrechten Unterweltskönig handelt. Es ist dann auch kaum zufällig, dass er ihn den ' schrecklichen König' nennt " (5).

Historical considerations support this opinion. Such ancient Near Eastern literatures as those from Mesopotamia and Ugarit present a great number of inferior gods and demons : we can safely say that they were at home in the milieu of the OT. And, as the OT clearly affirms Yahweh's victory over death, a ' belief' in Death as an Enemy was by no means contrary to orthodox faith. Later developments also support our thesis. Maag continues : " Da unten herrschte also tatsächlich für eine vom Jahwismus nie ganz liquidierte landläufige Vorstellung ein König, den man, dachte man an Jahwä, als dessen Antagonisten auffassen konnte. ... Als aber die Apokalyptik das Thema des Antagonismus zu Jahwä aufnahm, war der Moment gekommen, in welchem der Herr der *sch^e'ol* mit den anderen Antagonisten zu einem einzigen Symbolkomplex verschmolz und in diesem Zusammenhang zu einem der Wesensaspekte des Satanischen wurde. Auch für die spätere Zeit soweit sie das Weltbild der Apokalyptik beibehielt, blieben Tod und Teufel in einer Symbiose verbunden " (6).

If Death as a person is found before and around biblical Israel and in later Judaism, it is reasonable to suppose that it was also present between both periods. As long as Death and Beyond were not integrated in Yahwism, their primitive meaning must have survived, although in a weakened form (as Yahweh had no equals).

G. A. Barton writes : " While but few individual demons can be traced in the canonical literature, the apocryphal writings bear witness to the fact that the popular thought abounded with them " (7). We

---

(5) " Tod u. Jens. " 31.

(6) *Ibid.* ; D. S. Russell writes about one of the " other antagonists " : " Those tendencies toward evil, which appear in the biblical references to " the Satan " reach their full extent in the apocalyptic writings where Satan and his legions are presented as the arch-enemies of God, bent on controlling and so ultimately destroying not only the human race, but even the cosmos itself ". (*The Methods and Message of Jewish Apocalyptic* 238). " Later Death is identified with ' Satan ', ' the Devil ' (' Death ' and ' Hell ", Rev 1,18 ; 20,13 f. ; ' Devil ' and ' Hell ': Heb 2,14) ; he is also the ' enemy ' who spoils the sower's crop (Mat 13,39) ". (Kosmala, " Mot and the Vine ... " *ASTI* 3 [1964] 148). See Mt 13,19 (the evil one), Eph 6,12 ; Col 1,13 ; Rev 26,18 (rulers of darkness, etc.) 2 Cor 6,15 (Belial), Rev 12,9 (dragon), 2 Tim 2,26, 1 Tim 6,9 ; 3,7 (nets), 1 Petr 5,8 f. (lion). This evolution Death – Devil is borne out by the transition Sheol – Hell, below, pp. 190 f.

(7) In Hastings, *Encyclopaedia of Religion and Ethics* IV (Edinburgh 1911) 598 B.

11

will now consider some other " individual demons " connected with Death.

3.2 Associates

When Mot has been recognized as a person, the interpretation of *bᵉkôr māwet* in Jb 18,13 offers fewer difficulties. Our solution was proposed by Sellin already in 1933 ([8]). In Pope's translation, v. 13b runs : " Death's first-born feeds on his (the wicked's) limbs. " Because Ugaritic myth does not contain any reference to Death's offspring, which no doubt is an expression of his sterility, it is hard to determine the impact of this " firstborn ". When in v. 14 the " king of Terrors " is understood " as a folkloristic allusion to the demonic king of the nether world " ([9]), it is not likely that " his firstborn " is a mere poetical metaphor, standing for " any death-dealing force like disease or pestilence " ([10]). And as the author of Job knew mythology very well, the Firstborn is hardly a clumsy invention of his. This is about all that our evidence permits us to say about the import of Jb 18,13 ([11]).

In Babylonian literature Nergal, the king of the nether world, disposes of a messenger, a god of illnesses ([12]). Ancient practice and Semitic mythology, however, suggests that messengers generally came in pairs ([13]). Prv 16,14a shows that Death also was thus equipped : " The wrath of the king is Death's two messengers " ([14]). It is therefore striking that not rarely in the OT illnesses (or demons) come in pairs, and, it seems, in fixed combinations. It is doubtful whether parallelism alone can be held responsible for this. Deber and Reshep appear in Dt 32,23 and Hab 3,5 ; the latter is a well-known Semitic god of plague and pestilence ([15]), the former's identity is further illustrated by two other occurrences in the OT. Ps 91,6 reads :

([8]) *Theologie des Alten Testaments* (Leipzig 1933) 80. Quoted by Baumgartner, *TRu* 13 (1941) 172.
([9]) Gaster, *IDB* I, 821 A.
([10]) So Pope, *Job* 126.
([11]) For the tenor of the vs. see Sarna (in *JBL* 82 [1963] 315-318) ; certainly this son is an extraordinary phenomenon. In Greece Hades and Persephone have no children ; this " würde der allgemeinen Vorstellung von der Unfruchtbarkeit des Gottes widersprechen " (Roscher, *Lex. Myth.* I, 2, 1781)
([12]) Dhorme, *RB* 5 (1907) 65.
([13]) Gaster, *Thespis* 157 f., note.
([14]) Dahood, *Prov.* 36.
([15]) See e.g. Gaster, *IDB* I, 819A ; Maag, in Schmökel, *Kulturgesch.* 584 (*Ršp* is connected with Sheol).

(You will not fear) the *deber* that stalks in the night,
nor the *qeṭeb* devastating at noonday.

According to Nicolsky, *dbr* and *qṭb* are " dämonische Wesen ... Sie
stehen in Verbindung mit Sheol ... und mit dem Tode (Maweth)
selbst " ([16]).

For this he refers to Hos 13,14 :

> Shall I ransom them from (*mîyyad*) Sheol,
> Shall I redeem them from Death ?
> O Death, where is your *dbr* ([17]) ?
> Where is your *qṭb*, O Sheol ?

It is obvious that Death and Sheol in the first two cola stand for a
personal reality ; in the latter two *dbr* and *qṭb* are apparently considered as his servants or messengers.

qṭb also occurs in Dt 32,24, this time accompanied by *ršp* and
others ; it is qualified as *mᵉrîrî*, a derivate from *mrr*, " to be bitter "
or " strong " ([18]).

As in Dt 32,24b, not rarely illnesses are said to be " sent "by
Yahweh ; as the same *šlḥ* is used for the sending of his messengers,
the prophets, it is not impossible that the use of this verb to denote
a punishment as inflicted by God, has its background in a mythical
world, where demons of illnesses were sent ([19]).

The trio *ḥrb – rᵉb – dbr* in Jeremiah also preferably has *šlḥ* with
it ([20]). As shown before, the latter two probably have a mythological
past ; the same may be argued for *ḥrb*. The sword has " hands "
and a " mouth " and sometimes the context suggests more than the
normal meaning : e.g., Ps 22,21 and 144,10 ([21]). So perhaps Jeremiah's triplet also has a mythological prehistory.

([16]) Nicolsky, *Spuren magischer Formeln* 16 ; the reference to Hos 13,14 is
is given by A. Jirku, *Die Dämonen und ihre Abwehr im AT* (Leipzig 1912) 44 ;
Briggs remarks : " G thinks of the pestilence as a demon, and it is possible
that H had the same idea ", C. A. Briggs and E. G. Briggs, *A Critical and
exegetical Commentary on the Book of Psalms*, II (ICC ; Edinburgh 1951 [=
1907]), 280.

([17]) For the sg. see *BH*, critical apparatus. Gaster (*IDB* 820B) translates
dbr as " catastrophe " (*dbr* = " to cast prone ") and derives *qṭb* from *qṭb* " to
cut off ".

([18]) Dahood, in *Bib* 39 (1958) 309 f.

([19]) See *BDB* 1018B *sub* 2 a + b. See the expression in Ps 78,49.

([20]) Object : the three : Jr 24,10 ; 29,17 ; the sword : 9,15 ; 49,37.

([21]) *ᵉl ydy ḥrb*, cp. *BDB* 391B ; *pî* .. : *ib.* 352B. Cp. above, pp. 107 f. See

Jb 18,11 f. reads:

> Round about terrors (*blhh*) affright him,
> and harry him at every step.
> Let the Hungry One face him,
> and Calamity be stationed at his side ([22]).

Referring to 22,10, where " snares " are balanced by " sudden dread ", Pope thinks that " terrors " here are some sort of demons ([23]). In view of the strong mythological colouring of v. 12 this is not unlikely. Nicolsky suggested that *'êd* also has a demonic background; indeed parallelism shows that " calamity ", just as in Ps 18,19, in fact stands for " Death " ([24]).

As to Ps 91,3.5, most commentators think that here demons are meant ([25]); Gaster is reserved, but, for the " faery arrow ", points to *ršp ḥs* ([26]). The " fowler " returns in Ps 124,7; he is either Death himself, who is often pictured as using nets (in casu *paḥ*) and in Greek is called ζαγρεύς, " Erzjäger " ([27]), or some inferior demon, to be compared with the Accadian " Netzdämon " ([28]). As to the lions and serpents in Ps 91,13, both are often associated with Death ([29]);

---

npl bḥrb, Hos 14,1. (For *npl* " to perish " see van Dijk, *Ezekiel's Prophecy* 90). Cp. Gunkel in Gn 3,24: " Die Flamme des sich drehenden Schwertes ... ist in Wirklichkeit ein Wesen für sich, eine Art Dämon " (*Genesis* 25).

([22]) Above, p. 109.

([23]) Pope, *Job* 125.

([24]) Nicolsky, *Spuren magischer Formeln* 16; Dahood, *Psalms* 111.

([25]) Gunkel, *Psalmen* 404; Duhm, *Die Psalmen* (2nd ed. 1922); H. Schmidt, *Die Psalmen* (1934) 192; Kraus, *Psalmen* 638; J. de Fraine, " Entmythologisierung " 101-105.

([26]) Kition, Cyprus; *KAI* 32 : 3 f.

([27]) See Roscher, *Lex. Myth.* I, 2, 1783. Cp. Rev 6,8 (Death as a rider).

([28]) Falkenstein – von Soden, *Hymnen* B 78 : 4 (p. 351); Widengren, *Accad. and Hebr. Pss* 198 f.; below, pp. 172 ff. Cp. Zandee, 233, B 19.1.

([29]) See also Sir 39,30; Is 30,6. See above p. 112, 118 (lion); the material resists uniform classification which therefore should be avoided, but sometimes there is a clear reference to the nether world or its agents. As to Ugaritic Leviathan, Kapelrud writes: " Lôtân ... represents destruction and death, as did serpents and dragons in Near Eastern Mythology " (*Baal in the Ras Shamra Texts* [Copenhagen 1952] 119); according to Gemser, Leviathan is " Oud-oosterse verpersoonlijking van de woede der chaotische watermacht " (*De Psalmen* [Groningen 1949] 115); indeed in the OT there is no direct connection between human death and that monster. See Jr 51,34: the swallowing dragon (*tnn*; *bl'*). The serpent is closely related to the dragon; it has the same connection: " Le serpent symbolisant presque partout ce qui est latent, préformel, indif-

Satan is associated with a serpent in *Apoc. Moses* 17 : 4 and in Rev 12,9 and 20,2.

This identification also appears in Wisd 2,24, where the temptation by the serpent (Gn 3) is rendered thus :

> ... Through envy of the devil death came into the world (cp. KJ) ([30]).

Very suggestive is the reference to Lk 10,19, given by Kraus ([31]). Parallelism is to be noticed here ; it seems that Ps 91,13 is quoted :

> Behold, I have given you authority
> to tread upon serpents and scorpions,
> and over all the power of the Enemy.

férencié " and consequently chaotic (Eliade, *Mythe* 110) ; this might be relevant for the exegesis of Gn 3. It seems that Hebrew *šḥl* originally stood for serpent-dragon (Mowinckel ; " šaḥal ", in D. Winton Thomas and W. D. McHardy, editors, *Hebrew and Semitic Studies to G. R. Driver ...* [Oxford 1963] 85-103) ; the word may may still have that meaning in Job 28,8 (and Ps 91,13) where there is connection with chaos again. It is remarkable that an intimate relation between dragon and lion was suggested also : see Pope, *Job*, 179 f. In Ugaritic mythology a *klb ilm* appears, which might be a Semitic hellhound : " Conceivably, the ' mighty bitch ' was some Semitic counterpart of Cerberus " (Gaster, *Thespis* 239, n.). This beast is found in the company of other monsters : Dragon, Serpent, Seven-headed Monster, Mighty Calf (Anat III : 37 ff.), but translations are rather divergent (*Thespis* 240 ; Driver, *CMAL* 87 ; Gordon, *IL* 20). See Ps 22,13 (bulls compared with a lion with wide-open mouth) and 35, 16 (dust of death) 17 (dogs) 17 (lions) 21 (mouth wide-open as Sheol's) 25 (*blʿ*). Cp. Ps 140,4. For dogs see p. 112 and Lagrange, *Religion des Sémites* (2nd ed. ; 1905) 221, n. 1, etc. Further perhaps the jackals in Ps 44,20 (another interpretation with Dahood, *Psalms I*, 267) and 63,11 (cf. Heidel 155 f.). Snakes are prominent in Egyptian literature, too. " As an animal of the earth it houses in the darkness of the realm of the dead " (Zandee, 98). A devouring serpent is mentioned (*ibid.* B. 6, e, p. 160). Further we find the crocodile, lion, and dog (*ibid.* B. 12, pp. 192 ff.). In Rev 12,9 serpent and dragon are identified : they stand for the devil (cp. Kittel *ThWHT* II [Stuttgart 1935] 284, 2-4). Scandinavian Hell is a sister of the serpent and the wolf. The latter monsters belch fire and deadly smoke. The serpent is thrown into the sea, which he moves with his tail. The gate of Hell is guarded by the bloody dog, called Garm (Guerber, 178 ff.). " Der Drache (ist) das Bild des Meeresungeheuers, der Urschlange, das Symbol für die kosmischen Wasser, die Finsternis, die Nacht und den Tod — kürz für das Amorphe und Virtuelle, was noch keine ' Form ' hat " (Eliade, *Das Heilige* 29 ; *RGG*³ II, 259 f.).

([30]) Courtesy of my friend E. C. John.

([31]) Kraus, *Psalmen* 638 ; Russell, *Methods and Message* 256.

The same phenomenon is observed in Coptic Christian literature. The devil approaches Judas in the shape of a snake and Judas prays : " Lord, he came to me in the shape of a snake, while his mouth opened, while he wanted to devour me " [32].   The language is characteristic.   And Mary prays : " May the dragon flee for me " (*ibid*).

These summary remarks show that the number of demons connected with Death is rather restricted ; and as these allusions are generally short and vague, some doubt remains as to their number and quality.   This proves that officially, demons did not play a role of any importance in Israel ; popular belief, of course, is another matter [33].

---

[32] Zandee, 334.

[33] On demonology : B. Duhm, *Die bösen Geister im AT* (1904) ; A. Jirku, *Die Dämonen und ihre Abwehr im AT* (Leipzig 1912) ; L. Köhler, *Der Hebräische Mensch* (Tübingen 1953) 121 f. ; also W. O. E. Oesterley, *An Introduction to the Books of the Apocrypha* (2nd ed. ; London 1937) 190 f. ; for Is 19,3 : H. Wohlstein in *BZ* 5 (1961) 35 f.

CHAPTER 4 : ENTERING INTO SHEOL

4.1 šûb (" to return ") halak (" to pass away ")

4.1.1 *šûb* (" to return ")

The transition from the land of the living to the region of the dead can be called a " return " on the basis of the conception that man comes forth from the womb of the earth, from the nether world. Ps 139,14 reads :

> My bones were not hid from thee :
> when I was made in secret, and woven in
> the depths of the nether world. (RP)

Further see *BDB* 997 *sub* 4a and above, pp. 86 ff. and pp. 122 ff..

4.1.2 *halak* (" to pass away ")

Jb 7,9 runs :

> As the cloud fades and vanishes (*hlk*),
> so he who goes down to Sheol does not come up.

Ps 78,39 proclaims :

> He remembered that they were but flesh ;
> a wind that passes (*hlk*) and comes not again.

Man is " transient " as the driven cloud and the driving wind ; he disappears and is no more. In Hebrew as well as in other languages ([1]), the verb " to go, to depart, to pass away " has become an " euphemistic substitute for dying " ([2]). Sometimes this meaning appears from local modifications : " to Sheol " (Qoh 9,10), " to one Place " (*ibid*. 3,20 ; 6,6), " to the eternal house " (12,5) ; " in dark-

---

([1]) Dhorme, *Job* 186 refers to Arabic ; Latin " perire ", etc. In Egyptian also *šm*, " to go away " means " to pass away, to die " (Zandee, 54.A.2.1.).

([2]) Pope, *Job* 105 ; for texts see *BDB* 234A, *sub* II, 1 and Dhorme, *Job* (Jb 14,20 ; 16,22 ; 19,10). For *'br* see *BDB* 718 A, 5 h. and Ps 48,5.

ness " (6,4) ; " the way of no return " (Jb 16,22) ; " to him " (a deceased son ; 2 S 12,23).

Sometimes this connotation is elucidated by other additions : " to the way of all the earth " (Jos 23,14 ; 1 K 2,2) ; " a generat'on goes, and a generation comes " (Qoh 1,4) ; " just as he came, he shall go " (*ibid.* 5,15) ; " before I go and be no more " (Ps 39,14) ; " before I go, not to return " (Jb 10,21).

Sometimes the general context suggests this interpretation : Jb 14,20 runs : " You overwhelm him for ever and he passes " (Pope) [3] ; Jb 19,10 : " He breaks me down on every side and I am gone " (RSV) ; but also Ps 81,13 (with due reserve) :

I let them go in the stubbornness of their heart,
that they might walk / perish according to their own devices [4].

And finally Gn 15,2, as quoted before [5].

Childless I pass away ... [6].

4.2 To be gathered to one's kinsmen

The formula *n'sp 'l 'myw* has been carefully analysed by B. Alfrink [7]. He came to the conclusion that this is the authentic wording of an archaic expression which refers to the union of the deceased with his forefathers in Sheol ; this fact is followed by the burial from which it is clearly distinguished in some texts. In view of the antiquity of the formula this distinction between descent to Sheol and the burial is an important indication for the historical evolution. It is to be noticed that it occurs in prose.

It is generally believed that the idea of an abode common to all dead developed from the family grave, a resting-place common to the member of a clan. Indeed, the facts at our disposal point to that conclusion [8]. Now the use of our formula, as clearly distinguished from the mention of the burial, shows this development to have taken place before the biblical texts came into existence.

A short summary of Alfrink's article will be given here.

— The formula is found ten times, exclusively in the Pentateuch (in the priestly tradition).

---

[3] Dhorme, *Job* 186 refers to 4,2 and 20,7 for parallels.
[4] We think of the facts related concerning Num 14, pp. 26 f.
[5] Cf. above, p. 77.
[6] For Hebrew *yrd* cf. above, pp. 32 f., Ps 22,30.
[7] B. Alfrink, " L'expression *ne'esap el-'ammāyw* ", *OTS* 5 (1948) 118-131.
[8] Above, p. 133 etc.

— ʿām, " kinsman " is mainly found in the Pentateuch ; moreover in technical formulas with the verbs krt and 'sp and in archaic names [9].

— Sometimes (Gn 25,8 ; 25,17 ; 35,29) the sequence is : gwʿ, died, was gathered ". This shows that gwʿ originally had a neutral sense ; according to Driver [10] this was " to gasp for breath ", as appears from Ps 88,16 and Lam 1,19.

— The third person sg. niphal of 'sp in narrative prose is found in Genesis ; the only exception is Gn 49,29, in the history of Joseph, where also gwʿ is found without the additional mwt. In the latter case the formula is probably used for solemnity's sake. Elsewhere the formula is found as spoken by God ; here it is exclusively applied to the great national figures Moses and Aaron : Nu 20,24.26 ; 27,13 ; 31,2 ; Dt 32,50. This is probably due to its archaic ring : it is a solemn expression. In a later period (Sir) it is also said of women and non-Israelites.

— In its oldest use it is distinguished from death and burial. Gn 25,8-9 : " Abraham breathed his last and died ... and was gathered to his kinsmen. Isaac and Ishmael ... buried him ". Cp. Gn 35,29 ; 49,33 f.

— The formula does not apply to the family grave (Moses and Aaron).

— Burial in the family grave is normal ; see the exceptions in 1 K 13,22 ; 2 C 26,33. The fact is explicitly mentioned where the contrary might be expected (Jud 16,31 ; 2 S 2,32, etc.).

— Further evolution : a) " to be gathered to one's fathers " (normally : to sleep with one's fathers) : Jud 2,10 and 2 K 22,20 ; b) " To be gathered to one's grave " (2 K 22,10) ; c) Equivalent to ' to die ' : Ps 26,9 (qal) ; stands in parallelism with 'bd in Is 57,1. d) Said of bones in 2 S 21,13 ; Jr 8,2, etc. For Jb 27,19 see above [11].

4.3 To sleep with one's fathers

The formula škb ʿm 'btyw should by no means be confused with the expression studied in the preceding paragraph ; its meaning is distinctly different and it is at home in other books : in Kings and Chronicles mainly. The genre is the same : narrative prose.

This expression was studied by G. R. Driver ; the result of his analysis will be summarized here [12]. The verb škb, used absolutely,

[9] Cp. KB 710A.
[10] JSS 7 (1962) 15 ; see also G. R. Driver, " Plurima Mortis Imago ", Fs Neuman 141-43.
[11] Pp. 74 f.
[12] G. R. Driver, " Plurima Mortis Imago ", in Fs Neuman 137-143. Prof. Driver kindly sent me a copy of his article.

means both " to be dead " and " to lie in the grave " ([13]). The expression " to sleep with one's fathers " may originally have stood for the interment in the family grave; this is not true, however, for its biblical use. In fact this is excluded, where the formula is applied to Joseph and Moses ([14]) and expressly denied in some other cases ([15]). Its import is clearly suggested by the combinations in which it is found. We find two fixed formulas : " And X slept with his fathers; and they buried him ... " ([16]) ; and : " And X slept with his fathers and was buried " ... ([17]). In four texts we read : " and X slept with his fathers and was buried with his fathers " ; consequently there cannot be any doubt as to the formula not standing either for interment in the family grave or for burial in general. Apparently " to sleep with one's fathers " refers to death ; it is never preceded or followed by the verb *môt* or an equivalent, and where *môt* is used, there our formula is found missing. Therefore it is evident that the use of either expression depends upon (the quality of the subject and) the way a person died. " To sleep with ... " is exclusively said of kings ; the preposition *'m* indicates the " common lot " ([18]), so that the expression may be paraphrased as " to die a customary, usual death ", " to die normally ". And as pointed out by Alfrink also, in practice this means a " natural " death and excludes a violent one ([19]). Consequently the solemn obituary notice is kept from kings who died in battle, or in a *coup* ; other exceptions are Athalia's sons (because of their mother's impiety) and Joram in 2 C 21 (who dies of an illness which is a punishment for his wickedness).

In view of the latter two categories the present writer ventures the conclusion that the fixed formula is an indirect *testimonium pietatis* : in Israel an untimely death was considered a certain consequence of a bad life ([20]). Simple " to die ", applied to kings in Kings and Chronicles, as a rule implies a violent death ; said of other per-

---

([13]) Cp. *BDB* 1012, 4 a-c.
([14]) Gn 47,30 ; Dt 31,16. " Ich glaube ... nicht dass die Scheolverstellung an die Stelle der lebendigen alten Vorstellung vom Familiengrab getreten sei in die Weise, dass die Scheol nur die Gesamtheit der Erbbegräbnisse des Stammes oder Volkes wäre ", F. Nötscher, *Altorientalischer und alttestamentlicher Auferstehungsglauben* (Würzburg 1926) 211.
([15]) 2 K 16,20, cp. 2 C 28,27 ; 2 K 21,18 ; cp. 2 C 33,20.
([16]) 1 K 15,8 ; 2 K 10,35, etc.
([17]) 1 K 2,10 ; 11,43, etc.
([18]) Cp. *BDB* 676 F, *sub* e.
([19]) B. Alfrink " L'expression *šăkab 'im ăbôtāyw* ", *OTS* 2 (1943) 106-118.
([20]) Cp. Nu 16,30 ; 1 S 2,32 ; Jr 28,16 ; Prv 10,27.

sons, however, it does not connote a judgment about the way of death.
As a clear example of this use we might quote 1 K 11,21 :

> Hadad heard ... that David slept with his fathers and that
> Joab had died.

In fact the king died the death of the just, and Joab had been executed (2 K 2,34) ; but the latter cannot be deduced from the formula
used by the Deuteronomist.   He could not possibly have written that
David and Joab " had died ", because the king died peacefully.   The
distinction would have been imperative even if the army commander
had passed away because of old age.

4.4   To be planted in Sheol

In *UT* 76 : II : 24 f. Baal tells his sister Anat that he has conquered his enemies and will return to power :

nṯ'n bars iby We have planted my foes in the nether world	*wb'pr qm aḫk* those rising up against your brother in the dust ([21]).

The discovery of this theme proved fruitful for the translation of Ps
73,18, where instead of doubtful TM *baḥălāqôt tāšît lāmô* should be
read : *baḥălāqôt tišt^elēmô* ; " you transplanted them in Perdition " ([22]).
   This eschatological interpretation of *štl* may be reinforced by
its occurrence in Ps 1,3,   " So shall he be like a tree transplanted near
the streams of water ", if it is interpreted correctly by M. Dahood
as referring to the transference of the just to the Elysian Fields ([23]).

([21]) Gordon, *UL* 50 ; Dahood, " HULex ", *Bib* 45 (1964) 408 s.v. *ḫlq*.
   ([22]) M. Dahood, *Psalms* 3 ; for *nt'*, to transplant : *KB* 1015A ; for *ḫlq*, cp.
above, pp. 83 f.   The present writer quite surprisingly came across the same use
of words, here applied to burial, in Mark Twain's *Huckleberry Finn*.   In view
of the author's knowledge of dialects (see his Explanatory) we have reason
to believe that the expression belongs to the idiom of some negro dialect, spoken by Jim : " He said that a man that warn't buried was more likely to go
a-ha'nting around than one that was planted and comfortable " (Samuel Clem-
ens, *The Adventures of Huckleberry Finn* [New York 1952] p. 57 ; ch. 10,
initio).
   ([23]) For this theme see Dahood, *Psalms* 3 ; also 33 f. ; 222 f. ; it is not discussed here.   See also Ps 52,7 : " He shall uproot you from the land of the living ".

4.5 Other ways and instruments used

4.5.1 *blʿ*

As set forth above (²⁴) *blʿ* " to swallow ", is a favourite word for characterizing the way Sheol receives the dead. The term evokes the unquenchable appetite and voracious muzzle of Sir Death.

Against this background the subtle irony of Is 25,8 becomes apparent : " He (Yahweh) engorged Mot for ever " (²⁵).

Because of the apparent allusion to the rapacious jaws of the victim the measured language should not be overlooked here.

Gaster finds the same theme in *UT* 67 : I : 5 where Mot says : *ank ispi uṭm ḏrqm amtm*, which he translates (²⁶) :

> (As things are), I am the one that has been swallowed up ;
> a stopper, as it were, has been placed upon me ;
> drained of strength (?) as I am, *I* am the one that is dying.

Indeed *ispa* is said of being eaten by Death in *UT* 49 : V : 20 ; but " this passage is one of the most difficult in the entire poem, and our interpretation is therefore tentative ", as Gaster himself confesses. This uncertainty is stressed by Aistleitner's translation : " Fressen werde ich frischblutende Bissen " (²⁷). Final *amtm*, however, recommends an understanding of *ispi* as passive.

4.5.2 For *dḥh*

" to thrust ", see above (²⁸).

4.5.3 Ropes and nets

In Accadian literature every god is said to have his net to drag his enemies into the nether world (²⁹) ; Widengren affirms that in Sumerian texts also gods know the use of nets and snares (³⁰) and the same is ascertained by Kristensen for Egyptian texts (³¹). Eliade collected an impressive amount of evidence about this motive (³²).

(²⁴) See above, pp. 125 ff.
(²⁵) Dahood, *Psalms* 134 ; Gaster, *Thespis* 203 n.
(²⁶) Gaster, *Thespis* 202 ; see 203, note. See above, p. 8.
(²⁷) *WUS* 2724.
(²⁸) Cf. above, pp. 93 f.
(²⁹) Dhorme, *RB* 4 (1907) 64.
(³⁰) *Accad. and Hebr. Pss*, 238, cp. the demon's name Alluḫappu, " hunting net " (*ANET* 109B ; Falkenstein–von Soden, B 78 ; 4, p. 351).
(³¹) *Leven uit den Dood* 165 ; Zandee, B. 19 (226 ff.).
(³²) M. Eliade, *Images et Symboles* 124-152.

Vedic mythology knows two binding gods of death, Nirrti and Yama; the expression " snares of death " occurs ; snares, ropes, and knots are essential attributes of these gods. In Persia the demon of death binds his victims. In the Pacific the god Vaerua drags the deceased with ropes into the nether world (Dangu Islands); the souls of the dead are caught in the nets of gods or demons (Harvey Islands ; Aranda); Death is called " Fisher of Souls " on San Cristobal. In the Semitic area, Tammuz is " Lord of the snares " ([33]); Widengren mentions the Accadian god Alluḫappu, " hunting net ". The Scandinavian sea-goddess Ran, a rapacious and miserly being, is said to draw her victims into the depths by means of a strong net ([34]).

The same motive appears in Goethe's *Iphigenie auf Tauris*:

> Hat ein klein Geschick
> Mit des Avernus Netzen ihn umschlungen? ([35]).

Both Kristensen and Eliade, however, stress the ambivalence of this motive ([36]). There is a fatal binding, there is also a roping which means protection ; sometimes fetters express cosmic world-order, the harmonic coherence of human life and universe (a net spread over a mummy ensures victory over death), at other times they are instruments of forces undermining life.

In its favourable sense this motive is alluded to in Jb 7,6 and Ps 2,3 and the like, but most often it means a danger for man.

Ps 18,6 reads :

> The cords of Sheol surrounded me,
> the traps of Death confronted me. (Dahood)

In other words, the psalmist feels drawn into Sheol; so the torrents of Belial in v. 5 most likely stand for the Styx surrounding the citadel of Death, rather than for the Land of Darkness itself. The motive

---

([33]) *Enuma eliš* I, 60-74 ; IV, 49. 95. 111 f.

([34]) Widengren, *Accad. and Hebr Pss* 198 f. ; C. Barth (*Errettung* 78) connects our motive with Sheol as a prison, but our evidence shows that Death as a hunter is in the background. For Ran, see Guerber, 184.

([35]) *Werke*, V (Hamburg 1958) p. 34, 979 f.

([36]) W. Brede Kristensen, *Symbool en Werkelijkheid*, (Zeist–Arnhem–Antwerpen 1961) 116 f. ; Eliade, *loc. cit.*

returns in 2 S 22,6 and Ps 116,3. It is also found in Jb 18,7-10, in a context, clearly referring to the nether world:

> His (the wicked's) mighty strides are narrowed,
> His own schemes trip him.
> He is thrown by his feet in the net.
> His steps upon the webbing.
> The snare seizes him by the heel,
> The bands tighten on him.
> His noose is hid on the ground,
> His trap upon the path. (Pope)

Compare Eliphaz' description of Job's condition:

> Therefore snares surround you,
> And sudden dread terrorizes you (22,10) [37].

In Ps 42, the psalmist " compares his wretchedness to the cheerless existence of Sheol " [38]. V. 7 reads:

> .. I remember you,
> from the land of descent and of nets [39].

The motive does not surprise in an IL; see the collective ThPs 124 which describes the dangers in terms of chaotic waters (vv. 3 ff.), and concludes (v. 7):

> We have escaped as a bird
> from the snare of the fowlers;
> the snare is broken,
> and we have escaped.

  In the guise of human enemies Hunter Death caught the pious Israelites, but these were miraculously saved by their God, who made heaven and earth, i.e., by the God who creates cosmos, life and fertility, the victor of Death.

  Obviously Qohelet starts from the same conception of Death's instruments where he writes:

> And I found stronger than Death the woman

---

[37] See above, p. 75.
[38] Dahood, *Psalms* 255.
[39] Cf. above, pp. 145 f.

whose heart is snares and nets, and whose
hands are fetters (Qoh 7,26) ([40]).

It would not be surprising if this imagery were transferred to Yahweh,
Lord of life and death. This might be the case in Ez 32,3:

I will throw my net over you
with a host of peoples;
and I haul you up in my dragnet ([41]).

The language of Hos 7,12 is reminiscent of Ps 124,7:

As they go, I will spread over them my net;
I will bring them down like birds in the air..

Here it seems certain that descriptions of Hunter Death have been
applied to Yahweh. This is also true for Jb 19,6 where Job says:

But know 'tis God who has subverted me,
Has thrown his net around me ([42]). (Pope)

Not unlikely the attributes of former gods and demons passed to
the enemies of the psalmist in the IL. Ps 140,6 reads:

Arrogant men have hidden a trap for me,
and with cords they have spread a net,
by the wayside they have set snares for me ([43]). (RSV)

In 2 Tim 2,26 the motive is transposed to the Devil: " They may
escape from the snare of the devil... "

Many Hebrew words clearly relate to the conception of Sheol as
a prison and to Death as a fowler. In Jb 18 we find: 8. *rešet* " net "
(for catching game and birds) — *śᵉbākâ*; 9. *paḥ* (" bird-trap ") —
ṣammîm; 10. *ḥebel* (" rope ") — *malkōdet* (" snare "). Ps 2,3: *môsērâ*
(" bands ") and *'abôt* (" rope "). Further: *ḥerem* (" dragnet "; Ez
32,3); *māṣôd* (" hunting-net ") and *'ēsûr* (" fetter ") in Qoh 7,26;
môqēš (" bait, bird-trap "; Ps 140,6); *mikmōr* (" net, snare "; Ps
141,10). The essential common element is the idea of binding ([44]).

([40]) For *mar*, " strong " see Dahood, *Bib* 39 (1958) 309 f.

([41]) According to Gunkel (*Schöpfung und Chaos*) however, this is an allusion to the Drachenkampf (72 ff.); indeed Eliade (*Images et Symboles*) confesses
that it is hard to obtain a clear impression of Mesopotamiam idea on the point.

([42]) Eliade, *Images et Symboies* quotes Hos 7,12; Ez 12,31; 17,20; 32,3.

([43]) Cp. Ps 64,6; 124,7; 141,9; 142,2; Hab 1,15 f. etc.; cf. above, pp. 110 ff.

([44]) Cp. Ps 91,3, Qoh 9,12, and p. 164, above.

5.1 The Rephaim and Elohim

Though there was little doubt as to the common meaning of Rephaim in biblical usage, its etymology remained uncertain in pre-Ugaritic exegesis. No doubt expectations ran high when the Ugaritic texts, now known as *UT* 121, 122, 123 and 124, appeared to be dealing with *rpum*. Partially because of the fragmentary condition of these tablets, however, widely varying translations of the texts are proposed, so that little certainty can be obtained as to biblical *rp'ym*. The difficulty of this fascinating problem is reflected by the numbers of studies devoted to the theme in recent years ; they were, written by scholars such as Gaster, Ginsberg, Gray, Jirku, Ryan, van Selms, and Worden ; the most intensive studies of recent date were composed by A. Caquot and Jörg Jeremias (¹). We will try to summarize the results of this research here without pretending to give a full survey of all opinions put forward, and as to Ugaritic texts we will limit ourselves to the elements essential for our argument.

The relation of the *RPUM* to the nether world can be established in this way.

a. *UT* 62 : 16-18 ff. runs : *tbkyn. tbqrnh. tštnn. bḫrt.ilm.arṣ* : " You will weep for him, bury him, and put him in a cave of the gods of the earth ". As to *ilm.arṣ*, the combination apparently is the status constructus of plural *ilm* with enclytic -*m*, as often in construct chains (²) ;

(¹) H. Ginsberg, " The Legend of King Keret " 41 ; Th. Gaster, *JQR* 37 (1946-1947) 288 f. ; J. Gray, *PEQ* (1949) 127-139 and (1952) 39-41 ; A. Jirku, *ZAW* 77 (1965) 82 f. ; D. Ryan, " *Rpum and Rephaim*. A Study in the Relationship between *rpum* of Ugarit and the *Rephaim* of the Old Testament " (National University of Ireland 1946) ; van Selms, *Marriage* 131 ; T. Worden, *VT* 3 (1953) 281 ff. ; see also Virolleaud, " Les Rephaim, Fragments de poèmes de Ras Shamra ", *Syria* 22 (1941) 1-30 ; A. Caquot, *Syria* 37 (1960) 75-93 ; Jörg Jeremias, *Rephaim in the OT and RPUM in the Ugaritic Texts* (Master Paper, Yale University, unpublished). I am much indebted to Dr. Jeremias for kindly talking the problem over with me and for placing his paper at my disposal.

(²) H. D. Hummel, " Enclitic Mem in Early North-West Semitic ", *JBL* 76 (1957) 85-107 ; Dahood, *Psalms* 109, etc.

arṣ stands for the nether world.   Van Selms comments: " The grave as a hole in the ground is part of the domain of the earth-gods " ([3]).

b. Probably these " gods of the nether world " are identical with the *rpum.*   Text 128 : III : 13-15 reads : *mid.rm (krt).btk.rpi.arṣ. bpḫr.qbṣ.dtn* : " Be most exalted Krt, in the midst of the *rpum* of the earth, in the gathering of the assembly of Datan ".

Here the connection between *rpum* and *arṣ* is clear and the tenor of the text justifies the assumption that the *rpum* belongs to the class of the *ilm arṣ* in text 62.

These texts also suggested that the *rpum* are a kind of gods.   This fact can be specified : Ugaritic *ilnym* ([4]), but for one exception, is always applied to the *rpum.*   This clearly appears from *UT* 62 : 44 ff. :

> *špš rpim. tḥtk*
> *špš. tḥtk. ilnym*
> *ʻdk. ilm hn. mtm*
> *ʻdk* ([5]).

Unfortunately the meaning of these words is uncertain ; but parallelism between *rpim* and *ilnym* is obvious.   If the last two lines are synonymous with the former, the *rpum* are identified with the dead ; this, however, is less certain ; *ilm* might stand for " gods " and *mtm* for " mortals ".   Chiastically parallel structure of a-b and c-d suggests that *rpim-ilnym-ilm-mtm* are on a par with each other.   The pattern is :

> (A) — B — C
> (A) — C — B′
>   D — E
> (F) — E′ — D

That is, if *tḥtk* = *ʻd* :   A - B
>   B′ - A
>   B″- A
>   A - B″

The divine character of these beings can also be deduced from the proper name *abrpu* (311: 10).   The word *ilnym* is not rarely found in North-West Semitic texts ; scholars think it is used for inferior

---

([3]) Van Selms, *Marriage* 131.
([4]) See *UT* Gloss 194.
([5]) Driver translates *tḥtk* by " kept company " and *ʻd* by " round " (*CMAL* 115) ; this is relevant in view of the following argument.   Other occurrences of *ilnym* and *rpum* : *UT* 122, 4.12 and 123,5 f.

gods, which would account for this by-form of *ilm* (⁶). This corresponds with its always having a plural meaning (there is one certain exception) (⁷). Very interesting for our purpose is a New-Punic text, beginning with the words: *l'l(nm) 'r'p'm*, translated: *d(is) m(anibus) sacrum* (⁸).

This use is reflected in 1 S 28,8 where Saul asks the woman: " Divine for me by a spirit (*'lhym*) ".... See also Is 8,19.

Both this title and the extraordinary knowledge attributed to this spirit show that there was an ancient tradition according to which the spirits of the dead were somehow more than human beings (⁹). In the OT this view practically extinct, at least officially (cp. Lv 19,31; Dt 18,11, etc.).

It cannot be doubted that the *rpum* are related to fertility. In 121 : II the *rpum* come to the threshing floors and plantings : to restore fertility, it seems. In this context scholars often refer to biblical *rp'*, in some cases meaning " to give back fecundity ". The texts quoted are Gn 20,17 and 2 K 2,21; the former runs:

> God healed Abimelek and also healed his wife
> and female slaves so that they bore children.

This is further explained in v. 18:

> For Yahweh had closed all the wombs of the house of Abi-
> melek (¹⁰).

In his commentary on 128 : III. 13 ff., Ginsberg points to the parallelism between *rp'* and *qbṣ* in that text (¹¹). (Of course *btk*, " in the midst ", is balanced by *bpḥr*, " in the assembly "). He remarks that Hebrew *bqṣ* means to " gather " and consequently defines *rp'* thus:

(⁶) See *KAI* II, 14 f. The *Rpum* do not travel walking or flying; they are more progressive and use chariots. This shows that they are less tied to tradition than higher gods (Jeremias).

(⁷) Jean–Hoftijzer 15; *KAI* III, 2B.

(⁸) *KAI* I, 117,1; II, p. 122.

(⁹) *GB* 40B *sub* 3; see E. König, *Geschichte der alttestamentlichen Religion* (Gütersloh 1915) 88; Maag, " Tod u. Jens. " 18; H. Wohlstein " Zu den altisraelitischen Vorstellungen von Toten- und Ahnengeistern " (*BZ* 5 [1961] 30-38) 36 f. In Egypt also the dead are deified, cp. Kristensen, *Leven* 30 f., 54. For the degree of knowledge possessed by the dead see the name *yiddeᵉ-ōnî*.

(¹⁰) In 2 K 2,19-22, bad water, sterilizing the land, is made wholesome by Yahweh; " henceforth neither death nor miscarriage shall come from it ". For " making wholesome " the verb *rp'* is used.

(¹¹) *The Legend of King Keret* 41.

" to join, *ergo*: to mend, to heal ". *Rpum* is then to be rendered as
" those gathered ". For confirmation, Ginsberg refers to Prv 9,18:

> But he does not know that the Rephaim are there, that her
> guests (*qr'ym*) are in the depths of Sheol [12].

And to Prv 21,16:

> A man who wanders from the way of understanding will
> rest in the assembly of the Rephaim.

In the former text the " invited " guests are apparently represented
as gathered in Sheol, and the latter even approaches *UT* 128 by the
combination *qhl rp'ym*. This is a tempting suggestion, but it seems
Ginsberg is straining the evidence ; in view of extra-biblical testimo-
nies a direct connection with healing and fertilizing looks more likely.
Several authors state the fact that in ancient Greece local heroes were
considered as protectors, as minor deities especially acting as healers [13].
In Greek mythology, all chthonic deities dominate death and life,
flowering and fading [14]. The same fact is attested for Babylonia [15].

Certainly this healing character of the Rephaim does not appear
in the OT. This is by no means surprising ; J. Barr's words, quoted
before [16], are to the point : " It is quite wrong to suppose that the
etymology of a word is necessarily a guide to its ' proper ' meaning
in a later period or to its actual meaning in that period " [17]. In
our case this shift is historically quite understandable : Yahweh " kills
and brings to life ; he brings down to Sheol and raises up " in Israel
(1 S 2,6).

The name Rephaim remained connected with Sheol and occurs
eight times in this sense ; historical development from *rpum*, however,

---

[12] According to van Dijk (*Ezekiel's Prophecy* 83) *b⁶* is emphatic here,
the depths themselves being guests. In view of the parallelism an interesting,
but all the same curious, interpretation. More convincing is this meaning in
Ps 88,19 : " For friends I have darkness ".

[13] Albright, *VTS* 4 (1957) 253 ; M. Nilsson, *Les croyances religieuses de la
Grèce antique* (Paris 1955) 16 f. ; J. E. Harrison, *Prolegomena to the Study of Greek
Religion* (Cambridge 1908) 340-349; O. Kern, *Die Religion der Griechen*, I (Berlin
1926) 122 ; A. Brelich, *Gli eroi greci* (Roma 1958) 113-118.

[14] Pauly–Wissowa, III, 2 (1899) 2524.

[15] A. Jeremias, *Hölle und Paradies* (Leipzig 1903) 24.

[16] Cf. above, p. 23.

[17] J. Barr, *Semantics* 109.

explains that their character is rather vague ([18]). In this view the
etymology of Rephaim is of no use for better understanding of the
term, or rather : of little use. For it does at least rule out a derivation
from the root *rph*, " to sink, relax ". The conception of a shadowy,
flaccid existence of the dead cannot be associated with the title Rephaim.

5.2   Local distinctions

Several times already we were confronted with the adjective *tḥty* ;
its implications will be studied here. There are two clear examples
of its proper meaning. Gn 6,16 reads : " Make it (the ark) with lower
(*tḥty*), second, and third decks ". And Jb 41,16 uses the same adjective in " the nether millstone ", i.e., the lower and stationary mill-
stone ([19]). This evidence shows sufficiently that the word means " the
lower " (of the two) or " the lowest " (of more than two). As an adjective with *'rṣ*, and consequently in the feminine singular, it is found
in Ez 31,14.16.18 only. In the same book it occurs also in the feminine plural after *'rṣ* ; elsewhere the formula is *taḥtiyôt 'rṣ*. Somehow
this looks like the gradual disintegration of a fixed formula.

Taking the ambiguity of *'rṣ* as a starting-point, we suppose that
the adjective in question served to remove the ambiguity inherent in
'rṣ by specifying it as the " nether " world, just as it does with the
two millstones in Jb 41,16. If this is correct, most likely a tripartite
division of the universe is behind this : heaven – earth I (the " upper ")-
earth II (the " nether "), and *'rṣ* may have a cosmological sense (" earth")
rather than an anthopological one (" land "). The latter statement is
supported by the fact that *'rṣ* may have a purely cosmological sense,
when consequently the idea of human habitation, as implied by the
translation " land " is less likely ([20]).

It is hardly surprising that a corresponding " upper earth " does
not exist. This shows that earth-*simpliciter*, is the primary and evi-

([18]) Conclusion of J. Jeremias *loc. cit.* ; cp. Martin-Achard, *From Death*
35. Rephaim occurs in Is 14,9 ; 26,14.19 ; Ps 88,11 ; Jb 26,5 ; Prv 2,18 ; 9,18
and 21,16. But for Is 14,9 (cp. H. Schmidt, *RGG*[3] VI, 912), there is no indication for the Rephaim being the aristocrats among the dead.

([19]) Pope, *Job* 286.

([20]) See above, pp. 44-46. According to Tallqvist, the Accadians distinguished *irṣitu elītu*, " the upper earth ", inhabited by man, from *irṣitu qablītu*,
" the middle earth ", where Ea resides, and from *irṣitu šaplītu*, " the under
world " (*Namen der Totenwelt* 11 f.). When simple *irṣitu* stands for the nether
world this is a secondary meaning, as in *arallū*, " Länderberg, Erde ; Unterwelt " (*ibid.* 7) and in *ekurru*, " Berghaus, Erde ; Unterwelt " (*ibid.* 25).

dent meaning of the word *'rṣ*, while " nether world " is only a secondary extension of it. This seems to correspond with man's experience of reality, in which the Beyond does not come first.

This is also suggested by the more recent appearance of Sheol in North-West Semitic. As, however, this type of development does not necessarily obey common logic, our suppositions are not unexceptionable. Anyway, the combination *'rṣ tḥtyt*, as found in Ez 31, just means " nether world " (RSV), or " das Land drunten " ([21]).

It may be doubted, however, if this is also true for the alternative formulas. We will limit ourselves here to the expression *'rṣ tḥtywt* in Ez 26,20 and 32,18.24. We quote 32,24:

> Elam is there...; all of them slain, fallen by the sword, who went down uncircumcised into *'rṣ* etc..., and they bear their shame with those who went down to the pit.

The expression under discussion is used literally here of Sheol. As the end of the verse shows there is talk of a shameful lot here. Indeed, O. Eissfeldt has shown that the expression " fallen by the sword " does not refer to ordinary soldiers, killed in action, but to those executed or murdered ([22]). So in Nu 19,16 *ḥll-ḥrb 'w...mt* must mean " somebody murdered or perished " ([23]); and the sword is not rarely a judicial instrument ([24]). For our text this is underlined by added " uncircumcised ", for this condition is a despicable one among peoples who practise circumcision.

In view of the parallelism of our verse with 22 f. we may maintain that the formula under discussion is equivalent to *yark^e tê bôr*, occurring in v. 23. *Yark^e tê bôr* occurs in Is 14,15, where it is contrasted with *yark^e tê ṣāpôn* of v. 13c. Apparently the two extremes of the universe are indicated in this way here. As to *yar^e kâ*, M. Dahood points to parallel Ugaritic *ṣrrt ṣpn*, which is parsed by Accadian *ṣurru*, " heart " ([25]); Hebrew *yārēk* also means " loins, inward parts"([26]). Consequently *ṣrrt* and *yrkh* join in the meaning " inward part "; this can be applied to heaven ([27]), and to Sheol as in our text. This cer-

---

([21]) Zimmerli, *Ezechiel*, 621 f.

([22]) O. Eissfeldt, " Schwerterschlagenen bei Hesekiel ", in: H. H. Rowley, (editor) *Studies in OT Prophecy* 73-81.

([23]) A. Drubbel, *Numeri uit de grondtekst vertaald en uitgelegd* (De Boeken van het Oude Testament, Deel II, Boek II; Roermond–Maaseik 1963) 99.

([24]) Eissfeldt, *loc. cit.* and Jr 21,9; Is 34,5; Lv 26,25; Jb 19,29.

([25]) Dahood, " HULex ", *Bib* 44 (1963) 105; cp. Driver *CMAL* 150, n. 18.

([26]) Gn 46,26; Ps 128,3.

([27]) See O. Mowan " Quatuor montes sacri in Ps 89,13 ? " (*VD* 41 [1963] 11-20) 14, n. 1, where a bibliography is found.

tainly sounds better than a derivation from " two thighs ", i.e., fig.
" angle, recess... " ([28]).

It should be noted, however, that the interpretation " inward
part, recesses " is less succesful in accounting for the Hebr. dual form.
In Is 14,15, we may conclude, the expression stands for the extreme
depths of Sheol.   Returning to Ez 32,24, we may also refer to v. 21,
where " the mighty chiefs " are said " to speak to him" (Egypt,
who is in the extreme depths, v. 18), " out of the midst of Sheol " :
this formulation again suggests a distinction between Sheol proper
and these depths, for the heroes speak from the midst of the nether
world to what apparently is another part of it.

This conclusion is reinforced by v. 27 where other uncircumcised
peoples are said not to lie with the mighty fallen men : *ergo* in a place
more shameful than the midst of Sheol itself ([29]).   Eissfeldt concludes,
with a reference to Is 14,18 f. (where he reads *npl* instead of the vexing *nṣr*), that abortions and uncircumcised, murdered, or executed
people were interred in a separate place and consequently were considered to be in a special part of Sheol also.

This squares perfectly with the relation between the grave and
the nether world as studied above, p. 133.   We may also add that
people who were not buried properly, were located with the categories
mentioned above : such is the lot of the king in Is 14,19 f.   For this
reason it was thought a serious misfortune to remain deprived of sepul-
ture ([30]).   These conceptions are found among other peoples as well ([31]).
As to the feminine plural of *tḥty* before (*h*)'*rṣ* the conclusion reached
above is also valid : in all three occurrences the intention of connoting
the furthest extreme is present.

The other combinations with the adjective must be understood
in the same way.   We find *š'wl tḥtyh* in Ps 86,13 (IL) as an expression of utmost need :

([28]) So *BDB* 438A. J. de Fraine, " Entmythologisierung " 98 : " cuisse,
la partie la plus éloignée ".

([29]) See Jahnow, *Liechenlied*, BZAW 36, 237 ; she thinks that conquered
enemies are put on a par with those uncircumcised. " Later ... dook de ten-
dens op om in de onderwereld een diepere kuil te onderscheiden, waarheen de
booswichten werden verwezen " (Coppens, *Onsterfelijkheidsgeloof* 6).

([30]) For references see Stade, *Geschichte des Volkes Israel* I, 185 and ency-
clopaedias. The exceptions in Jb 3,16.19 and Is 14,10 ff. are probably due to
the sentiments prevailing there.

([31]) Eissfeldt, *op. cit.* 81, refers to Greek evidence and Virgil's *Aeneid*, VI,
426-41 ; see also Fr. Jeremias, in Chantepie de la Sausaye, *Lehrbuch der Reli-
gionsgeschichte* I (Tübingen 1925) 585 f. (dead who have not been buried find
no rest).

> Great is thy steadfast love, O Most High,
> Thou hast delivered my soul from the deep Sheol (³²).

The phrase returns in Sir 51,6. Finally *bôr taḥtîyôt* for the same purpose in Ps 88,7 and Lam 3,55 (both laments). As *bôr* itself is a certain name of the nether world, the latter expression confirms our theory: additional *tḥty* does not serve to take away any ambiguity of the noun, but must be interpreted as denoting its extreme depths.

All these formulas are probably secondary extensions of the use of *tḥty* with *'rṣ* (³³).

5.3 Sleep

When the abode of the dead is pictured as a dormitory (³⁴) it is not surprising to find its inmates described as comatose. As texts will show, this passed from the grave to the nether world, a fact ascertained time and again.

5.3.1 *šākab*

This verb both means " to lie down in death " and " to be lying in the grave, in Sheol " (³⁵). A clear trace of its origin is found in Ps 88,6:

> Among the dead is my couch;
> among the slain, buried (*škb*) in the grave (³⁶).

The transition is perceptible in Ez 32,26 f.:

> Mescheh and Tubal are there, and all their multitude,
> their graves round about it (i.e. the people) ....
> And they do not lie with the fallen mighty men ....

Here the graves are sunk into the common dwelling of the dead, Sheol; the condition of the deceased is identical with the one in the grave. See also Ez 31,18.

(³²) *'ālāy* is read as the divine name here, cp. Dahood, " The Divine Name 'Elî in the Psalms ", *Theological Studies* 14 (1953) 452-457. So the dubious *gādôl ālāy* disappears and an eloquent opposition (most High – deepest Sheol) comes to light.

(³³) Although *'rṣ* with fem. pl. *tḥty* looks like a late differentiation; Zimmerli (*Ezechiel* 611) notes that LXX always render sg. but for 26,20.

(³⁴) Above, pp. 156 ff.

(³⁵) *BDB* 1012, 4a-c; above, pp. 169 ff.

(³⁶) See above, pp. 157 ff.

In Ps 3,6 also its contrary appears; moreover the implications of this *škb* are explicitly expressed through the verb *yšn*:

> If I lie down to sleep,
> I shall wake up (*qyṣ*); for Yahweh sustains me ([37]).

A correct interpretation of the first colon is vital for the understanding of this " waking up ": as opposite to the sleep of death it appears to contain the idea of resurrection ([38]). The true impact of this revival of course corresponds to the nature of the death it is opposed to; we know that " death " in IL often stands for utmost danger or distress: consequently " resurrection " should be understood ⸢accordingly there. The idea of resurrection is denied not less than three times in Jb 14,12:

> And man lies down and never rises (*qûm*).
> They wake (*qyṣ*) not till the heavens decay;
> They rouse (*'ûr*) not from their sleep (*šnh*) ([39]). (Pope)

5.3.2 *yašan*

UT 1 Aqht: 150 f. reads:
> *hm t'pn 'l qbr bny*
> *tšḫṭann b šnth,*
> If they fly over the grave of my son,
> if they disturb him in his sleep ([40]).

The condition of a person lying in the grave is described as " sleep " here (*šnh*, as in Hebrew). An example from Egypt: in parallel sequences for dying and resurrection it reads: " You go away and return, you sleep and wake up, you land and you revive " ([41]); " Hupnos and Thanatos are twins ... The ancients saw congeniality in them: full life was suspended " ([42]). Consequently, resurrection is expressed there in this way: " Osiris wakes up. A tired god awakes " ([43]).

The same use of words is current in Hebrew. Ps 13,4 reads:

([37]) Dahood, *Psalms* 15.
([38]) Dahood, *Psalms* 99.
([39]) Cp. Is 26,14.
([40]) Dahood, *Psalms* 78; Driver, *CMAL* 63, n. 5.
([41]) Zandee, 82, a. 8. c. Similarly in biblical individual lament, as need is described as death, so relief may be expressed in terms of rising. This should not be understood as a resurrection in our sense.
([42]) Zandee, 84, 8.A.j.
([43]) Zandee, 81 f.

Look at me, answer me, Yahweh my God.
Enlighten my eyes
lest I sleep the sleep of death / avert the sleep of death ([44]).

Job, cursing the day of his birth, says:

Why did I not die at birth ...
Like a stillbirth would I were hidden ([45]) ...
For now I would be lying quiet;
I would be asleep and at rest (Jb 3,11a. 16a.13; Pope).

The contrasting appreciation of this sleep in Ps 13 and Jb 3 is symptomatic for OT conceptions about the nether world which to some degree are conditioned by the emotional attitude of the speaker. Job is depressed to such a degree that anything seems better than his present condition, even the empty sleep of Sheol looks desirable ([46]); the psalmist, however, clings to life, as he has not yet given up hope that things will be better for him ([47]).

5.3.3 *lîn*

The dead are said " to stay the night " in Sheol: here the thought of night and darkness, descriptive of Sheol, are added to the idea of sleep, studied above. Jb 17,2 runs:

Surely the two nether-world hills are with me,
and my eyes will pass the night in the twin miry depths ([48]).

([44]) Translations of RSV and Dahood (*Psalms* 78) respectively. Reading *pannē* (ipt piel of *pnh*) yields a fine balance between the two imperatives of colon a with these of colon b; the apocopated form is quite normal: Jouön, 79 i; moreover Jb 33,21 (*ykl*; cf. app. crit.) and 36,10 [*id.*]; Jb 24,8 [*śd*] and Cross–Freedman, EH *Orth.* 17, etc. The substantive *'îsôn* is also found in Prv 20,20: " His lamp shall go out in the sleep of darkness ". In view of Ps 13 " sleep of death " the combination in Prv 20 is perfectly normal. As to *'yšn* in Prv 7,9, this may be the same word or identical with Aramaic *'ešwan*, " time ", as suggested by *BH*[3] in the critical apparatus and Driver in *JSS* 10 (1965) 112. For full argumentation see Dahood, *Prov.* 14 f. The *genitivus explicativus* of *māwet* is not uncommon: see 1 S 15,32 " bitterness of death " and Ps 55,5 " terrors of death "; also *ṣalmāwet* (See above pp. 140 ff.).

([45]) *ṭāmûn* is an allusion to the identical name of Sheol used in Jb 40,13; cp. pp. 46 f. above.

([46]) The same appreciation in Sir 30,24; " Only in the eyes of a Lebensmüde death is something favourable " (Zandee, 45).

([47]) For Jr 51,39 cf. below. Ps 90,5 may also use *šnh* in this sense.

([48]) See above, pp. 54 f.

Ps 30,6b uses the verb as equivalent of " dying " :

> In the evening one falls asleep (*lyn*) crying,
> but at dawn there are shouts of joy ([49]).

It is to be noted here that the evening is the threshold of the night, a well-known epithet of Sheol. The Hebrew compactly says : " In the evening one enters the night, to be passed in tears ".

The frontier between grave and Sheol is indiscernible in Ps 49,13 :

> For man in the Mansion will pass the night indeed ([50]).

" Now they lie / grovelling and prostrate on yon lake of fire " ([51]).

The three expressions discussed here indicate the condition of the dead in the Beyond : they lead a reduced existence, as condemned patients in a gloomy ward, emaciated figures with languid looks, who are in and out of bed all day.

They are dozing away the centuries : " a perpetual sleep " (Jr 51,39).

In Is 14,9-11, the king is addressed this way :

> Sheol beneath is in commotion,
> awaiting your arrival ;
> He (Sheol) arouses the shades because of you,
> all the leaders of the earth ;
> He raises from their thrones
> all the kings of the earth.
> All of them begin to speak and say to you :
> " You, too, you have become weak as we,
> like us you have become !
> Your eminence is brought down to Sheol,
> the sound of your harps ;
> a bed of maggots is spread beneath you,
> and worms are your covering !... "

Here, in spite of their confessed weakness, the shades are patently not totally passive ; they react in a human way. It is, however, hard to tell how far the poet took this as literal truth himself. Again we see that OT conceptions of the nether world are hardly consistent ;

([49]) Dahood, *Psalms* 181, 183.
([50]) Dahood, *Psalms* 295 ; above, p. 78.
([51]) Milton, *PL* 1 : 279 f.

are we to imagine the lamented king in his gruesome bed while his colleagues are sitting on their thrones?

The relation described between the grave and the nether world is very remarkable also within the OT. The king is admitted into the company of the other deceased kings; he has become " like one of them " ([52]).

5.4   The multiple negation

As, among others, H. Renckens has remarked, Gn 1 tries to represent chaos by drawing a negative picture of the cosmos, and the naught as the reverse image of the existing world: thus an idea of chaos is obtained by subtracting all that is positive, well arranged, and good from well-known reality ([53]).

Along the same *via negationis* the condition of the dead in their abode is often described in the OT.

5.4.1   No possessions

An Egyptian harpers' song reads: " Behold, nobody is allowed to take his possessions with him. Behold, there is nobody who has gone, who has returned " ([54]).

Ps 49 considers the value of wealth and pleasure in the light of the beyond. Verses 17 f. run:

> Be not envious when a man grows rich,
> when the wealth of his house increases;
> For when he dies, nothing he will take,
> his wealth will not descend with him ([55]).

A Dutch consolation for the poor just: in a windingsheet there are no pockets! The theme returns in Jb 15,29, where the same problem is under discussion:

> 28   He will dwell in ruined cities,
>   Tenantless houses will be his,
>   Which are ready to go to heaps.
> 29   He will not be rich, nor his wealth endure,
>   Nor his possessions reach the nether world.
> 30   He will not escape from darkness.... (Pope)

([52]) See further above, pp. 181 f.
([53]) H. Renckens, *Israels visie* 45 f. (German translation, 49 f.).
([54]) Zandee, 55.
([55]) Dahood, *Psalms* 296; see Ps 39,7.

There are three allusions to the nether world in this fragment: "ruins" ([56]), "darkness" ([57]), and *'rṣ*, which in this connection quite naturally stands for "underworld" ([58]). As to Hebrew *mnlm*, this is compared with Arabic *manal* by Zorell ([59]); Pope interprets the final *-m* as a enclitic, which follows the possessive suffix ([60]).

5.4.2   No memory

The dead lose their memory: they lose their historical individuality and are reduced to the impersonal archetype of the "forefather". Thus this well-known motif in the history of religions is explained by M. Eliade ([61]). Its echoes are heard in the OT as well; Ps 88,13 reads:

> Shall thy wondrous works be known in the dark: and they righteousness in the land where all things are forgotten? (RP)

Parallelism strongly suggests that RP's paraphrase of "land of forgetfulness" is a correct one. God does not work wonders for the dead (Ps 88,11), nor is there memory of his wondrous works among them: the connections have been severed ([62]). The dead are altogether forgotten, says Qohelet (9,5): they simply are absent, out of sight and out of mind ([63]).

5.4.3   No knowledge

There is a tradition according to which the dead are Elohim, disposing of a knowledge hidden from common mortals. As necromantic practice shows, this conception was deeply rooted in popular belief ([64]).

It is hardly orthodox, however.

A more pessimistic view appears in Job and Qohelet. Job 14,21 runs:

([56]) Ruins, see above, pp. 72 ff.

([57]) Darkness, above, pp. 142 ff.

([58]) Cf. above, p. 42; Dahood, *Job* 60 f.

([59]) *Lexicon* 450A *m^eⁿōlām*: "possessio eorum".

([60]) Dahood, *Job* 112; see also Sir 11,18 f.

([61]) *Mythe* 78; Zandee, 63, A.4.O.

([62]) Schottroff, *Die Wurzel zkr in A.T.* 184: "Aufhören des Lebensbezuges".

([63]) *Ibid.* 292; Barth, *Errettung* 64; see also Qoh 1,11 and 2,16.

([64]) Dt 18,11; 1 S 28; 2 K 21,6; 23,24; Is 8,19; 29,4; 54,4. Cf. above, p. 178.

His (the dead's) sons achieve honor, but he never knows;
They are disgraced, but he perceives not. (Pope)

And in 21,21 Job confesses:

What cares he for his family after him,
When his quota of months is spent?

The same fact is attested by Psalm 49,21 in more general terms:

Man in the Mansion will nothing sense, become
like beasts that cease to be. (Dahood)

Indeed, in Sheol there is black negativity only:

There is no work or account or knowledge
or wisdom in Sheol (Qoh 9,10) ([65]).

5.4.4 No joy

Jesus Sirach summarizes all these negative statements about the
nether world, where he repeats Qohelet's *carpe diem*: " Give and
take, yea, indulge thy soul; For in Sheol there is no delight " (14,16) ([66]).

5.4.5 No return

Everybody returns to the nether world, but nobody returns from
it. The latter truth is found in prose also. After his child's death,
David groan: " Now he is dead; why should I fast? Can I bring him
back again? I shall go to him, but he will not return to me " (2 S
12,23). As the king is unable to bring back his son, he cannot do
anything at all for him; compare 2 Mc 12,43 ff. Sheol is the " Land
of No Return "; although the OT knows the conception of the nether
world as a womb, it stubbornly rejects the optimistic consequence
that death is identical with potential life ([67]). Death is irrevocable;
this thought is prominent in the book of Job:

([65]) For *ḥešbôn*, " account ", see Dahood, " ULex, " p. 89 *sub* 990. For
Jb 36,12 see p. 150.

([66]) R. H. Charles, *The Apocrypha and Pseudepigrapha of the Old Testament* I (Oxford 1913) 368 (H: " no seeking of delight " = G), cp. Sir 38,21.

([67]) For this concept in Egypt see Kristensen, *Leven uit den dood* 7-36;
in Greece, *ibid.* 227 ff.; in Mesopotamia, see Tallqvist, *Namen der Totenwelt* 15 f.

— The way of no return I go (16,22, cp. Prv 2,19)
— Let me smile awhile
Before I go, never to return,
To a land of darkness and gloom (10,22).
— He that goes down to Sheol...
returns to his house no more (7,9 f.) ([68]).

5.4.6   No end

If nobody comes back from Sheol, man remains there for ever:
They will sleep a perpetual sleep,
and not wake, says Yahweh (Jr 51,39).

Jb 14,12 reads:

Man lies down and never rises.
They rouse not from their sleep. (Pope)

The same thought may be found in Jb 16,22:

For years beyond counting will come,
and I will go the way of no return.

In this case *mspr* is vocalised *miss^epor*, which seems the obvious solution for the interpretation of this line ([69]).   In this interpretation, the parallelism is synonymous.   The same theme is alluded to by Qohelet, who contrasting " darkness " with " life " writes:

... let him remember that the days of darkness will be many (11,8).

5.5   Two limitative negations

5.5.1   No torture

Sheol is the reign of negativity, the triumph of chaotic forces over life and order; death is the summation of all evil.   It is therefore the worst disaster which can happen to man; it is the negation of all that is good, attractive, and desirable.

The thought of premature death fills the Israelite with great horror ([70]) and his urgent desire for life without end, for the acces-

---

([68]) Cp. Jb 14,21 (above, pp. 188 f.). In Ez 26,20 we read *tāšubî* so that the same theme appears there; see p. 68, n. 215.

([69]) For *min*, " beyond, above ", see *BDB* 582 ff. See Jb 15,20.

([70]) R. Taylor wrote (*Ephemerides Theologicae Lovanienses* 42 [1966] 80):

sibility to the tree of life, does not come true. Most descriptions of Sheol are borrowed from the grave, as noticed again and again in this study. By way of example the " bed of worms " may be mentioned (Is 14,11) ; it returns in a late text, Is 66,24, where the worms serve to show the punitive character of the condition described :

> And they shall go forth and look on the dead bodies of the men that have rebelled against me ; for their worm shall not die, their fire shall not be quenched, and they shall be an abhorrence to all flesh ([71]).

The " fire " mentioned in this text does not belong to the classical description of the nether world ([72]), but it quite fortunately illustrates the new significance which Sheol has in this text : Sheol has become Hell, the instrument of God's wrath, where the wicked are punished for their sins. For this phenomenon, the traditional representation of God's ire is to be kept in mind ; see Ps 21,10 which looks like a transitional stage in this evolution :

> You put them as into a blazing furnace,
> at the time of your fury, O Yahweh !
> In his wrath he engorged them,
> and his fire devoured them ([73]).

The imagery of this verse is very pregnant ; it is a suggestive example of the development found in the Hebrew use of words and images concerning Sheol. On the one hand this " blazing oven " is reminiscent of later Hell ; on the other hand the use of bl^c suggests that Yahweh has adopted a characteristic trait of Sheol ([74]). Yahweh appropriates a quality of Death ; the fire, currently an expression of his anger, becomes also the instrument of his wrath, chastisement which is inflicted in Hell on those who resisted his holy will.

As to the use of pouring libations into the grave, this also shows

"Ideally death could be considered in the Old Testament as a well-deserved peace ". This statement seems exaggerated ; all we can say is that normal death, the end of a long life, was generally accepted as a natural phenomenon in Israel.

([71]) Worms : Sir 7,17 ; 10,11 ; 19,3 ; fire : Jud 16,21 ; Sir 21,9.

([72]) Dahood, *Psalms* 130 ; cp. Ps 78,21.50 ; 79,5 ; Am 7,4-6, etc.

([73]) But see Ps 140,11a.

([74]) Above, pp. 125 ff. ; Dahood. *Psalms* 134, Related imagery in Ps 37,20. Cp. Jb 20,26 : " An unfanned flame shall consume him " (parallel : total darkness ; translation by Pope) ; Jb 15,30.

that the traditional thirst of the dead derives from the same
" source " (⁷⁵). An Egyptian text attests the same fact. The dead man
is unable to drink and therefore suffers thirst though he is in the deep
waters : " I am thirsty, though there is water on my side " (⁷⁶). The
Babylonians also call the nether world " the field of thirst ", and according to Gaster the same motif is found in Is 5,13. Here the people
who " run after strong drink, who tarry late into the evening, till
wine inflames them " (v. 11) are threatened with the words :

> Therefore my people go into exile for want of knowledge ;
> their honoured men are dying of hunger,
> and their multitude is parched with thirst.

Certainly the thought of final disaster is not far away in this
text, and the sway of approaching Death makes itself felt in this need,
but that is about all that can be said. In fact the following verse
suggests that Death's appetite is aroused by this languor of the people ;
the poet with subtle irony sets the hunger and thirst of the displaced
Israelites on a par with the appetite of Sheol. This, however, hardly
proves that the thirst of death is meant in v. 13 ; at most this want
is the herald of " perpetual thirst " to be suffered in Sheol (⁷⁷).
    With more probability the thirst of the dead is found in Jr 17,13 :

> Those that turn away from the shall be enrolled in hell, for
> they have forsaken Yahweh, the fountain of living water (⁷⁸).

In other words : abandoning the Lord implies being delivered to the
perpetual thirst of the nether world, which cannot be assuaged by the
libations poured into the grave. The theme is resumed by our Lord,
when He says :

(⁷⁵) For Ugaritic evidence, see van Selms, *Marriage* 102 ; Gray, *Canaanites*
116 ; for Israel see Maag in Schmökel, *Kulturgesch.* 568 ; *id.*, "Tod und Jens".
21 (Sir 30,18 Gr.) ; Noth, *Die Welt des AT* 134 ff. See Eliade, *Traité* 175-177.
    (⁷⁶) Zandee, 67, A.5.b ; cp. 5.d-e.
    (⁷⁷) Gaster, *Thespis* 204 n. Allusions to thirst we found in Ps 63,2 and
143,6 ; see also Ps 22,16 in its general context and 102,5.12.
    (⁷⁸) Interpreting *miqwê* as " pool " (*GB* 455B) and deriving *yēbōšû* from
ybš, Dahood obtains a consistent metaphor throughout the verse : " The pool
of Israel is Yahweh, all who abandon Him will surely wither. Those who turn
from Him... ". Severing -*k* from ʿōzᵉbê and reading it as emphatic *ki*, Dahood
interprets the -*y* ending of both participles as a third person sg. suffix (see
Phoenician). Indeed, the shift from second to first, and then to third person
is troublesome.

If any one thirst, let him come to me,
and let him who believes in me drink.   As the scripture has
said, " out of his heart shall flow rivers of living water "
(John 7,37 f.).

A source of water, symbol of divine life, will spring up in the
faithful and thus fulfil man's desire for immortal life :

Whoever drinks of the water that I shall give him will never
thirst ; the water that I shall give him will become in him
a spring of water welling up to eternal life (John 4,14) (⁷⁹).

In some texts belonging to the area of our research there is talk
of corporeal pain in Sheol.   Both the phrasing of these texts and the
general tendency of descriptions of conditions in the nether world
suggest that this also is a transposition of ideas, at home in the sphere
of the grave, to the beyond : according to Jb 14,22, man after his
death does not know about the fate of his sons ;

Only his own flesh pains him,
And his own soul mourns itself. (Pope)

And Jb 18,13 pictures this fate thus :

His skin is gnawed by disease ;
Death's first-born feeds on his limbs. (Pope)

A third category of texts considers the evils of after-life as pro-
longations of the vicissitudes of this life ; besides, the dead remain
in substantially the same status they occupied on earth (⁸⁰).   The
latter statement should not be generalized : it cannot be applied
to texts according to which people go down to Sheol " in sorrow ",
" mourning ", " not in peace " (⁸¹). These expressions apparently bear
upon the way a man dies ; they are opposed to a peaceful death, in old
age, when one is full of days (⁸²).   This is vital for a correct understanding of the phrase : " they go down alive into Sheol " (⁸³).   Cor-

(⁷⁹) See note a) in the *La Sainte Bible* traduite... sous la direction de l'École
Biblique de Jérusalem, p. 1402.
(⁸⁰) E.g., see 1 S 28,14 ; Is 14,9 ; Ez 32,27. A different conception in Jb
3,13-19, where the fundamental equality of all men in death is stressed.
(⁸¹) Gn 42,38 ; 37,35 ; 1 K 2,6.
(⁸²) Gn 35,29 ; 1 C 29,28, etc.
(⁸³) Nu 16,30.

nelius a Lapide interpreted the expression in this way, that Dathan *cum suis* arrived living in the abode of the dead, and Sutcliffe dryly remarks they must have been dead after the earth closed its mouth ! ([84]) Obviously the phrase means : " They die in full vigour ".

The third category of texts, alluded to above, is happily illustrated by Is 5,14, as interpreted by G. R. Driver : " Their splendid ones ... shall go down and suffer pangs therein " (i.e., in Sheol). Driver correctly comments that this does not mean punishment after death, which is a more recent idea, but " a mere continuation of the consequences of surfeit on earth into the next world ; as they were here, so they shall be there " ([85]).

5.5.2 No annihiliation

Water is the domain of the " non formé ", water remains in the sphere of the virtual, water precedes any form, Eliade writes ([86]). And about Gn 1,2 Renckens says : this is the " plastische Darstellung des absoluten Nichts " ([87]).

In view of the essential affinities between chaos and the nether world we may ask if biblical statements about Sheol do not imply the idea of the annihilation of the dead. It might seem that the minimalism, the utter negativity of these descriptions are a primitive attempt to picture the Nothing the dead are reduced to.

Other indications seem to support this interpretation. At the end of his first speech, Job sighs :

> ... now I shall lie in the Dust ;
> and Thou wilt seek me, but I shall not be (7,21).

Here, however, " to be " has definitely not the metaphysical meaning we are inclined to understand by it : it rather denotes an existence worth while living, a way of being which constitutes a human value. " To be " means to be living on earth, where happiness is within reach. Just as " das biblische Sein ist ein lebendiges, effektives Sein, ein wahrnehmbares Dasein " ([88]), so " '*ēn* sometimes denotes : he is not

---

([84]) Sutcliffe, *The OT and Future Life* 23.

([85]) G. R. Driver, in : J. Hempel, *Von Ugarit bis Qumran*, *BZAW* 77 (Berlin 1958) 43 ; '*lz* is interpreted according to its basic sense " quivering, vibrating " (cp. Prv 23,16 ; 1 Mc 2,24) which can apply both to pain and joy. For Jb 18,14 see pp. 119 f.

([86]) *Mythe* 26 ; *Images* 199 f.

([87]) *Urgeschichte u. Heilsgesch* 75 (Dutch text 70).

([88]) Renckens, 75 ; T. Boman, *Das hebräische Denken* 43 ff.

present " ([89]).   This is illustrated by Jb 7,8 where the words " ... the eyes are upon me, but I am no more ", are explained in the following statement :

> A cloud fades and vanishes :
> so he who goes down to Sheol does not come up any more ([90]).

So searching eyes will be unable to find Job, because he disappeared into the darknesses of the nether world, not because he simply stopped being.   A dead man " departs and is no more " (Ps 39,14).   That *'ênennû* has this purely relative content is shown beyond any doubt by Jb 23,8, where it is applied to God and where parallelism is to be noted :

> Behold, I go forward, but He is not ;
> and backward, but I cannot perceive Him.

A similar parallelism is found in Ps 37,36 :

> He passed away and, lo, he was no more ;
> I sought him, but he could not be found. (Dahood)

Compare Jb 20,7 f. :

> He shall perish forever like dung ;
> They who saw him will say : " where is he ? "
> Like a dream he flies, none can find him ... ([91]). (Pope)

As remarked before : " The dead lose their memory ; they lose their historical individuality and are reduced to the impersonal archetype of the forefather " ([92]).   For the archaic mentality, however, this does not mean that there is no personal survival, for the archetype as extra-temporal event is in fact the only and fundamentally real pheno-menon ([93]).

In other cases it is to be kept in mind that descriptions of Sheol were on a large scale borrowed from the grave ; the corruption and ruin they refer to in fact apply to the corpse.   Quite a few other elements point to an ancient belief in immortality : see the possibility

---

([89]) Dahood, *Psalms* 117. See Gen 5,24.
([90]) Cp. Wisd 2,4.
([91]) Cp. Jb 24,24 ; 27,19 ; Dhorme, *Job* 100.
([92]) Above, p. 188.
([93]) Eliade, *Mythe* 78 f.

of revival and resurrection, however exceptional, in the early period, and burial customs (gifts and libations) ([94]).

5.6   The impact of Yahwism

5.6.1   Yahweh and Death

" Zu den am längsten beiseite geschobenen und darum vom Jahwä-glauben lange nicht durchgestalteten kanaanäischen Elementen gehören die Vorstellungen von Tod und postmortalem Dasein ". " Und.. nach der Einschmelzung der kanaanäischen Bauernbevölkerung in den israelitischen Volkskörper ... war die Antwort : Jahwä hat nichts damit zu tun und will nichts damit zu tun haben " ([95]). In other words : the OT has " no formal doctrine concerning the destination and fate of the dead ; all that it says on the subject belongs to the domain of popular lore " ([96]). No doubt myth is broken also here in the OT ; but it survives in as far as it is " ahnendes, dichterisch eingeklei-detes Begreifen des Göttlichen und der Welt " ([97]). Death and Beyond belong to the realities " which can be understood and expressed in a mythical-symbolical way only " ([98]). This is hardly a secondary and inferior kind of knowledge ; " It is not like this, that I ' properly ' mean a concept, when I use an image, but rather the reverse : when I apply a concept, I properly and originally mean an image, a living ' mythical ' reality ... The whole world of the abstract concept exists by grace of the imagination only " ([99]).

In fact this type of knowing is necessary here ; Death and Beyond are realities which present themselves in contrasting ways they consequently cannot be expressed fully in concepts ([100]).

([94]) See Noth, *Die Welt des AT* 134 ff. ; Heidel, 150-156 ; for immortality, Dahood, *Psalms*, index 326.

([95]) Maag, " Tod und Jens. " 17.

([96]) Gaster, *IDB* I, 787A.

([97]) L. Rademacher, quoted by A. Anwander, *Zum Problem des Mythos* 37.

([98]) O. Casel, *Glaube, Gnosis, Mysterium* (1941) 124. A " demythologiza-tion ", i.e., a removal of characteristically primitive thinking (which considers existence and phenomena of this world to be utterly dependent replicas of a kind of perpetually present primordial events, taking place outside our time and space and being represented in sacred rites) is imperative ; but " demythi-sation ", which would try to take away all symbols from our speaking, is impossible. For the terminology : P. Barthel, *Interprétation de language mythique et théologie biblique...* (Leiden 1963). For mythology and Death in the Psalter see the balanced exposition of C. Barth in his *Einführung Pss*, 56-62, esp. 61 f.

([99]) v.d. Leeuw, *Primitieve Mensch* 98.

([100]) Eliade, *Images* 17.

5.6.1.1 Yahweh's might

In a way Yahwism during the greatest part of the OT period kept aloof from Sheol, which was " ein aussergöttliches Bereich " ([101]). This statement, however, should be specified, for this very " dediviniz- ation " is due to the influence of Yahwism and consequently implies some degree of penetration of Yahweh into the former reign of Mot. Although the historical development cannot be traced here, we can safely say that Gunkel's statement is too general and consequently false, where it refers to " (Israelitisches Denken), wonach Jahwes Macht nicht in die Unterwelt reicht " ([102]).

We think that the situation is less inadequately expressed by Y. Kaufmann, who writes : " To be sure, JHWH rules Sheol, yet there is no relation between him and the dead " ([103]). In other words : Sheol is not beyond Yahweh's power, but in fact it is beyond his saving activity as unfolded in history. Yahweh has full control over Sheol as well as over death and life. As to the latter, the true Israelite knows that death is in God's hands : the Lord only can give this solu- tion, when man feels unable to cope with life any longer. A sorely tried Moses prays :

> I am not able to carry all this people alone, the burden is too heavy for me. If Thou wilt deal thus with me, kill me

---

([101]) Maag, " Tod u. Jens. " 20.

([102]) *Psalmen*[4] 94. There are traces of dualism in the OT. According to Ps 49,16 God will pay a ransom to Sir Death ; this colon shows at least that the Israelite reckoned with the possibility of a ransom being paid by Yahweh to Death (Barth, *Errettung* 135) : strictly speaking the verb *pdh* stresses the payment of purchase-money (*ibid.* 134). This would imply a certain dualism. (Other occurrences of *pdh npš* may have a similar connotation of deliverance from death, though the person (or situation) one is taken from is not men- tioned : see Ps 34,24 cp. death in v. 23 ; Ps 71,23 cp. nether world in v. 20.) Vriezen (*Hoofdlijnen der Theologie van het Oude Testament* [2nd ed. ; Wagenin- gen 1954] 203) sees traces of a dualism in Ps 115,17 (the dead do not praise Yahweh) ; and indeed it is only logical to suppose that the radical separ- ation between Yahweh and the dead implied his being impotent in this re- gard. God's attitude as described in the OT can be defined as a neutral one : Yahweh's power is unlimited, but *de facto* He does not normally exercise it in favour of the deceased. Possibly the latter idea is a later mitigation of Yahweh's former limited authority over Sheol. We do not dispose of sufficient evidence to trace the historical development and the existence of divergent opinions in early Judaism. For Ps 88,6 see below, pp. 201 f.

([103]) Y. Kaufmann – M. Greenberg, *The Religion of Israel*. From Its Be- ginnings to the Babylonian Exile (2nd ed. ; Chicago–London 1963) 314.

> at once, if I find favour in thy sight, that I may not see my
> wretchedness (Nu 11,14 f.; E).

Here weariness of life does not lead to an attempt at suicide, but
to a prayer to the Master of Life and Death.

The same sentiment is expressed by Elijah in 1 K 19,4 (surroundings of E) [104]:

> But he himself went a day's journey into the wilderness
> and he came and sat down under a broom tree; and he asked
> that he might die, saying: " It is enough; now, O Lord, take
> away my life... ".

The prophet knows no way out but the one God offers. " In solchen
Abgründen der Verzweifelung gibt es nur den Weg den Gott eröff-
net " [105].

This belief finds its classical expression in the words of Hannah:

> Yahweh kills and brings to life;
> He brings down to Sheol and raises up (1 S 2,6).

As Sheol and Death refer to a situation of diminished life, this text
should not be understood as referring to resurrection, or transposition
into an eternal life [106].   In fact its tenor is explained in other texts;
Ps 68,21, most likely very ancient, reads: " With Yahweh, the Lord,
is escape from Death. "

The thought often returns in the Psalter; e.g., in Ps 33,17 f.:

> Mark well: The eye of Yahweh
>   is on those who fear Him,
>   on those who rely on his kindness,
> To rescue them from Death,
>   to preserve their lives from the Hungry One [107].
>   (Dahood)

Ps 16,10 expressed a less common conviction. " The psalmist ... is
convinced that God will assume him to himself, without suffering the
pains of death " (cp. Ps 49,16; 73,24) [108].   The verse runs:

[104] Th. C. Vriezen, *De Literatuur van Oud-Israel* 146.
[105] Von Rad, Seminar University Heidelberg, 11.2.1966.
[106] Cp. Maag, " Tod u. Jens. " 24 f.
[107] See also Jb 33,28; 30,23.
[108] Dahood, *Psalms* 91.

.. You will not put me in Sheol,
nor allow your devoted one to see the Pit. (Dahood)

Sheol also acts as the excutioner, appointed by Yahweh:

But if the Lord creates something new, and the " ground "
opens its mouth, and swallows them up ..., and they go down
alive into Sheol, then you shall know that these men have
despised the LORD ([109]). (RSV)

Job is provoked by Yahweh to prove his right to discuss with God
by an act of divine power:

Bury them (the proud an wicked ones) in the dust together;
Bind them in the infernal crypt ([110]). (Pope)

So Yahweh is Lord and Master of Sheol; His are the keys of the nether
world; " he shall open, and none shall shut; and he shall shut, and
none shall open " (Is 22,22).

Ps 139,8 runs:

If I ascend to heaven, thou art there!
If I make Sheol my bed, thou art there!

This verse is commonly understood as referring to Yahweh's omni-
presence. This, however, can hardly be correct. Old Testament
Sheol is a region of death and darkness, just because Yahweh is not
there. The living God and the abode of the dead essentially exclude
each other; just as the fullness of life implies the presence of Yahweh,
so the stay in Sheol connotes his absence ([111]). Sheol is Sheol because
the living God is not there ([112]). It is clear that this conception creates
a theological problem: it looks like a restriction of Yahweh's omnipotence and so a menace to monotheism.

As to Ps 139, here the psalmist, accused of idolatry, confesses his

[109] Nu 16,30. Cp. Is 5,14; Prv. 22,14.
[110] Jb 40,13; for Jb 12,22, cp. above, p. 143.
[111] With Maag we can say " dass, sofern alles Leben von Jahwäs Gegenwart ausgeht, jede Abwendung ... Gottes vom Menschen diesen der Seinsweise
des Toten ausliefert " (" Tod u. Jens. " 25).
[112] Barth, *Errettung* 41-44; G. von Rad, " Gerechtigkeit und Leben "
428-437.

belief that he is unable to escape the God of Israel [113].   In Maag's words : " Diese Texte (Ps 139 and Am 9,2) reden von der Unentrinn-barkeit des lebenden (!) Menschen gegenüber Jahwä " [114].   Both Heaven and Sheol stand here " bildlich ... um ein vollendetes Versteck zu bezeichnen " [115].   The psalmist confesses : whereever I go, I can-not escape you ; I can hide myself where I like, I will not be hidden for you.   This meristic phrase should not be taken literally, it appar-ently is a " stylistic survival ", used for its vivacity and expressivity [116]. In fact quite a few of these phrases are found in the OT and outside it.   Pope quotes " The dialogue of Pessimism ", an Akkadian poem, where we read :

> Who is tall (enough) to ascend to heaven ?
> Broad (enough) to compass the nether world ? [117].

And Kroll quotes a similar phrase, in El Amarna texts applied to a king :

> " Ob wir aufsteigen zum Himmel,
> ob wir niederfahren zur Hölle :
> so ist unser Haupt in deinen Händen "

And he comments that in Ps 139 " Stilzwang antithetisscher Formu-lierung (ist) ... viel wichtiger als eine bewusste Absicht, die Allmacht des Gottes zu umschreiben " and characterizes the formula as " Pathos-formel " [118].   Kroll then quotes several similar phrases occurring in the OT, which he labels " pathetische Formulierung der Allmacht Gottes " [119].

The correctness of this judgment is illustrated by Jb 26,6 as com-mented upon by 26,14 :

> 6   Naked is Sheol before Him,
> Perdition has no cover.

---

[113] See E. Würthwein, " Erwägungen zu Psalm CXXXIX " (*VT* 7 [1957] 165-182) 173.   Moreover he writes : " Es geht ... nicht um philosophischen Spe-kulationen über Allwissenheit und Allgegenwart Jahwes " (175).

[114] Maag, " Tod u. Jens. " 26.

[115] Fohrer on Jb 14,13 (p. 258).

[116] A. M. Honeyman, *JBL* 71 (1952) 17.

[117] Pope, *Job* LXIII (*ANET* 437 f.).

[118] J. Kroll, *Gott u. Hölle* 328 ; cp. Dt 30,12 f.

[119] *Ibid.* 330 ; he refers to Is 7,11 ; ... Ps 22,28 ; Jb 26,5 ; 14,13 ; Prv 15,11 ; see also Dt 32,22 ; Jb 34,22 ; 11,7.

14   Lo, these are but bits of his power ... ([120]).

In other words : where texts affirm that Yahweh fathoms Sheol, this should not be understood in our intellectualistic sense of knowing. When Yahweh knows Sheol, it is in his hands (Ps 95,4). The same statement can be made as to the relation between Yahweh and chaos : God is not there, but he controls it ([121]).

Now Ps 88,6b can be studied. It reads :

5b   I have become as a man without strength ;
6a   Among the dead is my couch,
       among the slain, lying in the grave ([122])
 b   whom you do not remember any more,
       but they are separated from your hand.

Although v. 6b immediately seems to apply to the " slain ", this probably is not essential for the interpretation, as their difference from other deceased is only gradual. The problem to be solved is the understanding of ' hand ' in this verse. In view of the tenor of the preceding section it very likely does not mean " power " ([123]). We will try to establish its meaning first by means of parallelism.

" Memory is not identified with the action, but it is never divorced from it " ([124]). So here " to remember " means a " tathaftes Eingehen der Gottheit auf den Menschen der sich in Not befindet " ([125]). God's *zkr* is " Aufnahme und Erhaltung des Lebenbezuges zwischen Jahweh und seinem Verehrer ([126]), it results in blessing and salvation. Consequently " not remembering " means " Aufhören des Lebensbezuges ". Schottroff then paraphrases the second colon in this way : they are separated from your " Machtsbereich ". And he quotes

---

([120]) Dhorme comments : " Dieu est partout, au Shéol comme aux cieux " (*Job* 339). Coppens' correction of this phrase is to the point : " More accurately, God's knowledge and omnipotence extend as far as the underworld " (" Men precisere : Gods kennis en almacht strekken zich tot de onderwereld uit ", *Onsterfelijkheidsgeloof* 26, n. 4). Würthwein (*VT* 7 [1957] 177) points to vs. 10 in this connection.

([121]) See Reymond, " L'eau ", and Gn 1,2.6-10 ; 7,11 ; 8,21 ; 9,11 ; Ps 36,7 ; 95,4 ; 135,6b ; 148,7.

([122]) See above, pp. 157 ff.

([123]) As often suggested ; Maag's " Hilfe " (" Tod u. Jens. " 26) looks like a solution *ad hoc*.

([124]) Childs, *Memory and Tradition in Israel* (London 1962) 33.

([125]) Schottroff, *Die Wurzel zkr* 191.

([126]) *Ibid.* 184 ; Childs, *op. cit.* 34.

von Rad, who, however, is essentially more prudent: " Die Toten standen ausserhalb des Kultus und seines Lebenskreises. Darin bessteht eigentlich ihr Totsein " [127]. Elsewhere the same author writes: " Der Tod beginnt da wirklich zu werden, wo Jahweh einen Menschen verlässt, wo er schweigt, also da, wo immer sich die Lebensbeziehung zu Jahweh lockerte " [128]. And further: " Die Toten stehen ausserhalb des Geschichtshandlens Jahwehs, und in diesen Ausgeschlossensein lag für Israel die eigentliche Bitterkeit des Todes " [129].

So v. 6a does not refer to Yahweh's power, but rather to his attitude towards the dead. They are out of view, out of mind. He does not remember them any more and here " remember " (as implying a lasting knowledge) may have the strong affective connotation of Hebrew " knowledge ". This tendency of v. 6a points to the interpretation of *yad* as " love, attachment ", a meaning it clearly has in Ugaritic texts. *UT* 51 : IV : 38 reads:

> Why, the love (*yd*) of El will take care of thee, the affection of (*ahbt*) of the Bull-God protect thee [130].

ʿnt : III : 3 f. runs thus:

> A feeling of affection (*yd*) for Pdraya ...
> of love (*ahbt*) for Ṭlaya ...
> of endearment (*dd*) for Arṣaya ... [131].

We think this meaning perfectly fits into verse 6:

> whom you do not remember any more,
> but they are severed from your love [132].

5.6.1.2 Yahweh Victor

Is 25,8 uses characteristic *blʿ* [133] to describe Yahweh's victory over Death: He will swallow Death up for ever.... In Ugaritic texts

---

[127] von Rad, *Theologie* I, 386.
[128] *Ibid.* 401.
[129] *Ibid.* 386 ; this is exactly the import of Ps 88,11-13.
[130] Translation from Gaster, *Thespis* 184 (Gordon, *UL* 32 ; Driver, *CMAL* 97).
[131] Translation from Gaster, *ibid.* 238 (*UL* 18 ; *CMAL* 87).
[132] " A cura tua " (*Liber Psalmorum cum Canticis Breviarii Romani*, ... a Professoribus Pontificii Instituti Biblici [Roma 1955] 175).
[133] Above *s.v.* Belial, pp. 125 ff. ; see Ps 21,10, p. 191.

Baal is often called " Victor " (*aliyn*) ; he is the god of life who over-comes his adversaries Mot and Sea (chaos).

> I knew that the victor Baal was alive,
> that the prince of the earth existed ([134]).
> " O Mot son of El, how canst thou fight
> with the victor Baal ? " ([135])
> The victor Baal is our king,
> our judge, and one above whom there is none ([136]).

Another derivative of the verb *l'y*, " to be strong, to prevail " ([137]) is *lan*, " strong " ([138]) ; it occurs in *UT* 127 : 13 f. : *š'tqt dm lan*, " Truly Shataqat was victorious ! "

The root also appears in Accadian and Phoenician. Harris mentions *l't*, " The Strong One " as an epithet of Istar and refers to biblical *l'h* (Leah) ([139]). Biblical Hebrew presents two derivatives of the root : *lē'ōn*, to be compared with Ugaritic *lan*, and *lē'*, " a stative participle, like *gēr*, or Ugaritic *ib*, foe " ([140]) Against the Ugaritic background it is not surprising, that both titles, applied to Yahweh, are often associated with questions of life and death. Relevant examples will be quoted here ([141]).

Hab 1,12   My holy God is the Victor over Death (*lē'ōn māwet*)
               Art thou not from everlasting Yahweh?

Ps 22,30c   *wnpš wl' ḥyh* : The Victor (*lē'*) himself restores to life.

Ps 85,7   You are the Victor (*hallē*), you will again revive us.

Jb 13,15   If the Victor (*lē'*) would slay me...

The victory of Yahweh not only means that Mot's power is a broken one, but also that it passed to Yahweh. The OT offers some interesting suggestions of this fact.

Ps 50,22 reads :

> Consider this well, you who forget God,. (Dahood)
> lest I snatch and there is none to rescue

([134]) 49 : III : 8 f. (Driver, 113).
([135]) 49 : VI : 24 f. (Driver, 115).
([136]) 51 : IV : 43 f. (Driver, 97).
([137]) *UT* Gloss. 1342 ; *WUS* 1430.
([138]) *WUS* 1430.
([139]) Z. Harris, *Grammar* 114.
([140]) Dahood, *Psalms* 144.
([141]) *Ibid.* 144 and 146.

TM: *pen-eṭrōp wᵉ'ên maṣṣîl*. Here we find two elements belonging to a *Wortfeld* which is strongly related to danger and death. A third element is the "lion"; the complete set is found four times in the OT, in the literary genres individual lament, threat, and *Unheilsprophetie* which are closely allied.

Ps 7,3, containing a reference to Death, runs:

> Rescue me lest he tear apart (*ṭrp*) like a lion
> rending my neck with none to rescue me. (Dahood)

So also Hos 5,14; Is 5,29 (subject Yahweh); Mi 5,7. Ps 22,13 shows the Lion and *ṭrp*. The phrase *'ên maṣṣîl* occurs also in Dt 32,39; Is 42,22; Jb 5,4; 10,7. By way of conclusion we remark that the *Wortfeld* is more naturally to be expected with Death than with Yahweh; in fact it is found with widely different subjects in the OT (the enemies in Is 5; the Remnant in Mi 5, which, however, reflects a later use of the phrase also in as far as it is in a Heilsprophetie). The correspondance between Ps 7,3 (subject: Death) and Ps 50,22 and Hos 5,14 (subject: Yahweh) is at least striking for the relation between Yahweh and Mot [142].

In Hab 3,5 Yahweh appears as an ancient oriental god, accompanied by two servants, one before and one after him [143]; these demythologized demons [144] are *dbr* and *ršp* (the latter is a well-known inferior god):

> Before Him Pestilence marched,
> and Plague went forth at His feet [145].

Both demons belonged to the sphere of Death. In Accadian incantations persecution is one of the favourite occupations of demons [146]. The Angel of Yahweh has a similar task in Ps 35,5:

[142] We saw before that the "lion" not rarely appears in connection with Death. If the *Wortfeld* originally was proper to Death, it is not surprising that in Israel it was used of Yahweh in the threats.

[143] For parallels see Gaster, *Thespis* 157 f. note.

[144] E.g., cp. K. Elliger, *Buch der zwölf kleinen Propheten* II. *Die Propheten Nahim, Habakuk. Zephanja, Haggai, Sacharja, Maleachi* (ATD 25;; Göttingen 1951) 49 and above, pp. 162 f.

[145] Translation by Albright, in Rowley (editor), *Studies in OT Prophecy* 12.

[146] Cp. Falkenstein – von Soden, *Hymnen* B 49: 11 (p. 312); B 67: 5 f. (p. 340); B 70,8; (p. 345).

Let their destiny be Darkness and Destruction,
with the angel of Yahweh pursuing them. (Dahood)

In Ps 66,11 Yahweh handles nets, elsewhere so popular among Death
and demons. Similarly Jb 19,6 ([147]). Moreover Yahweh is equipped
with the arrow, the characteristic weapon of Resheph, another god of
the nether world ([148]).

In Lam 2,4 Yahweh also hurls his fire, another weapon of Resheph,
at his enemies:

He has bent his bow like an enemy,
with his right hand set like a foe; ...
he has poured out his fury like a fire ([149]). (RSV)

Fohrer correctly concludes: " Das Bild von Jahwe als einem Bogen-
schützen rührt aus mythologisch-dämonologischen Vorstellungen her.
Wenn Gott in dieser Gestalt Krankheit und Unheil sendet, wird ihm
eine Funktion übertragen, die in älterer Zeit den Dämonen oder
bestimmten Göttern zugeschrieben wurde. Vor allem ist der Syrische
Gott Resef mit dem Pfeil ... zu nennen, der als Pest- und Kriegsgott
ein Bogenschütze ist (vgl. auch Ps 76,4) " ([150]).

5.6.1.3 Yahweh Rock

The cosmic mountain is a well-known phenomenon in the history
of religions. It is the centre of the universe, starting-point of creation,
highest place in the world, *axis mundi*, connecting heaven and nether
world. It signifies the victory of cosmos over the chaotic forces of
the nether world ([151]). " Rock " is applied to Yahweh, mainly in the
Psalter, in a sense closely related to some aspects of the cosmic mountain ([152]).

([147]) See above, p. 175.
([148]) See above, pp. 107 f. and 164.
([149]) Further Ps 38,3; 64,8; Jb 6,4; 7,20; 16,12 f.; Lam 3,12 f. For Dt
32,23 see above, pp. 107 f.
([150]) Fohrer, *Hiob* 169. A similar change takes place when Ps 42,8, etc.
refers to " Thy breakers ", as if Yahweh were the god of chaos and nether world.
([151]) M. Eliade, *Mythe* 33-37; Kristensen, *Leven uit den dood* 77-87; F. Heiler, *Erscheinungsformen und Wesen der Religion* 38.
([152]) For the relation between Yahweh and the Temple-rock, see H. Schmidt,
" Der heilige Fels in Jerusalem " (Tübingen 1934); H. W. Herzberg: " Der heilige Fels und das A. T. ", *JPOS* 12 (1932) 32-42 (= *Beiträge zur Traditions-
geschichte und Theologie des A.T.* [Göttingen 1962] 45-53). Cp. commentaries on Mt 16,18, e.g. de Vaux, *Les Institutions de l'Ancien Testament* II (Paris
1960) 157; Joh. Ringger, " Das Felsenwort ", in M. Roessle – O. Cullmann,

Most often there is a clear opposition with the quicksand of Sheol (cp. Ps 69,3), with waters, with death, and danger. Of course the occurrences are mainly found in individual laments, where danger is described in terms of death : see the first colon of Ps 78,34 :

34 When he killed them, they sought for him ;
    they repented and sought God earnestly.
35 They remembered that God was their rock,
    the most high God their redeemer.

The first colon is reminiscent of the use of " to die " in Ugaritic texts. In *UT* 68 : 1 a goddess (probably Anat) exclaims in despair : *yd* (.) *ḫtt.mtt*, " My power is broken ; I am finished ! " ([153])   In v. 35 parallelism is eloquent : where Yahweh is called " Rock " there the Israelite spontaneously seems to think " Rock of our Salvation " (Ps 95,1). Sometimes the texts suggest that the Temple-rock is meant ([154]) :

One thing I have asked a hundred times,
    Yahweh himself do I seek ([155]) :
To dwell in Yahweh's house
    all the days of my life,
Gazing upon the loveliness of Yahweh,
    awaking each dawn in his temple.
Indeed he will treasure me in his abode,
    after the evil day ;
He will shelter me in his sheltering tent,
    will set me high upon his mountain (*ṣûr*).
    Ps 27,4 f. (Dahood)

Perhaps also Ps 61,3 :

From the edge of the nether world I called to you
when my courage failed.
On a lofty rock you led me from it ([156]).

Begegnung der Christen. Fs. O. Karrer (Stuttgart – Frankfurt am Main 1960) 271-347, etc.

([153]) Cp. *CMAL* 13B ; Gaster, *Thespis* 160. See above, p. 136.

([154]) Barth, *Errettung* 137.

([155]) Cp. Dahood, *UHPh* 14 *sub* 8.3 ; reading *'ōtô* for TM *'ōtâ*. Dahood obtains a third person throughout in this verse. The balance of the two cola is evident.

([156]) Dahood, *Psalms* 260.

In other cases Yahweh is identified with the rock; here surrounding titles and descriptions should be noticed: Ps 18,3 ff. reads:

> Yahweh is my rock (*sl'*) and my fortress;
>   my deliverer is [my God,
> My mountain (*ṣûr*) where I take refuge:
>   my shield and my horn of salvation,
> My stronghold, worthy of praise.
> I called Yahweh,
>   and was saved from my Foe.
> The breakers of Death encompassed me....

Because in IL the enemies appear as the Archenemy, dangers as infernal dangers and distress as hellish distress, it is not surprising to find Yahweh-Rock opposed to the wicked pursuers of the just:

> ... save me!
> Be thou my rock and my refuge, that thou mayest preserve me:
> for thou art my strong rock and my castle.
> Deliver me O my God out of the hand of the ungodly ....
> (Yea, thou wilt bring me from the deep of the earth again
> (Ps 71, 3 f. 20) (RP).

The idea of the Miry Deep where one's feet find no hold, is on the threshold in Ps 62,3:

> He (God) only is my rock and my salvation,
>   my fortress: I shall not be greatly moved (*mṭ*) (157). (RSV)

5.6.2   The dead and Yahweh

Biblical evidence suggests that Sheol was not always considered unclean in Israel: in Gn 50,1, Joseph's corpse is kissed, Joshua is

---

(157) For *mṭ*, above pp. 92 f. a) On basis of *UT* 51 : II : 32 f. : *qḥ rṭt bdk / rbt 'l ydm* (" Take a net in thy hands, a large [mesh] in thy hands ", *Thespis* 178), Aistleitner (*WUS* 2482) translates *rbt* as " grosses Netz "; this might apply to *rabbâ* in Ps 62,3. In the present writer's opinion this is very uncertain; the meaning of *rbt* in *UT* 51 may entirely depend on parallelism, its general sense " a big one " being determined by parallel *rṭt* (Hebr, *ršt*). b) See also Ps 42,8-10; 89,26 f. It is not certain if our interpretation accounts for the use in texts like Dt 32,4.15.18.30.37. For *'ēl šadday*, see Frank Cross, Jr. " Yahweh and the God of the Patriarchs ", *HTR* 55 (1962) 225-259 (esp. 244 ff.); see also Dahood, *Psalms* 118.

interred in his house (^{158}) and according to Ezekiel the kings were buried near the temple until the exile (^{159}). So it seems that the uncleanness of the sphere of death is not an ancient conception. This is the more striking because at the same time all territory outside Israel was considered unclean: Yahweh could not be worshipped there (^{160}).

It would seem that this uncleanness originally was not a ritual one; it rather had a theological basis: Sheol was unclean, as it belonged to the sphere of demonic powers opposed to the only God of Israel (^{161}). Perhaps this fact obtained a special weight in Israel, because the dethronement of Death implies that his kingdom is reduced to chaos, which is dominated by demons.

Maag stresses the fact that in Ugarit the nether world belongs to the cosmic building (^{162}): this would explain how the dead could be considered as minor deities in an early period. The " disappearance " of Mot would imply the degradation of both his domain and his former subjects: they became chaotic, withdrawn from the true Creator-God, or, in other words, not consecrated, *ergo* unfit for cult (^{163}). " Das Heilige ... gründet ... die Welt " (^{164}). So ritual uncleanness immediately follows from the " theological " one.

(^{158}) 1 S 25,1; 1 K 2,34; Theoretically, " house " could stand for " grave " here (cp. *byt 'lm*); so indeed the recensio Luciana of the LXX. Archeology, however, establishes the practice of interring in the house (see J. A. Montgomery – H. S. Gehman, *Kings* [ICC; Edinburgh 1951] 95; Heidel, 160-166).

(^{159}) Ez 43,7; Stade, *Geschichte des Volkes Israel* I, 138 f.; A. van den Born, *Bijbels Woordenboek* 362, 1421.

(^{160}) 1 S 26,19; 2 K 15,27; Am 7,17; Ez 4,13; Ps 137,4 (Noth, *Geschichte Israels* 268).

(^{161}) L. E. Toombs, art. " Clean ", *IDB* I, 643 f.

(^{162}) V. Maag, " B^{e}lija'al im AT ", *TZ* 21 (1965) 296 f. " Trafen sich Totengott und Chaosungeheuer am gleichen gottfernen Ort, so verschmolzen sie dort zu einer Symboleinheit " (*ibid.* 298). Two supplementary remarks seem imperative: 1) Being cosmic powers, Ugaritic gods have no dealings whatsoever with the dead (see Cazelles, in: *Le Jugement des Morts* (Sources Orientales; Paris 1961) 103-142, esp. 106 f.); so it is hard to say what is to be understood by " Totengott " in Ugarit. 2) Time and again in this study this *Verschmelzung* appeared to be a universal phenomenon.

(^{163}) Compare Maag, " Tod u. Jens. " 18; Eliade, *Das Heilige* 18 ff.

(^{164}) Eliade, *ibid.* 18; in the Ugaritic Baal-cycle there is a clear distinction between Baal's struggle with Mot and with Yam; the latter only is chaotic, and his defeat means the victory of cosmic powers. For Gaster the overthrow of Yam also belongs to the myth which relates Baal's victory over Mot (*Thespis* 137 ff.); according to Maag (Schmökel, 579) the latter is part of the " Vegetationsmythus ", the former the " Drachenkampf " belonging to the Creation

Then the uncleanness of the nether world may also be used as a weapon against the cult of the dead ([165]). As a consequence of these views other ideas may have developed. The dead are far from the loving-kindness of Yahweh and consequently far from his saving activity. They feel oppressed by his anger, do not even remember his past benefits any more:

> Dost thou work wonders for the dead:
> or shall the dead raise up again and praise thee?
> Shall thy loving-kindness be told in the grave:
> or thy faithfulness in the pit of destruction?
> Shall thy wondrous works be known in the dark
> and thy righteousness in the land where all things are for-
> [gotten? (Ps 88,11-13) (RP)

The psalmist knows: as long as there is life, there is hope; after death there is no hope whatever, no hope of return, no hope of Yahweh's intervention. Without contesting Yahweh's power, the psalmist expresses his conviction that *de facto* Yahweh will not intervene any more ([166]). It seems, however, that to reinforce his appeal, he pictures the situation in Sheol in the darkest colours he disposes of. Where, in Ps 6,6, the psalmist complains:

> ... no one in Death remembers you,
> in Sheol, who praises you?

parallelism makes it clear that " the problem arises from the failure of the dead to share in the praise of Yahweh which characterizes Israel's worship "; " he suffers not because of the inability to *remember* Yahweh in death " ([167]).

Here we have to confess our ignorance; we do not know if this " no memory, no knowledge " tradition was an independent trend, existing next to a less gloomy one, or is just an expression of sentiment (it is found in Job, Qohelet, and Ps 88) ([168]). This question may more often be asked in view of the different conceptions, studied in

---

Myth. The *Drachenkampf* left clear traces in Psalter and Prophecy; vestiges of the *Vegetations mythus* are less certain in the OT.

([165]) Rendtorff, *RGG*[3] V; 942.

([166]) Von Rad, *Theologie* I, 386; Maag writes: " Der Sterbende (musste) nicht nur von dieser Welt und seiner gewohnten Umgebung, sondern auch von seinem Gott Abschied nehmen " (" Tod u. Jens. " 20).

([167]) Childs, *Memory and Trad.* 71.

([168]) See Rowley, in *From Moses to Qumran* (London 1964) 179.

this dissertation.   Moreover the historical development, which might be another explanation for this *Nebeneinander*, remains very obscure throughout our study.

But this much is certain : " *Nur* dort, wo Tod ist, gibt es Lob nicht.   Wo Leben ist, gibt es Lob.... Wo der Tod characterisiert ist darurch, dass es in ihm nicht mehr das Loben gibt, so gehört zum Leben das Loben.... Wirkliches Leben kann es ohne das Loben nicht geben [169].   The cruel darkness after death was not suppressed in Israel.   The remembrance of death remained living among these people.   " There is no practice which so intensifies life.   Death, when it approaches, ought not to take one by surprise.   It should be part of the full expectancy of life.   Without an ever-present sense of death life is insipid " [170].   We may conclude that Israel's passionate concern with death is a symptom of its passionate experience of life.

[169] Westermann, *Loben Gottes* 121.
[170] Muriel Spark, *Memento Mori* (Penguinbooks 1963) 150.

CONCLUSION

Old Testament scholars commonly seem to believe that speculation about the hereafter in Israel was mainly limited to poets. This may be true as far as they were able to express this overwhelming reality in really penetrating speech (¹). But a vital experience of this kind can hardly be the monopoly of " the men of letters ". The artist is affected by the same reality as the ordinary person; the difference consists in his being more impressionable as to its deeper dimensions and in his possession of a more refined instrument to express this experience. Moreover biblical poets were by no means marginal figures in their environment, constituting a kind of caste, as is not rarely the case in modern society.

If this view is correct, the frequent poetical reflection on the nether world shows that this theme was not a peripheral phenomenon in Hebrew thought (²). This is particularly true for the psalter, which as a book of common prayer may be thought to voice the daily emotions and the vital anxieties of the Israelite. It can hardly be disputed that the psalms, merely because of their frequent use, must have exerted a great influence on Hebrew thinking. The references to the hereafter in the psalter are extraordinarily numerous and they seem to imply that the people's conceptions of after-life were not so elementary and primitive as often believed. Even if this range of ideas was not originally popular, it must have become so through the psalter.

An important consequence of this poetical approach of our theme should not pass unnoticed. According to Noordmans the Psalms constitute the greatest miracle of the world: without giving an explanation of death, they helped successive generations to face it (³).

This indeed is the miracle of poetry: " the efforts to give a name to reality are efforts to name oneself and in that way to maintain

---

(¹) " Die Zeit ist vorbei, worin man die Poesie als spielerischen Vergleich, die Religion als spielerischen Begriff abtun konnte ". G. v. d. Leeuw, *Phänomenologie* 627.

(²) The poet discovers the way to the most profound experiences: " Nur der Dichter kann ... den Weg zurückfinden in das primitive Empfinden " (*ibid.* 70).

(³) See Barth, *Einführung Pss* 56.

oneself; the struggle of language is a vital struggle " ([4]).   These words of a noted critic about a modern poet obtain a special meaning in view of Israel's many names for the Beyond: always new words are called up to conjure the unavoidable and infernal reality of Sheol.   Thus, on the purely human level, man tried to rise above the inescapable: by exorcising it, by overpowering it by the power of the word.

In spite of the analytical nature of this study some general lines will stand out in synthesis.   The close relation between the grave and the nether world is a striking phenomenon; and, although the relation between the two cannot be explained satisfactorily in abstract terms, it is clear that Sheol owes much to the grave.   Both this and the frequent identification with Chaos explain the import of Sheol's location under the earth.

It appears that Sheol is described as a negative counterpart of the earth; being chaotic, it is approached by the *via negationis*.   It is furnished with negative experiences, opposed to the favourable ones on earth and corresponding to the griefs of this life.   In fact misery here is considered as a real anticipation of the stay in the reign of Death.

It is remarkable that the Bible, when it reflects on death, is generally occupied with a personal being and post-mortal conditions rather than with total ruin and the radical end of life as such.   Of course there are some expressions designating death as a kind of transition: " to be gathered to one's kinsmen " refers to the union of the dead with their forefathers in Sheol; " to sleep with one's fathers " denotes dying itself; " to be transplanted " signifies the transition from the earth to the underworld; the way this happens is suggested by the " cords and snares of Death " or by the verbs " to be thrust " and " to be swallowed ", and, more peacefully, by " return ", " descent ", and simple " way ".   But all these expressions conceal the existential aspect we expect to find.   It occurs, but generally in descriptions of serious illness and the like, which were considered as an anticipation of death.   In this way the phenomenon of death itself, too, is touched upon, in so far as it is a painful process threatening human life.   Similarly we moderns experience illness as a kind of death, but then the feeling of the cessation of life prevails.   The Old Testament however, evokes the miserable conditions of diminished life by terms denoting the stay in Sheol.   So a dynamic process is rendered in a static way,

([4]) Kees Fens, on the poetry of G. Kouwenaar, " Taalstrijd als Levens-strijd ", *De Tijd*, zaterdag, jan. 15 1966.

which shows that the Hebrew mind was especially ¡captivated by the lasting conditions man is subject to after this life (⁵).

Besides, Death was experienced, not as an abstract power or an inexplicable fate, but as a personal reality, the Arch-enemy, the King, the Shepherd, etc.; as a threatening demon. This explains why he is alluded to rather than discussed. No doubt there exists some connection between mythological Death and the biblical figure of Sir Death, who, despite some traces of dualism in the Old Testament, is generally subject to Yahweh. The pedigree then continues with the devil, personification of moral evil. The use of the same symbols in these three cases (e.g., the devouring lion) suggests an intimate relation between them. As these realities remained outside Yahwism for a considerable time, popular custom must have kept up the ancient mythological traditions, although the OT shows that already in an early period Mot was subdued to the God of Israel.

Sir Death is the enemy *par excellence*, death is the summary of all evil. So persecution, oppression, need, and illness are felt as forms of partial but real death, and their originators as manifestations of the Arch-enemy, as his visible representatives and, because of his affinity with Chaos, as connected with chaotic forces. But though these destructive forces remain a threat for human happiness, they are fundamentally broken: they are subject to the living and only God. The power of Yahweh over Death and Sheol is affirmed throughout the OT.

(⁵) See Dr. C. Verhoeven. " Als een dief in de nacht ". *Het grote gebeuren* (Utrecht 1966) 269-289.

Index of Subjects

Numbers in brackets refer to the classification of motifs according to Stith Thompson, *Motif-Index of Folk-Literature*, 6 vols. (Bloomington, Ind., 1932-1936).

Abaddon 80 f., 130
Abyss : see Depths
Accadian 15, 21 f., 23, 44, 76, 77, 110, 113 f., 116, 132, 149, 172, 200 (See also Index of Accadian Words.)
Adonis 15
Amarna 149, 200
Ambiguity – poetical device 11, 45 f., 56, 61, 108, 117
Anat 10, 12 f., 14, 53, 59, 99, 206
Angel 204 f.
Annihilation 194-196
Apocalyptic 113, 161
Apollyon 81
Apophis 110
Appositional waw 16, 81
Arabic 126
Aramaic 21, 78, 185
Archetype 99, 188, 195
Arrow 19, 108, 205
to ascend (F. 101) 27, 38, 90, 115, 125, 134, 167
Ash 75, 91
Athtar 6, 13, 15, 53, 85, 153, 203

Baal (A.430) 6, 9, 10, 11, 12 f., 15, 16, 17, 57, 59, 61 f., 82, 99, 102, 104, 110, 149, 203, 208
Bed (F.165) 67, 143, 156-159, 183, 199, 201
Belial 66, 125-128, 150, 161
Binding : see Ropes 47, 66, 199
Bitterness of death 202
Breakers (A.672, F.162) 63, 65 f., 82, 136, 146, 207

Bridge (F.152) 150
Burial (E.412.3) 13, 17, 73, 157, 168 f., 171, 176, 182, 196

Casting of metal 147 f.
Chaff 93
Chains : see Nets 155
Channel (Styx, A.672) 147-151
Chaos (A.650, F.160) 63, 122, 127, 132, 190, 194, 205, 208, 213
Cistern 66-69
Clay : see Mud 86 f.
Cloud (symbol of transiency) 167, 195
Contraction (grammatical) 34 f.
Coptic 166
Cords : see Nets
Corn – spirit (A.433.1) 14 f., 31
Corruption 69-71, 158
Cosmic conversation 42, 59
Cosmic mountain (A.875.1) 206
Covenant (with Death) 9 f., 102
to be covered 39, 61, 80
Crocodile (B.11) 165
Curse 32, 53, 54, 75, 84, 93, 94

Danel 16 f.
Danger : see Need
Darkness 17, 40, 41, 57, 60, 66, 74, 75, 77, 78, 84, 90, 93, 94, 95, 98, 114, 118, 124, 140-144, 153-155, 157, 161, 167 f., 173, 187 f., 190, 195, 199, 205, 209 f.
Death : see Mot 16, 129 f., 135-140, 193 f.

Index of Scripture References

I. Old Testament

II. New Testament

Index of Ugaritic References

Index of Hebrew Words

Index of Ugaritic Words

aliyn	203	*mk*	7
arṣ	7, 13, 23 f.	*mr*	56
arṣy	27	*mt wšr*	16, 80 f.
ib	209	*nhr*	63
ilnym	177 f.	*nṭʿ*	17
edom	27	*ʿpr*	17
bl	92	*ʿrʿr*	18 f.
bṯn	57, 62	*ġṣr*	15, 146
d-	34	*ṣrrt*	181
dbr	10 f.	*rb tmtt*	106
dmt	76	*rpum*	176-180
dry	14	*ršp*	19, 108
hmry	7 f., 54	*šbm*	57
ḥmr	9	*šd*	52
ḫḫ	7	*šdmt*	16, 52 f.
ḫlq	11 f., 83	*šḫlmmt*	10 f.
ḫpṯṯ	7, 157 ff.	*šḫt*	18 f.
ḫtr	14	*šlḫ*	147 ff.
yd	100	*šnh*	184
ym	63	*šʿtqt*	18, 116, 203
yrd	32	*šr*	16
klb	165	*thm*	54
lʿy	203	*tḫpṯṯ*	7, 157 ff.
lan	203	*tl*	55
ltn	62	*tnn*	62
mhmrt	8, 54	*ṯbb*	57

Index of Accadian Words

Index of Authors

DATE DUE